MW00909542

The Vision of Six Sigma

A Roadmap for Breakthrough

Mikel J. Harry, Ph.D.

President & CEO
Six Sigma Academy, Inc.

1997

Tri Star Publishing

Phoenix, Arizona, USA
(800) 350-6350

Ordering Instructions

"The Vision of Six Sigma:
A Roadmap for Breakthrough"

Mikel J. Harry, Ph.D.

Fax: 602/269-1469
Call:602/269-2900
National: 1-800-350-6350
Write:
Tri Star Publishing
3110 North 35th Avenue, Suite 4
Phoenix, Arizona 85017
USA

Please Include:
Title of Publication, ISBN#
Your Name, Phone, Fax, Company, Address

Library of Congress Cataloging in Publication Data

Harry, Mikel J.
    The Vision of Six Sigma.

    Includes Bibliography and References
    1. Quality control - Statistical methods. 2. Six Sigma
I. Title

Eight Book Boxed Set: ISBN 0-9643555-7-4
Current Printing (last digit)
5 4 3 2

Cover Design & Printing By:
Tri Star Visual Communications
Phoenix, Arizona

To the Memory of Bill Smith

Preface

History of Quality

The need for quality was first recognized after humankind's initial efforts to produce a duplicate of an object. Those initial efforts at object duplication resulted in rather crude copies that were in all probability functional, but rather frail with regard to dimensional stability and applicability of use. Examples of this are clearly seen in arrow flints, stone hammers, and early cooking utensils. Although such efforts at quality control resulted in reproductions which appeared to be relatively similar, there were, however, considerable variations in one or more of the quality characteristics which, in turn, resulted in large differences in performance. In some instances the variations were of enough magnitude to negate any possible use of the reproduction; for example, a weapon made from a stone that was too large or a "food stick" that was too big for the user's mouth.

Over much time, these assertive, if not exasperating, efforts to gain control over the quality of a reproduction gave impetus to the rise of craftsmen. These individuals became quite skilled at duplicating specific types of objects. As demand for their skills increased, craftsmen that produced similar objects slowly banded together to form what became known as guilds. Essentially, guilds allowed craftsmen to further specialize and solidify their skills. Although these craftsmen were highly skilled they still were not capable of duplicating an object accurately enough to create replacement parts in advance of a probable repair. When a repair was necessary, the original object was required. It was not until Eli Whitney conceived the idea of interchangeable parts that this situation was turned around.

Eli Whitney's idea was to have each worker make one specific part, or perform a limited number of operations on a given part to exact specifications so that all of the individual parts would be identical and could be assembled into a product. Although the idea was sound in theory and basically applicable, as evidenced by the production of rifles during that era, it became readily apparent that a human being simply could not produce an "exact" copy of an object. This remained true no matter how skilled the worker was or how simple the part or operation. The recognition of this dilemma led to the development of "tolerances."

The Essence of Six Sigma

Since that time, the need for process control has increased at an astounding rate. The idea of quality control has yielded to the notion of quality assurance. From this perspective, the practice of statistical process control and experimental design has flourished. Yet in spite of these advances, the customers that form the enormous base of today's world market are sending a clear and undeniable message -- produce higher quality products at lower costs with greater responsiveness. Companies are hearing this message and are again rising to the challenge. For many, the stalking of Six Sigma has led to the development of new and exciting approaches for the improvement of business, engineering, manufacturing, service, and administration performance. The purpose of this book is to present the Six Sigma strategies, tactics, and tools which have been successfully used to achieve a world-class level of business performance.

In essence, Six Sigma advocates that there are strong relationships between product defects and product yield, reliability, costs, cycle time, inventory, schedule, and so on. As the number of defects increase, the number of sigmas decreases. In other words, the larger the sigma value, the better the product quality – and visa versa. Although the ultimate aspiration is zero defects, the threshold of excellence is Six Sigma performance. This target holds for all processes related to the operation of a business.

Interestingly, Six Sigma quality is estimated assuming "typical" shifts and drifts in process centering. In this sense, 99.99966 percent capability at the "part" and "process step" levels is an intermediate target toward the ideal of perfection. This may be illustrated by considering a product that contains 300 unique purchased parts and a related manufacturing process that consists of say, 500 independent operations. A Six Sigma capability at the part and operation level would ensure an aggregate or "rolled" yield of 99.73 percent. This would be to say, out of every 10,000 units of product manufactured, there would be 9,973 units that would be produced completely free of defects.

Aim of the Book

Throughout this book, variation is viewed as the number one enemy of quality, yield, and costs. It must be arrested and ultimately eliminated in order to achieve "best in class." By attacking variation during the design phase, within suppliers' processes, and within our own processes, Six Sigma capability can be achieved. In doing so, the foundation of excellence is laid.

Based on the statistical perspective, the product and process engineering viewpoints are brought into focus by means of analytical examples. Through the discussion and examples, insights are developed as to the objectives of the Six Sigma initiative; enhanced product quality, yield, and cost – all of which, in turn, improve customer satisfaction.

Again, this book has been specifically designed to structure an in-depth overview of the fundamental strategies, tactics, and tools necessary for achieving Six Sigma product designs, manufacturing processes, service quality, and quality of administration. Up front, the basic tenets of Six Sigma will be revealed in a nontechnical manner and then illustrated in more technically oriented discussions. Specifically, the book will explore:

- *The Driving Need for Six Sigma Quality*
- *The Fundamental Objective of Six Sigma*
- *The Customer's Perspective of Six Sigma*
- *The Basic Tenets of Six Sigma*
- *Advanced Six Sigma Concepts*
- *Key Business Conclusions Resulting From Global Benchmarking*
- *Six Sigma as a Target for Total Quality Management (TQM)*
- *The Primary Tools for Achieving Six Sigma*
- *The Impact of Product and Process Complexity on Quality*
- *The Impact of Six Sigma on Product Reliability*
- *The Impact of Six Sigma on Manufacturing Cycle-Time*
- *The Impact of Six Sigma on Inventory*
- *The Impact of Six Sigma on the Bottom Line*
- *How to Create and Maintain Six Sigma Product Designs*
- *How to Create and Maintain Six Sigma Manufacturing Processes*
- *Strategies and Tactics for Implementing Six Sigma*

In addition, several "real life" case studies from Asea Brown Boveri, Texas Instruments (DSEG), and Motorola, Inc. are presented and thoroughly discussed. The case studies are configured to demonstrate many of the how tos, implementation issues, deployment tactics, and lessons learned with respect to Six Sigma. In particular, the cases will highlight the "Six Nuggets of Six Sigma." Those experience-based nuggets are as follows:

1) The same questions most often produces the same actions and, as a consequence, the same result. If we are to break out of this relative stagnation, we must formulate new questions so as to provide new directions and vision. Such action constitutes leadership.

2) We don't know what we don't know and we won't ever know until we measure. As we learn and apply new tools, we will begin to discover new relationships of a technical and/or business nature. The discovery of new relationships creates insight. In turn, insight breeds fresh questions which, in turn, kindle the mind and lay the path for breakthrough and continuous improvement. Naturally, this requires a process focus, or "mind-set" as some would say. This is the fundamental belief which underlies the Six Sigma paradigm -- management of our processes is management of the business.

3) Process capability is the secret of manufacturing success. If we do not know the capability of our processes, we can not design for manufacturability. This would be like trying to bake a good pie without knowing the temperature range of the oven.

4) One of the key performance measures of process capability is Sigma. The sigma scale of measure can be applied to anything which is considered important by the customer or producer. Sigma can be calculated using actual measurements or defect data. The Sigma scale of measure factors out complexity so that homogeneous or heterogeneous comparisons can be made. When this is done, we can directly contrast dissimilar things on a level playing field, so to speak. This is called quantitative benchmarking. By knowing the defect rate of any characteristic, we can use a benchmarking chart to determine the corresponding sigma level of capability. This is because the sigma scale is perfectly correlated to defects. Once the sigma of a process is known, we can readily understand what we do well in addition to what must be improved. In short, the sigma scale is to management as the stopwatch is to racing.

5) Theoretical calculations and massive amounts of data from numerous companies demonstrate that quality is a function of the interaction between the design and its related processes. As the efficacy of interaction increases, so does the quality. As quality improves, costs and cycle-time decrease. A singular focus on the improvement of process capability can typically reduce manufacturing costs by 30% and cut cycle-time in half. An interactive focus can decrease costs by as much as 25% of revenues.

6) The attainment of Six Sigma requires new tools which, in turn, demand the application of new knowledge. To consistently identify new tools, create roadmaps for their use, and ensure the propagation of value added know-how, a supporting infrastructure must be put in place. Such an infrastructure consists of Black-Belts. These are the in-house Six Sigma experts who know how to make improvement happen. People can only apply what they know how to do. If the knowledge is insufficient, chances are that the resulting action will be insufficient. In order to improve a process, we must go beyond experience. We must collect data so as to "let the product do the talking."

Special Acknowledgments

The quest for Six Sigma is a step beyond conventional thinking. It provides us a means to look over the horizon -- at new ways of doing things with bold levels of expectation. In this spirit, the author has explored a nonconventional format for structuring and presenting the vision and underlying concepts of Six Sigma. The format is based on the time proven belief that "a picture is worth a thousand words." In this sense, it is a graphic "story board" of ideas, experiences, and practices. It provides the reader with visual cues and, where necessary, reinforces or clarifies those cues with text. From this perspective, it is a "thinking" book versus a "reading" book. The intent is to stimulate additional questions, not just to provide answers and information. Naturally, when such questions are formed and diligently pursued, the result is discovery -- the core of profound knowledge. This represents the difference between understanding something versus knowing it. The richness of a picture far exceeds the limited budget of words.

Reducing the underlying concepts of Six Sigma to pictures initially appeared to be a fairly easy and straight forward task. Little did this author know that such an approach would prove to be so time consuming. The author discovered (first-hand) that while it is true a simple picture is worth a thousand words, it is far easier to just type the thousand words. Of course achieving the aims of this book required the input of many organizations and people.

The author would like to extend many thanks to Asea Brown Boveri, Texas Instruments (DSEG), and Motorola. These fine organizations cheerfully provided much of the information and data to support the aims of this book. Their experiences down the path of Six Sigma should serve as key landmarks in the pursuit of total customer satisfaction. For they have learned that to focus on the customer is to focus on the business. As a result, these organizations lead the way in quality improvement and business performance.

Naturally, an organization is only as good as its people. With this in mind, the author would like very much to extend a deep sense of gratitude and heart felt appreciation to those individuals who played a key role in the support, creation, review and production of this book. First, the author would like to acknowledge Mr. Robert "Bob" Galvin, former CEO and Chairman-of-the-Board, Motorola Inc. His wisdom, leadership, and words of encouragement shall always be remembered. Truly, no one can give deeper meaning to Six Sigma.

The author would like express a personal thanks to Dr. Thomas Cheek and Mr. Rich Karm at Texas Instruments, DSEG. In the spirit of Texas, they were always eager to listen, share information, try new things, and strive for a "win-win" relationship. These men exemplify the meaning behind the phrases "paradigm shifters" and "change agents." Their willingness to reach out is remarkable.

A very special recognition to goes to Mr. Kjell Magnusson, Vice-President, Customer Focus, TPT, Asea Brown Boveri. For more than a year now, Kjell has successfully labored to implement Six Sigma within his area of responsibility. During this period of time, Kjell immersed himself into the deepest recesses of Six Sigma. Never before has a senior executive delved so deep into the topic -- from an organizational, operational, and technical point of view. As a result, he has had a profound effect on his organization's thinking, culture, and practices in a very short period of time. In every sense, Kjell has practiced quality leadership. Owing to this, Six Sigma has made yet another step forward in refinement -- it is now a "process" for breakthrough. His influence and friendship will be with this author for a lifetime.

On the home front, the author would like to extend a loving note of gratitude to his beautiful bride, Sherry. She provided the emotional electricity necessary to keep the keyboard running. Without her sparkling support and encouragement, this book would not be. Thank you sweetheart.

Of course, there were many others who provided critical feedback and review. In particular, the author would like to recognize the contribution of all the Six Sigma Black-Belts around the world. Their memos, faxes, correspondence, and discussions have been invaluable. In the final analysis, we must all understand that individuals, such as those acknowledged in this book, serve to the keep the idea alive and the vision in focus.

Mikel J. Harry, Ph.D.
President & CEO
Six Sigma Academy, Inc.

Table of Contents

Introduction

CHAPTER ONE

Breakthrough

Breakthrough

THE VISION OF SIX SIGMA

Cutting to the Core

Behavior is a function of Values

$$B = f(V)$$

Behavior

The way in which a person or group of people responds.

Values

The complex of beliefs, ideals, or standards, which characterizes a person or group of people.

. . . What are the "common beliefs" which characterizes your organization ?

Defining Our Values

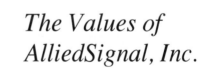

Teamwork
Customers Performance
Speed
Integrity Innovation
People

The Values of
AlliedSignal, Inc.

Source: "Total Quality Leadership: A Path To Excellence," AlliedSignal Inc., Morristown NJ.

THE VISION OF SIX SIGMA

 Six Sigma Academy, Inc.   1 . 3   ®1997 Sigma Consultants, L.L.C.

Exploring Our Values

Describe and prioritize the key values which characterize your organization.

P
Priority

Description of Standard

THE VISION OF SIX SIGMA

σ Six Sigma Academy, Inc.   1 . 4   ® 1997 Sigma Consultants, L.L.C.

Defining the Ideal Quality Value

1) List the 6 factors which you believe are the major determinants of quality.
2) For each factor, place a rating on the following statements:

M	Performance of the listed factor should ☐ be measured.	5 = Always
R	The performance measure should ☐ be reported.	4 = Often
R	Management should ☐ review the performance reports.	3 = Occasionally
I	Improvement actions should ☐ stem from the reviews.	2 = Rarely
		1 = Never

Factor	M Measure	R Report	R Review	I Improve	Total
Total					

THE VISION OF SIX SIGMA

σ Six Sigma Academy, Inc.   1 . 5   ®1997 Sigma Consultants, L.L.C.

Defining the Real Quality Value

1) List the 6 factors which you believe are the major determinants of quality.
2) For each factor, place a rating on the following statements:

M Performance of the listed factor is [____] measured in my organization.   5 = Always
R The performance measure is [____] reported in my organization.   4 = Often
R Management [____] reviews the performance reports in my organization.   3 = Occasionally
I Improvement actions [____] stem from the reviews in my organization.   2 = Rarely
                                                                                   1 = Never

Factor	M Measure	R Report	R Review	I Improve	Total
Total					

THE VISION OF SIX SIGMA

Six Sigma Academy, Inc.   1 . 6   ®1997 Sigma Consultants, L.L.C.

The Quality Value Grid

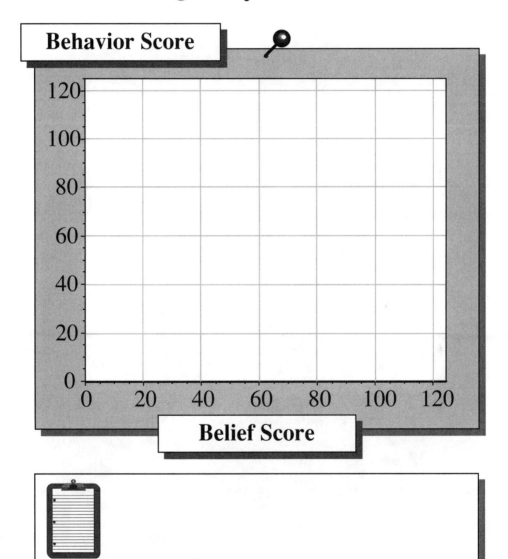

σ Six Sigma Academy, Inc.   1.7   ®1997 Sigma Consultants, L.L.C.

The Value of Measurement

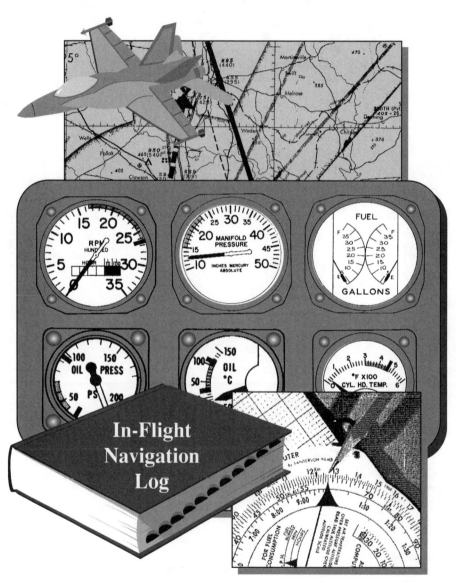

In-Flight Navigation Log

THE VISION OF SIX SIGMA

Measurements Get Attention

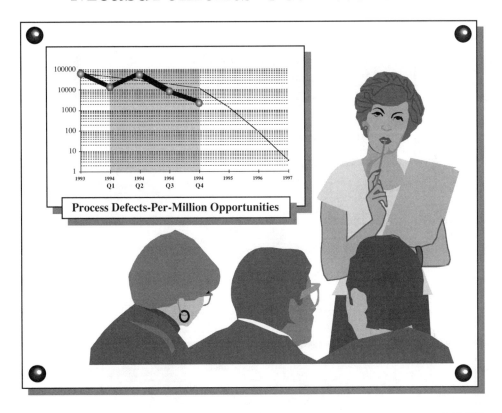

Process Defects-Per-Million Opportunities

[We don't know what we don't know.

[If we can't express what we know in the form of numbers, we really
   don't know much about it.

[If we don't know much about it, we can't control it.

[If we can't control it, we are at the mercy of chance.

THE VISION OF SIX SIGMA

σ Six Sigma Academy, Inc.   1 . 9   ®1997 Sigma Consultants, L.L.C.

Performance Metrics Reporting

We don't know what we don't know

We can't act on what we don't know

We won't know until we search

We won't search for what we don't question

We don't question what we don't measure

Hence, We just don't know

Dr. Mikel J. Harry

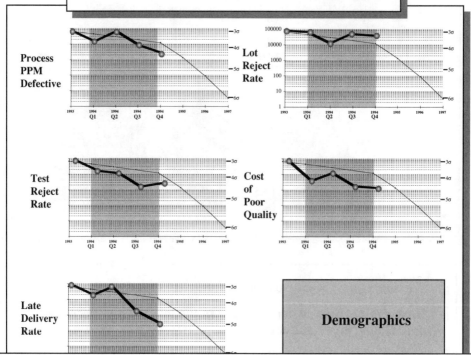

If we know what we should, then we know what to do.

Olle Burtus, ABB Transformers, Sweden

THE VISION OF SIX SIGMA

Six Sigma Academy, Inc.   1 . 10   ®1997 Sigma Consultants, L.L.C.

The Need for Knowledge

If we don't know, we can not act

If we can not act, the risk of loss is high

If we do know and act, the risk is managed

If we do know and do not act, we deserve the loss.

Dr. Mikel J. Harry

Therefore, we must conclude:

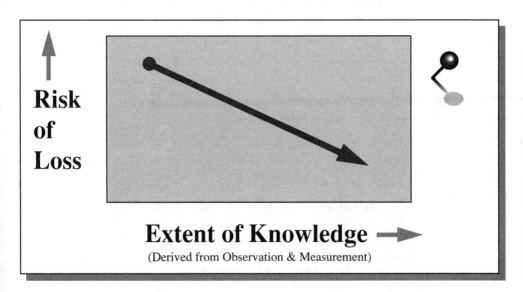

Risk of Loss

Extent of Knowledge →

(Derived from Observation & Measurement)

Ignorance is not bliss, it is the food of failure and the breeding ground for loss.

Dr. Mikel J. Harry

The Role of Questions

Questions lead and answers follow. The same questions most often lead to the same answers which, invariably, produce the same result. To change the result, means to change the question.

Management constitutes the leadership element in an organization. When focus is given to the measurement of standards, new questions will continuously arise.

As questions arise, vision emerges, direction becomes apparent, and ambiguity diminishes . In turn, people become organized and mobilized to common action.

When people take common action, the organization's ability to survive and prosper will increase, owing to the discovery of answers to problems heretofore not known.

Dr. Mikel J. Harry

 Six Sigma Academy, Inc.

Aims of the Discussion

Develop deeper insights into the many facets of Six Sigma. This will be done by discussing the concepts, interrelationships, and principles of Six Sigma. The intent is to further stimulate your questioning process which, in turn, will promote a more intensive pursuit of answers.

- What information do you need to know ?

- What concepts would you like to take back to the job?

- What would you like to see demonstrated?

- To what functional areas would you like to see it applied?

- What would motivate you to embody the principles ?

Questions Most Often Asked

❑ What is Six Sigma and how does it impact the bottom line?

❑ Why should I give Six Sigma serious consideration?

❑ Where and how does Six Sigma fit in my business?

❑ What makes Six Sigma different from other quality programs?

❑ How does Six Sigma help me focus my business operations?

❑ How is Six Sigma used in a low volume environment ?

❑ How does engineering use Six Sigma to improve?

❑ How does manufacturing use Six Sigma to improve quality?

❑ How do non-manufacturing organizations use Six Sigma?

❑ How does supply management use Six Sigma?

❑ What type of gains can I expect to see if I adopt Six Sigma?

❑ How long does it take to see financial benefits from Six Sigma?

❑ What does it cost to implement Six Sigma?

❑ What resources are required to implement Six Sigma?

❑ What kind of infrastructure is required to support implementation?

❑ What will my business look like after implementing Six Sigma?

❑ What are the implementation shortcuts?

❑ What are my first few steps to get the Six Sigma ball rolling?

THE VISION OF SIX SIGMA

σ Six Sigma Academy, Inc.   1 . 14   ®1997 Sigma Consultants, L.L.C.

The Role of Training

Undoubtedly, the single most important aspect of Six Sigma is people and their knowledge. Without this golden asset, all is for nothing. At the risk of redundancy , you don't know what you don't know, and if you don't know something, nothing will happen. Obviously, the key is knowledge. Successful change and improvement can not occur without it.

Today, the best-in-class companies provide a tremendous amount of training and education to their employees. Many such companies have made significant investments in training, and are discovery the rewards. For example, Motorola Inc. has discovered a 10 to 1 return on their training budget. In fact, they require every employee to receive 40 hours or more of training annually, of which 40% must be in the area of quality.

The Learning Model

- Lecture
- Course Notes
- Course Material
- Handouts
- Examples
- Exercises
- Case Studies
- Self-Review
- Step-by-step approach
- Video (where appropriate)
- Hands-on computations
- Computer simulations
- Application projects
- Participant presentations

THE VISION OF SIX SIGMA

The Keys for Skill Development

- **You must want to do it**
- **You must learn the tools**
- **You must be willing to practice**
- **You must be allowed to practice**
- **You must have adequate resources**
- **You must have adequate coaching**

THE VISION OF SIX SIGMA

Six Sigma Academy, Inc.   1.17   ®1997 Sigma Consultants, L.L.C.

Instructional Support Resources

- ✓ Case Studies
- ✓ Computer Simulations
- ✓ Excel Spreadsheet
- ✓ MiniTab Software
- ✓ SSA Software
- ✓ Turbo Learning System
- ✓ SSA Navigator

THE VISION OF SIX SIGMA

Six Sigma Academy, Inc.   1 . 18   ®1997 Sigma Consultants, L.L.C.

The Champion Program of Study

The one week Six Sigma Champion program of study will provide key individuals with the managerial and technical knowledge necessary to facilitate the leadership, implementation, and deployment of Six Sigma. The instructional goal is to transfer and reinforce the fundamental Six Sigma strategies, tactics, and tools necessary for achieving breakthrough in key product designs, manufacturing processes, services, and administrative processes.

Each instructional session will concentrate on the underlying philosophy, supporting theory, conventional practices, and application dynamics related to the Six Sigma strategies, tactics, and tools. In addition, each session will focus on the critical implementation issues and mechanics which surrounds the instructional material.

Directly following each program session, the participants will synthesize the key points of instruction and then contribute to the progressive development of a model Six Sigma implementation plan aimed at their respective business. With this as a backdrop, knowledge is translated to action.

Through this program of study, the instructional material delivered within the classroom is smoothly blended into an implementation and deployment plan. In turn, such plans are translated to front-line practice within the targeted business.

The MBB Program of Study

The two week Master Black Belt (MBB) program of study will provide a select number of individuals with the knowledge and skills necessary to best guide, propagate, and mature the black belt infrastructure. The intent is to present the MBB candidate with those methods and techniques (both technical and nontechnical) which best exploit the full power of advanced problem solving and process improvement tools. Naturally, the ideal MBB candidate has a technical background, understands basic statistics, and has application experience with basic problem solving and quality tools.

Although the primary focus of the development process is tactical in nature, an array of Six Sigma methods and advanced improvement tools will be presented and thoroughly discussed from an application (as well as theoretical) point of view. In addition, several real-life application case studies will be spontaneously presented and carefully analyzed to reinforce understanding and use of the tools.

By end of the second development cycle, each candidate will have formulated a professional growth plan. Essentially, the plan guides the MBB candidate toward further skill development. In closing, it is worth noting that a Master Black Belt is fully capable of independent training and coaching of business unit Black Belts, as well as providing strategic and tactical assistance to business unit champions and management during the course of Six Sigma implementation and deployment.

THE VISION OF SIX SIGMA

σ Six Sigma Academy, Inc.   1 . 20   ®1997 Sigma Consultants, L.L.C.

Champion & MBB Agenda

Six Sigma Champion and Master Blackbelt Program Agenda

Week	Session	Day	Session Title
1	1.01	Mon	Introductions and Expectations
1	1.02	Mon	Questing for Six Sigma
1	1.03	Mon	Focusing on the Customer
1	1.04	Mon	Understanding Performance Metrics
1	1.05	Tues	Discovering the Hidden Factory
1	1.06	Tues	Assessing the Hidden Factory
1	1.07	Tues	Benchmarking Products and Processes
1	1.08	Wed	Understanding Process Capability
1	1.09	Wed	Achieving Process Entitlement
1	1.10	Wed	Designing for Manufacturability
1	1.11	Thurs	Creating the Deployment Roadmap
1	1.12	Fri	Presentation and Review of Implementation Plans
2	2.01	Mon	Revisiting Basic Six Sigma Concepts
2	2.02	Mon	Linking Six Sigma Concepts to Statistics
2	2.03	Tues	Translating Practical Problems into Statistics
2	2.04	Tues	Discovering the Statistical Confidence in Data
2	2.05	Wed	Unlocking the Power of Experimentation
2	2.06	Wed	Diagnosing a Single Process Variable
2	2.07	Wed	Isolating and Leveraging Multi-Variable Relationships
2	2.08	Thurs	Screening for Leverage Variables and Effects
2	2.09	Thurs	Designing for Robust Performance
2	2.10	Fri	Holding the Gains with Statistical Process Control
2	2.11	Fri	Identifying the Drivers of Customer Satisfaction

Week 1 - Champions and Master Blackbelts
Week 2 - Master Blackbelts Only

THE VISION OF SIX SIGMA

 Six Sigma Academy, Inc.   1 . 21   ®1997 Sigma Consultants, L.L.C.

Week	Book	Chapt	Session	Champion and MBB Instructional Objectives
1	1	1	1.01	Recognize the need for change and the role of values within a business
1	1	1	1.01	Recognize the need for measurement and its role in business success
1	1	1	1.01	Understand the role of questions in the context of management leadership
1	1	30	1.01	Provide a brief history of Six Sigma and its evolution
1	NA	NA	1.01	Understand the professional needs and expectations of the group
1	NA	NA	1.01	Rationalize the instructor's needs and expectations of the group
1	NA	NA	1.01	Interpret the instructional roadmap for this particular program of study
1	NA	NA	1.01	Understand the SSA instructional resources and how they will be used during the program of study
1	1	2	1.02	Understand the need for measuring those things which are critical to the customer, business, and process
1	1	2	1.02	Define the various facets of Six Sigma and why Six Sigma is important to a business
1	1	2	1.02	Identify the parts-per-million defect goal of Six Sigma
1	1	2	1.02	Describe the magnitude of difference between 3, 4, 5, and 6 sigma.
1	1	2	1.02	Recognize that defects arise from variation
1	1	2	1.02	Define the thee primary sources of variation in a product
1	1	2	1.02	Describe the general methodologies which are required to progress through the hierarchy of quality improvement
1	1	2	1.02	Define the four phases of breakthrough in quality improvement
1	1	2	1.02	Identify the values of a Six Sigma organization as compared to a four sigma business
1	1	2	1.02	Understand the key success factors related to the attainment of Six Sigma
1	1	3	1.03	Provide a definition of the term "customer satisfaction"
1	1	3	1.03	Understand the "need-do" interaction and how it relates to customer satisfaction and business success
1	1	3	1.03	Interpret the expression "y=f(x)"

THE VISION OF SIX SIGMA

eek	Book	Chapt	Session	Champion and MBB Instructional Objectives
1	1	3	1.03	Provide examples for the y and x term relative to the expression y=f(x)
1	1	3	1.03	Define the term "critical-to-satisfaction" characteristic (CTS) and its importance to business success
1	1	4	1.03	Understand why inspection and test is non-value added to a business and serves as a roadblock for achieving Six Sigma
	1	5	1.03	Construct and interpret a histogram for a given set of data
	1	5	1.03	Understand the difference between the terms "process precision" and "process accuracy"
	1	5	1.03	Provide a very general description of how a process capability study is conducted and interpreted
	1	6	1.03	Understand what a normal distribution is, how it is related to a histogram, and how it is used to estimate defect probability
	1	6	1.03	Explain the nature of a "leverage variable" and its implications for customer satisfaction and business success
	1	12	1.03	Provide a definition of the term "opportunity for defect" which recognizes the difference between "active" and "passive" opportunities
	1	12	1.03	Define the term "critical-to-quality" characteristic (CTQ) and its importance to customer satisfaction
	1	12	1.03	Define the term "critical-to-process" characteristic (CTP) and its importance to product quality
	1	12	1.03	Identify the four primary scales of measure and provide a brief description of their unique characteristics
	1	13	1.04	Define the nature of a performance metric
	1	13	1.04	Identify the driving need for performance metrics
	1	13	1.04	Explain the benefits of plotting performance metrics on a log scale
	1	13	1.04	Provide a listing of at least six key performance metrics
	1	13	1.04	Identify the fundamental contents of a performance metrics manual
	1	13	1.04	Recognize the benefits of a metrics manual
	1	13	1.04	Understand the purpose and benefits of improvement curves
	1	13	1.04	Explain how a performance metric improvement curve is used
	1	13	1.04	Explain what is meant by the phrase "Six Sigma rate of improvement"

THE VISION OF SIX SIGMA

Week	Book	Chapt	Session	Champion and MBB Instructional Objectives
1	1	13	1.04	Explain why a Six Sigma improvement curve can create a "level playing field" across an organization
1	1	13	1.04	Understand the basic elements of a "sigma benchmarking chart"
1	1	13	1.04	Interpret a data point plotted on a sigma benchmarking chart
1	1	13	1.04	Compute and interpret the "Cp" index of capability
1	1	13	1.04	Compute and interpret the "Cpk" index of capability
1	1	13	1.04	Explain the theoretical as well as practical differences between Cp, Cpk, Pp, and Ppk
1	1	10	1.05	Provide a rational definition of a "defect"
1	1	10	1.05	Recognize the difference between uniform and random defects
1	1	10	1.05	Compute the defect-per-unit metric given a specific number of observed defects and units produced
1	1	10	1.05	Compute the throughput yield (Y.tp) given an average first-time yield and the number of related defect opportunities (m)
1	1	10	1.05	Identify the circumstances under which the Poisson distribution could be applied to the analysis of product or transactional defects
1	1	10	1.05	Provide a rational explanation as to the differences between "product" yield and "process" yield
1	1	10	1.05	Understand the applied differences between the Poisson and binomial distributions
1	1	14	1.05	Identify the key limitations of the performance metric "final" yield (i.e., output/input)
1	1	14	1.05	Identify the key limitations of the performance metric "first-time" yield (Y.ft)
1	1	14	1.05	Explain why the performance metric "rolled-throughput" yield (Y.rt) represents the probability of zero defects
1	1	14	1.05	Compute the probability of zero defects (Y.rt) given a specific number of observed defects and units produced
1	1	14	1.05	Understand the impact of process capability and complexity on the probability of zero defects
1	1	14	1.05	Compute the "normalized" yield (Y.norm) given a rolled-throughput yield (Y.rt) value and a specific number of defect opportunities
1	1	14	1.05	Compute the total defects-per-unit (tdpu) value given a rolled-throughput yield (Y.rt) value
1	1	14	1.05	Provide a brief description on how one would go about implementing and deploying the performance metric "rolled-throughput" yield (Y.rt)

THE VISION OF SIX SIGMA

eek	Book	Chapt	Session	Champion and MBB Instructional Objectives
1	1	15	1.06	Understand the difference between the idea of benchmark, baseline, and entitlement cycle time
1	1	15	1.06	Provide a brief description for the outcome 1 - Y.rt
1	1	15	1.06	Recognize that the quantity 1 + (1 - Y.rt) represents the number of equivalent units which must be produced to extract on good unit from the process
1	1	15	1.06	Describe how every occurrence of a defect requires time to verify, analyze, repair, and re- verify
1	1	15	1.06	Understand that work-in-process (WIP) is highly correlated to the rate of defects
1	1	16	1.06	Define what is meant by the term "mean-time-to-failure" (MTBF)
1	1	16	1.06	Interpret the temporal failure pattern of a product using the classic bathtub reliability curve
	1	16	1.06	Explain how process capability impacts the pattern of failure inherent to the infant mortality period (reference: classic bathtub reliability curve)
	1	16	1.06	Provide a rational definition of the term "latent defect" and how such defects can impact product reliability
	1	16	1.06	Explain how defects produced during manufacture influences product reliability which, in turn, influences customer satisfaction
	1	17	1.06	Rationalize the statement that "the highest quality producer is the lowest cost producer"
	1	17	1.06	State at least three problems (or severe limitations) inherent to the current cost-of-quality theory
	1	17	1.06	Identify and define the principal categories associated with quality costs
	1	17	1.06	Compute the cost-of-quality (COQ) given the necessary background data
	1	17	1.06	Provide a detailed explanation of how a defect can impact the classical cost-of-quality categories
	1	18	1.07	Construct a benchmarking chart using the "product report" option in Mintab software
	1	19	1.07	Understand the fundamental nature of quantitative benchmarking on a sigma scale of measure
	1	19	1.07	Recognize that the sigma scale of measure is at the "opportunity" level, not at the "system" level
	1	19	1.07	Interpret an array of sigma benchmarking charts
	1	19	1.07	Understand that global benchmarking has consistently revealed 4 sigma as the average while best-in-class is contained within the 6 sigma region
	1	19	1.07	Draw first order conclusions when given a global benchmarking chart

THE VISION OF SIX SIGMA

Week	Book	Chapt	Session	Champion and MBB Instructional Objectives
1	1	19	1.07	Provide a brief description of the "5 sigma wall," what it is, why it exists, and how to get over it
1	1	19	1.07	State the general findings which tends to characterize or "profile" a 4 sigma organization
1	1	19	1.07	List at least five separate sources which could offer the data necessary from which one could estimate a sigma capability
1	1	19	1.07	Explain how the sigma scale of measure could be employed for purposes of strategic planning
1	1	19	1.07	Recognize the cycle-time, reliability, and cost implications when interpreting a sigma benchmarking chart
1	1	19	1.07	Understand that a Six Sigma product without a market will always fail; however, a Six Sigma product in a viable market is virtually certain to succeed
1	1	7	1.08	Provide a qualitative definition and graphical interpretation of the standard deviation
1	1	7	1.08	Provide a qualitative definition and graphical interpretation of the variance
1	1	7	1.08	Compute the sample standard deviation given for a set of data
1	1	7	1.08	Explain why a sample six of n = 30 is often considered ideal (in the instance of continuous data)
1	1	7	1.08	Compute and interpret the total, between, and within group sum-of-squares for an appropriate set of data
1	1	7	1.08	Explain what phenomenon could account for a differential between the short-term and long-term standard deviation
1	1	8	1.08	Provide a qualitative definition and graphical interpretation of the standard "Z" transform
1	1	8	1.08	Explain why a "Z" can be used as a measure of process capability and its relationship to such indices as Cp, Cpk, Pp, and Ppk.
1	1	8	1.08	Compute the corresponding Z value of a particular specification limit, given an appropriate set of data
1	1	8	1.08	Convert a Z value into a defect probability, given a table of area under the normal curve
1	1	8	1.08	Provide a practical explanation of what could account for a differential between a short-term Z value (Z.st) and the corresponding long-term Z value (Z.lt)
1	1	9	1.08	Explain the difference between "dynamic mean variation" and "static mean off-set"
1	1	9	1.08	Recognize that a 1.5 sigma shift (between two consecutive sampling periods) is typical and; therefore, can be used when quantification is not possible
1	1	9	1.08	Understand the general guidelines for adjusting a Z value for the influence of shift and drift (i.e., when to add or subtract the shift value)
1	1	9	1.08	Conduct a complete baseline process capability analysis (using Mintab software), interpret the results, and make valid action based recommendations

THE VISION OF SIX SIGMA

Week	Book	Chapt	Session	Champion and MBB Instructional Objectives
1	1	21	1.09	Understand the driving need for breakthrough improvement versus continuous improvement
1	1	21	1.09	Define the two primary components of process breakthrough
1	1	21	1.09	Provide a brief description of the four phases of process breakthrough (i.e., measure, analyze, improve, control)
1	1	21	1.09	Interpret each of the action steps associated with the four phases of process breakthrough
1	1	21	1.09	Explain why the 5 key planning questions are so important to "project success"
1	1	21	1.09	Explain how the "generic planning guide" can be used to create a "project execution cookbook"
1	1	22	1.09	Provide a synopsis what a "statistically designed experiment (DOE)" is and what role it plays during the improvement phase of breakthrough
1	1	22	1.09	Create a graphical explanation of how performance tolerances can be prescribed using the results of a 2 level factorial experiment
1	1	22	1.09	Understand the basic nature of statistical process control charts and what role they play during the control phase of breakthrough
1	2	3	1.09	Describe the role of measurement error studies during the measurement phase of breakthrough
1	1	14	1.10	Understand how product and process complexity impacts design performance
1	2	26	1.10	Demonstrate why "worst-case" tolerance analysis is an overly conservative and costly design tool
1	2	27	1.10	Describe what is meant by the term "Monte Carlo simulation" and demonstrate how it can be used as a design tool
1	2	28	1.10	Explain the concept of "error propagation" (from a linear and nonlinear perspective) and what role of product/process complexity plays
1	2	28	1.10	Compute the standard deviation for a linear sum of variances and explain why the variances must be independent
1	2	28	1.10	Compute the system level defect probability given the sub-system means, variances (of a linear model) and all relevant performance specifications
1	2	29	1.10	Describe how RSS method can also be used as a "design-to-cost" tool and how it can be employed to analyze and optimize process cycle-time
1	2	32	1.10	Describe how statistically design experiments (DOE) can be effectively used to identify leverage variables, establish sensitivities, and define tolerances
1	2	18	1.10	Understand the fundamental ideas underlying the notion of "manufacturability"
1	2	18	1.10	Provide a brief description of the term "robust design" and why/when process capability data must be factored into the design process
1	2	18	1.10	Recognize that such analytical phenomenon as heteroscedasticity, variable interactions, and nonlinearities can be used to reduce white noise

THE VISION OF SIX SIGMA

Week	Book	Chapt	Session	Champion and MBB Instructional Objectives
1	2	28	1.10	Describe how reverse error propagation can be employed during system design
1	2	28	1.10	Explain why process shift and drift must be considered during the analysis of a design and how it can be factored into design optimization
1	1	14	1.10	Describe how Six Sigma tools and methods can be applied to the design process in and of itself
1	2	28	1.10	Discuss the pro's and con's of the classical approach to product/process design to that of the Six Sigma approach
1	1	23	1.11	Provide a brief description as to the nature of a Six Sigma Black Belt (SSBB)
1	1	23	1.11	Describe the role and responsibilities of a Six Sigma Black Belt
1	1	23	1.11	Understand the Six Sigma Black Belt instructional curriculum
1	1	23	1.11	Recognize that the SSBB curriculum sequence is correlated to the Six Sigma Breakthrough Strategy
1	1	23	1.11	Recognize the importance of, and provide a description for, the Plan-Train-Apply-Review (PTAR) learning process
1	1	24	1.11	Provide a brief description as to the nature of a Six Sigma Champion (SSC)
1	1	24	1.11	Describe the role and responsibilities of a Six Sigma Champion
1	1	25	1.11	Provide a brief description of the key implementation principles and identify the principal deployment success factors
1	1	25	1.11	List all of the planning criteria for constructing a Six Sigma implementation and deployment plan
1	1	25	1.11	Construct a generic milestone chart which identifies all of the activities necessary for successfully managing the implementation of Six Sigma
1	1	NA	1.11	Create a set of criteria for selecting and scoping SSBB projects
1	1	NA	1.11	Define a SSBB project reporting and review process
1	1	NA	1.11	Provide a brief description as to the nature of a Si x Sigma Master Black Belt (SSMBB)
1	1	NA	1.11	Describe the role and responsibilities of a Six Sigma Master Black Belt
1	1	NA	1.11	Develop a business model which incorporates and exploits the benefits of Six Sigma
2	1	8	2.01	Compute the Cp and Cpk indices for a set of normally distributed data with upper and lower performance limits
2	1	14	2.01	Explain why Cpk values will often not correlate to first-time yield information

THE VISION OF SIX SIGMA

Week	Book	Chapt	Session	Champion and MBB Instructional Objectives
2	2	2	2.01	Understand that the term "sigma" is a performance metric and only applies at the "opportunity level"
2	2	2	2.01	Explain how throughput yield (Y.tp) and opportunity counts (m) can be employed to establish the "sigma capability" of a product or process
2	2	2	2.01	Illustrate how a system level DPU goal can be "flowed-down" through a product or process hierarchy to assess the required CTQ capability
2	2	2	2.01	Illustrate how a series of CTQ capability values can be "flowed-up" through a product or process hierarchy to establish the system DPU
2	2	4	2.01	Construct a histogram for a set of normally distributed data and locate the data on a normal probability plot
2	2	4	2.01	Construct a histogram for a set of non-normal data and isolate a mathematical transform which will force the data to a normal condition
2	2	6	2.01	Compute the mean, standard deviation, and variance for a set of normally distributed data
2	2	7	2.01	Compute Z.usl and Z.lsl for a set of normally distributed data with lower and upper performance standards and then determine the probability of defect
2	2	7	2.01	Compute Z.usl and Z.lsl for a set non-normal data with lower and upper performance standards and then determine the probability of defect
2	2	24	2.01	Understand, construct, and interpret a multi-vari chart, then identify areas of application
2	2	27	2.01	Create a series of random normal numbers with a given mean and variance
2	2	27	2.01	Create a k sets of subgroups where each subgroup consists of n samples drawn from a normal distribution with a given mean and variance
2	2	27	2.01	Create a series of random lognormal numbers and then transform the data to fit a normal density function
2	2	6	2.02	Provide a graphical understanding of the standard deviation and explain why it is so important to Six Sigma work?
2	2	9	2.02	Explain the difference between "inherent capability" and "sustained capability" in terms of the standard deviation
2	2	9	2.02	Describe the role and logic of "rational subgrouping" as it relates to the short- and long- term standard deviation
2	2	9	2.02	Explain why the term "instantaneous reproducibility" (i.e., process precision) is associated with the short-term standard deviation
2	2	9	2.02	Explain why the term "sustained reproducibility" is associated with the long-term standard deviation
2	2	9	2.02	Explain the interrelationship between the terms "process capability", "process precision," and "process accuracy"
2	2	9	2.02	Explain the difference between "static mean off-set" and "dynamic mean variation" and how each impacts process capability
2	2	9	2.02	Compute and interpret the within, between, and total sums-of-squares for a set of normally distributed data organized into rational subgroups

THE VISION OF SIX SIGMA

Week	Book	Chapt	Session	Champion and MBB Instructional Objectives
2	2	9	2.02	Compute and interpret Z.st and Z.lt for a set of normally distributed data organized into rational subgroups
2	2	9	2.02	Compute and interpret Z.shift (static and dynamic) for a set of normally distributed data organized into rational subgroups
2	2	9	2.02	Recognize the four principal types of process centering conditions and explain how each impacts process capability
2	2	9	2.02	Compute and interpret Cp, Cpk, Pp, and Ppk
2	2	9	2.02	Explain how Cp, Cpk, Pp, and Ppk correlates to the four principal types of process centering conditions
2	2	9	2.02	Show how Z.st, Z.lt, Z.shift.dynamic, and Z.shift.static relates to Cp, Cpk, Pp, and Ppk
2	2	10	2.02	Create and interpret the standardized MiniTab Six Sigma process characterization reports
2	2	13	2.03	Explain how a practical problem can be translated into a statistical problem and the related benefits associated with doing so
2	2	13	2.03	Explain what a statistical hypothesis is, why they are created, and show the forms they may take in terms of the mean and variance
2	2	13	2.03	Define the concept of "alpha risk" and provide several examples which illustrates its practical consequence
2	2	13	2.03	Define the concept of "statistical confidence" and explain how it relates to alpha risk
2	2	13	2.03	Define the concept of "beta risk" and provide several examples which illustrates its practical consequence
2	2	13	2.03	Provide a detailed understanding of what the "null distribution" is and how it relates to the "null hypothesis"
2	2	13	2.03	Provide a detailed understanding of the "contrast distribution" and how it relates to the "alternate hypothesis"
2	2	13	2.03	Explain what is meant by the phrase "statistically significant difference" and recognize that such differences do not imply practical difference
2	2	13	2.03	Construct a truth table which illustrates how the null and alternate hypotheses interrelate with the concepts of alpha and beta risk
2	2	13	2.03	Recognize that the extent of difference required to produce practical benefit is refereed to as "delta"
2	2	13	2.03	Explain what is meant by the phrase "power of the test" and describe how it relates to the concept of beta risk
2	2	13	2.03	Understand how sample size can impact the extent of decision risk associated with the null and alternate hypotheses
2	2	13	2.03	Establish the appropriate sample size for a given situation when presented a sample size table
2	2	13	2.03	Describe the dynamic interrelationships between alpha, beta, delta, and sample size from a statistical as well as practical perspective

THE VISION OF SIX SIGMA

eek	Book	Chapt	Session	Champion and MBB Instructional Objectives
2	2	13	2.03	List the 15 essential steps for successfully conducting a statistically based investigation of a practical "real world" problem
2	2	8	2.04	Understand what the t distribution is and how it changes as degrees of freedom is reduced or increased
2	2	14	2.04	Provide a conceptual understanding of what a "statistical confidence interval" is and how it relates to the notion of "random sampling error"
2	2	14	2.04	Understand what the "distribution of sampling averages" is and how it relates to "central limit theorem"
2	2	14	2.04	Explain what the "standard error of the mean" is and demonstrate how it is computed
2	2	14	2.04	Compute the tail area probability for a given Z value which is associated with the distribution of sampling averages
2	2	14	2.04	Compute the 95% confidence interval of the mean for a small data set and explain how it may be applied in practical situations
2	2	14	2.04	Rationalize the difference between a "one-sided test of the mean" and a "two-sided test of the mean"
2	2	14	2.04	Understand what the "distribution of sampling differences" is and how it can be employed for testing statistical hypotheses
	2	14	2.04	Compute the 95% confidence interval for the (null) distribution of sampling differences given data which were randomly selected from two normally
	2	14	2.04	Understand the nature of a one and two sample t test and then apply this test statistic to an appropriate data set
	2	15	2.04	Compute and interpret the 95% confidence interval for a sampling variance using the chi- square distribution
	2	15	2.04	Explain how the 95% confidence interval for a sampling variance can be employed to test the hypothesis that two variances are equal
	2	15	2.04	Understand what the F distribution is and how it can be used to test the hypothesis that two variances are equal
	2	14	2.04	Understand how to compute the standard deviation for a set of data randomly selected from a binomial distribution
	2	14	2.04	Compute the 95% confidence interval for a proportion and explain how it can be used to test hypotheses about proportions
	2	11	2.05	Explain how the competing settings (i.e., levels) associated with an experimental factor can significantly influence the outcome of an experiment
	2	16	2.05	Provide a general description of what a statistically designed experiment is and what such experiments can be used for
	2	16	2.05	Recognize the principal barriers to effective experimentation and outline several tactics which may be employed to overcome such barriers
	2	16	2.05	Describe the two primary components of an experimental system and their related sub- elements
	2	16	2.05	Explain the primary differences between a "random effects model" and a "fixed effects model"

THE VISION OF SIX SIGMA

Week	Book	Chapt	Session	Champion and MBB Instructional Objectives
2	2	16	2.05	Identify the four principal families of experimental designs and what each family of design is used for
2	2	16	2.05	Outline a general strategy for conducting a statistically designed experiment and what resources are required to support its execution and analysis
2	2	16	2.05	Provide a specific explanation of what is meant by the term "confounding" and identify several ways to control for this situation
2	2	16	2.05	Provide a specific explanation of what is meant by the term "blocking variable" and explain when such variables should be employed in an experiment
2	2	16	2.05	Provide a specific explanation of what is meant by the term "replicate" in the context of a statistically designed experiment
2	2	16	2.05	Explain why there is a need to randomize the sequence of order in which an experiment takes place and what can happen when this does not occur
2	2	16	2.05	State the major limitations associated with the "one-factor-at-a-time" approach to experimentation and offer a viable alternative
2	2	16	2.05	Explain how statistically design experiments can be employed to achieve the major aims of Six Sigma from a quality, cost, and cycle time point-of-view
2	2	16	2.05	Recognize that most powerful of modern statistics can not rescue a poorly designed experiment
2	2	16	2.05	Explain what is meant by the term "full factorial experiment" and how it differs from a "fractional factorial experiment"
2	2	17	2.06	Provide a general description of the term "experimental error" and explain how it interrelates to the term "replication"
2	2	17	2.06	Recognize that when the within-treatment replicates are correlated (i.e., dependent) there is an adverse impact on experimental error
2	2	17	2.06	Provide a general description of one-way analysis-of-variance and discuss the role of sample size
2	2	17	2.06	Demonstrate how the total variations in single factor experiment can be characterized analytically and graphically
2	2	17	2.06	Demonstrate how the experimental error (white noise) in an experiment can be "partitioned" from the total error for independent consideration
2	2	17	2.06	Demonstrate how the between group variations (black noise) in an experiment can be "partitioned" from the total error for independent consideration
2	2	17	2.06	Compute the total sums-of-squares, as well as the within treatment and between treatment sums-of-squares for a single factor experiment
2	2	17	2.06	Define how the degrees-of-freedom are established for each source of variation in a single factor experiment
2	2	17	2.06	Organize the sums-of-squares and degrees-of-freedom into an analysis-of-variance (ANOVA) table and compute the mean-square-ratio (MSR)
2	2	17	2.06	Determine the "random sampling error probability" related to any given MSR (i,e, F) value and show how sample size can impact the resultant probability
2	2	17	2.06	List the principal assumptions which underlies the use of ANOVA and provide a general understanding of their practical impact should they be violated

THE VISION OF SIX SIGMA

Week	Book	Chapt	Session	Champion and MBB Instructional Objectives
2	2	17	2.06	Compute all "post-hoc comparisons " (i.e., pair-wise t-tests) in the instance that an F value proves to be statistically significant
2	2	17	2.06	Compute the "relative effect" (i.e., sensitivity) of an experimental factor, interpret the resulting value, create a "main effects" plot, and set tolerances
2	NA	NA	2.06	Explain how a statistically designed single factor experiment can be employed to study and control for the influence of measurement error
2	2	18	2.07	Describe the overriding limitations of the "classical test plan" when two factors are involved and state several advantages of a full factorial design
2	2	18	2.07	Show at least four ways that a two-factor two-level full factorial design matrix can be displayed and/or communicated
2	2	18	2.07	Understand the added value of a "balanced" and "orthogonal" design and the practical implications when these properties are not present
2	2	18	2.07	Explain what is meant by the phrase "hidden replication" and understand that this phenomenon does not preclude the apriori consideration of sample size
2	2	18	2.07	Construct the vectored columns for a two-factor two-level full factorial design given Yate's standard order
2	2	18	2.07	Explain what is meant by the phrase "column contrast" and show how it can be used to establish the factor effect as well as the related sums-of-squares
2	2	18	2.07	Construct and interpret a "main effects plot" as related to a two-factor two-level experiment and display the 95% confidence intervals on the plot
2	2	18	2.07	Construct and interpret an "interaction plot" as related to a two-factor two-level experiment and display the 95% confidence intervals on the plot
2	2	18	2.07	Compute the sums-of-squares associated with each experimental effect as related to a two- factor two-level full factorial experiment
2	2	18	2.07	Create an ANOVA table and compute the MSR for each experimental effect resulting from a two-factor two-level full factorial experiment
2	2	18	2.07	Determine the "random sampling error probability" related to any given MSR (i,e, F) value resulting from a two-factor two-level full factorial experiment
2	2	18	2.07	Compute the relative effect for each experimental effect (which proves to be statistically significant) and display the results on a Pareto chart
2	2	18	2.07	Provide for a center point within a two-factor two-level design and then estimate whether or not any observable curvature is statistically significant
2	2	19	2.07	Design and conduct a two-factor multi-level full factorial experiment and interpret the analytical outcomes from a statistical and practical perspective
2	NA	NA	2.07	Explain how full factorial experiments can be employed to study and control for the influence of measurement error
2	2	20	2.08	Provide a general description of a fractional factorial experiment and the inherent advantages which fractional arrays offer
2	2	20	2.08	Understand why third order and higher effects are most often statistically and/or practically insignificant
2	2	20	2.08	Create a half fraction of a full factorial experiment by sorting the entire matrix on the highest order interaction and then discern the pattern of confounding

THE VISION OF SIX SIGMA

Week	Book	Chapt	Session	Champion and MBB Instructional Objectives
2	2	20	2.08	Recognize how an unreplicated fractional factorial design can be "folded" into a full factorial design with replication
2	2	20	2.08	List the unique attributes associated with fractional factorial designs of resolution III, IV, and V
2	2	20	2.08	Explain what happens to the experimental error term when a factor is "collapsed" out of the design matrix by way of folding
2	2	20	2.08	Explain how Plackett-Burman experiment designs are used and discuss their unique strengths and limitations
2	2	20	2.08	Construct and interpret a "main effects plot" for a fractional factorial design using the response mean as a basis for the plot
2	2	20	2.08	Construct and interpret a "main effects plot" for a fractional factorial design using the response variance as a basis for the plot
2	2	20	2.08	Compute the sums-of-squares associated with each experimental effect as related to an fractional factorial design
2	2	20	2.08	Create an ANOVA table and compute the MSR for each experimental effect resulting from a fractional factorial experiment
2	2	20	2.08	Determine the "random sampling error probability" related to any given MSR (i,e, F) value resulting from a fractional factorial experiment
2	2	20	2.08	Compute the relative effect for each experimental effect (which proves to be statistically significant) and display the results on a Pareto chart
2	NA	NA	2.08	Explain how fractional factorial experiments can be employed to study and control for the influence of measurement error
2	NA	NA	2.08	Utilize the Taguchi orthogonal arrays to study the influence of several key process variables on a given response characteristic
2	2	18	2.09	Explain what is meant by the term "robustness" and explain how this understanding translates to experiment design and performance tolerancing
2	2	18	2.09	Illustrate how a main effects plot, as related to a two-factor two-level experiment, can be used as a basis for tolerancing
2	2	18	2.09	Illustrate how an interaction plot, as related to a two-factor two-level experiment, can be used as a basis for achieving robust performance
2	2	18	2.09	Describe what an "outer array" is in relation to a full or fractional factorial experiment design
2	2	18	2.09	Utilize an "outer array" in conjunction with a factorial experiment so as to desensitize the response variable to the selected independent variable
2	2	18	2.09	Illustrate how an independent variable can be manipulated within an "outer array" of a factorial experiment to yield a robust operating condition
2	2	18	2.09	Provide a statistical explanation of what is meant by the term "heteroscedasticity" and discuss its practical implications
2	2	18	2.09	Illustrate how heteroscedasticity can be leveraged to achieve robust performance
2	2	18	2.09	Illustrate how a nonlinear effect correlates the mean to to the variance and describe how this effect can be leveraged to achieve robust performance

THE VISION OF SIX SIGMA

Week	Book	Chapt	Session	Champion and MBB Instructional Objectives
2	2	22	2.10	Provide a conceptual understanding of each step associated with the general cookbook for control charts
2	2	22	2.10	Explain how the use of rational subgroups forces the nonrandom variations due to assignable causes to appear between sampling periods
2	2	22	2.10	Explain how the control limits of an SPC chart are directly linked to the concepts associated with hypothesis testing
2	2	22	2.10	Construct and interpret an X bar and R chart for as set of normally distributed data organized into rational subgroups
2	2	22	2.10	Construct and interpret an individuals chart for a set of normally distributed data collected over time
2	2	22	2.10	Construct and interpret a P chart and explain how the control limits for this type of chart relates to the confidence intervals of the binomial distribution
2	2	22	2.10	Construct and interpret a U chart and explain how the control limits for this type of chart relates to the Poisson distribution
2	2	22	2.10	Develop a pre-control plan for a given CTQ and explain how such a plan can be implemented
2	NA	NA	2.10	Illustrate how an X bar and R chart can be employed to study measurement error and contrast this technique with that of the DOE/ANOVA method
2	2	22	2.10	Construct and interpret an X bar and R chart for as set of data (organized into rational subgroups) which is not normally distributed within groups
2	2	22	2.10	Construct and interpret an individuals chart for a set of non-normally distributed data collected over time
2	2	22	2.10	Construct and interpret an exponentially weighted moving average chart (EWMA) and highlight its advantages and limitations
2	NA	NA	2.10	Provide a detailed understanding of how to adjust a process parameter using the "method of bracketing" and contrast this technique to other methods
2	2	25	2.11	Provide a general explanation of the chi-square statistic and the conditions under which it can be applied
2	2	25	2.11	Understand how the probability of a given chi-square value can be determined using the chi-square distribution
2	2	25	2.11	Recognize that the chi-square statistic can be employed as a "goodness-of-fit" of test as well as a test of independence
2	2	25	2.11	Understand the nature of "discontinuity" and how to apply Yate's correction to compensate for this effect for the special case of df = 1
2	2	25	2.11	Recognize that the square root of chi-square is exactly equal to Z for the special case of df = 1
2	2	25	2.11	Recognize that the crosstabulation of two classification variables (each of which have two categories) is refereed to as a 2x2 contingency table
2	2	25	2.11	Explain how to establish the degrees of freedom associated with any given contingency table
2	2	25	2.11	Compute the expected "cell frequencies" for any given contingency table and explain the rules governing the use of expected frequencies

THE VISION OF SIX SIGMA

Week	Book	Chapt	Session	Champion and MBB Instructional Objectives
2	2	25	2.11	Provide a general explanation of the chi-square statistic and the conditions under which it can be applied
2	2	25	2.11	Understand how the probability of a given chi-square value can be determined using the chi-square distribution
2	2	25	2.11	Recognize that the chi-square statistic can be employed as a "goodness-of-fit" of test as well as a test of independence
2	2	25	2.11	Understand the nature of "discontinuity" and how to apply Yate's correction to compensate for this effect for the special case of df = 1
2	2	25	2.11	Recognize that the square root of chi-square is exactly equal to Z for the special case of df = 1
2	2	25	2.11	Recognize that the crosstabulation of two classification variables (each of which have two categories) is refereed to as a 2x2 contingency table
2	2	25	2.11	Explain how to establish the degrees of freedom associated with any given contingency table
2	2	25	2.11	Compute the expected "cell frequencies" for any given contingency table and explain the rules governing the use of expected frequencies
2	2	25	2.11	Compute the chi-square statistic for a 2X2 contingency table and then ascertain the probability of chance sampling error (i.e., alpha risk)
2	2	25	2.11	Compute the chi-square statistic for a 2X2 contingency table and then establish the extent of association using the contingency coefficient
2	2	25	2.11	Compute the chi-square statistic for an n-way contingency table and then ascertain the probability of chance sampling error (i.e., alpha risk)
2	2	25	2.11	Provide a general description of a "stratification variable" is and explain how it can be used in conjunction with an n-way crosstabulation
2	2	25	2.11	Illustrate how the chi-square statistic and crosstabulation can be utilized in the design and analysis of surveys
2	2	25	2.11	Explain why survey questions which utilize the 5 point "Likert" scale of measure must often be reduced to two categories during analysis of the data
2	NA	NA	2.11	List and describe the principal sections of a customer satisfaction survey and explain how the sections can be used to link the process to the customer

THE VISION OF SIX SIGMA

σ Six Sigma Academy, Inc.   1 . 36   ®1997 Sigma Consultants, L.L.C.

Understanding Six Sigma

CHAPTER TWO

Breakthrough

Breakthrough

THE VISION OF SIX SIGMA

Some Plain Talk About Six Sigma

World Class Quality

Mikel J. Harry, Ph.D.
Chief Executive Officer
Six Sigma Academy, Inc.
Phoenix, Arizona

Today, focusing on the customer is absolutely essential. Of course, we all recognize this. But do we really internalize the idea? Do we really believe that such a focus has the potential to drive business growth and impact the level of prosperity which we should come to expect?

Closely linked to the idea of customer satisfaction is the concept of operational excellence -- the kingpin of success. Without a focus on excellence, it becomes easy to accept the position of second or third best. Being the best means embracing change and reaching out for new and higher standards of performance. Only then can one break the chains of complacency and pave the way for breakthrough. The attainment of excellence is no longer a lofty goal or ideal, it is now a fundamental requirement -- the ante for entering the game of business.

As most of us already know, Japan has assumed this perspective and steadily acted upon it. The result of their focus has been staggering, as evidenced by their superb products and services, not to mention their tremendous position in the marketplace. Hence, smart money says we must view the idea of operational excellence as a major force in today's marketplace. For those who might doubt such an assertion, just ask a customer what they think. After all, what the customer thinks provides us with a strong indicator of what will be purchased -- and from whom.

Of course, it is widely recognized that the operational performance of an organization is largely determined by the capability of its processes. Another way of looking at this would be to say that our performance as a company is governed by the quality of our processes -- high quality processes delivers high quality products, at the lowest possible cost, on time. Therefore, a focus on operational excellence (in everything we do) translates to a focus on process quality. Of course, we can not focus on what we do not measure and if we do not measure, we can not improve.

Trying to improve something when you don't have a standard to measure against, is like playing a sports game without knowing the score. Can you imagine setting out on cross-country trip in an automobile without a fuel gauge? Just think of the personal grief, cost, and inconvenience which might result. Would you allow yourself to be placed in such a situation?

THE VISION OF SIX SIGMA

Six Sigma Academy, Inc.   2 . 2   ®1997 Sigma Consultants, L.L.C.

As we will discover, the measurement and improvement of our processes is absolutely essential if we are to achieve operational excellence and the ideals of total quality. To do this, we must bear in mind the old axiom -- let the product do the talking. In other words, the quality of our products can tell us how capable our processes really are. To measure product quality is to measure process quality because the two are correlated. It is very important to recognize that the inverse of this also holds true.

Perhaps we should now set the stage for our ensuing discussion by examining what some have called the "chain of causation:"

Our survival is dependent upon growing the business.
Our business growth is largely determined by customer satisfaction.
Customer Satisfaction is governed by quality, price, and delivery.
Quality, price, and delivery are controlled by process capability.
Our process capability is greatly limited by variation.
Process variation leads to an increase in defects, cost, and cycle time.
To eliminate variation, we must apply the right knowledge.
In order to apply the right knowledge, we must first acquire it.
To acquire new knowledge means that we must have the will to survive.

If you can't express something in the form of numbers you don't really know much about it. And if you don't know much about it, you can't control it. And if you can't control it, you're at the mercy of chance. And if you're at the mercy of chance, why bother with it? Hence, we must learn the language of numbers.

Such thinking represents a business philosophy -- a way of guiding our company. From this perspective, we will focus our discussion on an all embracing standard and methodology called "Six Sigma." As we shall see, Six Sigma can be used to measure the quality of our work processes -- in any field, from assembling a motor car to inspiring a classroom full of students.

Over the years, this writer has been asked a great many questions about Six Sigma -- most of which have been quite simple, practical, and straight forward. For the sake of simplicity and reading ease, we shall complement such questions with simple, practical, and straight forward answers. Of course, we recognize that more sophisticated and detailed answers do exist, as many students of Six Sigma will testify. However, there is no point in hooking-up a fire hose when all we want is a glass of water.

QUESTION: What is Six Sigma?

ANSWER: Six Sigma is several things. First, it is a statistical measurement. It tells us how good our products, services, and processes really are. The Six Sigma method allows us to draw comparisons to other similar or dissimilar products, services, and processes. In this manner, we can see how far ahead or behind we are. Most importantly, we can see where we need to go and what we must do to get there. In other words, Six Sigma helps us to establish our course and gauge our pace in the race for total customer satisfaction.

THE VISION OF SIX SIGMA

σ Six Sigma Academy, Inc.   2.3   ®1997 Sigma Consultants, L.L.C.

For example, when we say a process is 6 sigma, we are saying it is best-in-class. Such a level of capability will only yield about 3 instances of nonconformance out of every million opportunities for nonconformance. On the other hand, when we say that some other process is 4 sigma, we are saying it is average. This translates to about 6,200 nonconformities-per-million-opportunities for nonconformance. In this sense, the sigma scale of measure provides us with a "goodness micrometer" for gauging the adequacy of our products, services, and processes.

Second, Six Sigma is a business strategy. It can greatly help us gain a competitive edge. The reason for this is very simple -- as you improve the sigma rating of a process, the product quality improves and costs go down. Naturally, the customer becomes more satisfied as a result.

Third, Six Sigma is a philosophy. It is an outlook, a way that we perceive and work within the business world around us. Essentially, the philosophy is one of working smarter, not harder. This translates to making fewer and fewer mistakes in everything we do -- from the way we manufacture products to the way we fill out a purchase order. As we discover and neutralize harmful sources of variation, our sigma rating goes up. Again, this means that our process capability improves and the defects (mistakes) go away.

QUESTION: Can the Six Sigma approach be used as a benchmark to measure the capability of any work activity? If so, how does one apply the same system of measurement to, say, manufacturing a transformer or filling out a purchase order?

ANSWER: Yes, the Six Sigma approach allows us to benchmark any work activity. For example, if we were to say that a transformer is 3 sigma, this would characterize the product as having below average quality, because we know (from extensive benchmarking) that the average product, irrespective of complexity, is about four sigma -- with best-in-class at around six sigma.

The same can be said for filling out a purchase order. In this case, the order form itself is a unit of product and the number of boxes to fill in constitutes the number of opportunities for error, where an error is an incorrect or unreadable entry. With this information, the sigma level can be determined.

As you can see, the sigma scale of measure can be universally applied because the common denominator is defects-per-unit, where a unit can be, literally, any kind of task or physical entity -- an hour of classroom instruction, a customer's invoice, a person at a barber shop, a part on a machine, etc. Also recognize that an "opportunity " is anything on, within, or connected to the "unit" which must be right. Thus, an "opportunity for error or defect" is anything which would be considered undesirable.

As should now be apparent, the first step toward improving the sigma capability of a process is defining what the customers' expectations are. Next, you "map" the process by which you get the work done to meet those expectations. This means that you create a "box diagram" of the process flow; i.e., identifying the steps within the process. With this done, you can now affix success criteria to each of the steps.

THE VISION OF SIX SIGMA

Next, you would want to record the number of times each of the given success criteria is not met and calculate the total defects-per-unit (TDPU). Following this, the TDPU information is converted to defects-per-opportunity (DPO) which, in turn, is translated into a sigma value (σ). Now, you are ready to make direct comparisons -- even apples and oranges if you want.

Once the comparison is completed, you should ask the following question: "Why is the best-in-class characteristic better than the rest?" If the answer is obvious, then go for it; otherwise, you must track down the sources of variation and then implement a logical scheme of variation reduction. Following this, you should verify the fix and get on to the next big issue. Of course, you would want to keep repeating this cycle until the customer smiles again. When the smiles test reveals the warm glow of lips turned upward, keep doing it because it may not stay that way.

QUESTION: Give an example of how the sigma system could be applied to the activities of a teacher, for instance?

ANSWER: Let us first recognize that a teacher provides a unit of product to their students. Consequently, we could view this as a customer-supplier relationship. Naturally, the delivered product is knowledge. In this case, we would want to measure the quality of the knowledge transfer process because we know that an improvement in the process will translate into improved grades. Thus, the customer sees added value. Of course, the success criteria is given by the traditional grading scale -- be that good or bad, as the case may be.

Based on the grades and the number of steps in the instructional process, we might discover that one of the two teachers is operating a 4 sigma instructional process. This would be to say the 4 sigma teacher will make 6,210 instructional mistakes per million opportunities for process error, on the average. In contrast, we might know the other teacher is 3 sigma. This would translate to 68,807 instructional mistakes per million opportunities for process error. Notice the difference between the two teachers. From the facts, it is obvious - the process of the 4 sigma teacher is over 10 times more error free.

QUESTION: But a teacher can't be only measured against exam results. How does one measure things like enthusiasm, transference of the desire to learn, and so on?

ANSWER: A simple statement explains it all. If you can't express something in the form of numbers, you don't really know much about it. And if you don't know much about it, you can't control it. And if you can't control it, you're at the mercy of chance. and if you're at the mercy of chance, why bother with it?

More directly, a questionnaire can be created to surface subjective ratings. For example, one of the survey items could be worded as follows: My work environment is stimulating. Given this statement, the students would rate their feelings on a one to five scale - strongly agree to strongly disagree.

THE VISION OF SIX SIGMA

Six Sigma Academy, Inc.   2 . 5   ®1997 Sigma Consultants, L.L.C.

Yet another statement could be: Do you feel you have a "say" in what goes on in class? Here again, the students would rate the extent to which they agree or disagree with the statement, depending on the number they put after it.

By breaking things into elements, and breaking each element into behavioral questions, people can give a pretty accurate rating. If the scores of several people are grouped together, the results of analysis are even more precise, owing to the law of large numbers. Of course, once you have the numbers, computing the TDPU and DPO is quite easy.

QUESTION: There are other systems for measuring work quality. What makes the Six Sigma approach so good?

ANSWER: First, other systems for measuring quality have traditionally focused on the cost of quality, but with Six Sigma, the belief is that quality is free, in that the more you work towards zero-defect production, the more return on investment you'll have.

Every time you track down a harmful source of variation and eradicate it, you eliminate the related defects, decrease cost, and improve cycle time. Why? Because it takes time and resources to detect, analyze, and fix a defect. In fact, benchmarking has shown that, for the typical 4 sigma company, the cost due to internal and external repair exceeds 10% of revenues. In many cases, it is as high as 30%.

If you are operating on an 8% profit margin, and someone can undercut you by 10% or more, how long will you be in business? Simply stated, a focus on cost-of-quality will lead an organization to the conclusion that to go beyond 4 sigma is not cost effective. Of course, such a perspective is "penny-wise and pound-foolish." Thus, stagnation and complacency sets in and the 4 sigma company will remain just that, average.

Second, the Six Sigma method allows us to reduce things to a common denominator -- defects-per-unit and sigma. In turn, this provides us with a common language and the ability to benchmark ourselves against like products, processes, and practices. Only then can we discover new ways of doing things that help the business. Of course, the alternative is to wait for people within the company to invent new things -- we must take advantage of the superior practices that already exist. Following this, we can transfer those methods, practices, and technologies back into our business areas. In a nutshell, this is the way of Six Sigma.

QUESTION: What constitutes quality?

ANSWER: Quality is when the customer is totally satisfied. That's the overriding objective. Who is the customer? Someone who buys from us. What is satisfaction? Satisfaction is the extent of certainty which the customer has that their quality, reliability, performance, delivery, and cost standards will be met. How much certainty is needed? Until exceptional quality becomes an everyday expectation in the eyes of the customer -- until near-perfection is a habit on our part. Here again, this translates to operational excellence.

QUESTION: It's interesting that the criterion for measuring quality is the customer, not the thing itself. Can more be said about this?

ANSWER: We're talking quality control versus quality assurance. Quality control is *a posteriori* (after the fact). It's like a boat. You can steer a boat by looking at the wake - that's 'control' and it results after the fact - or you can steer by looking ahead - that's 'assurance' and constitutes what will happen if we keep going in same direction.

In the process of benchmarking, we discovered a typical company is around four sigma, a world class company is at six sigma. Based on such information, things become crystal clear - to compete in a world market, companies have to move toward a 6 sigma level of operational performance. But here again, you don't know what you don't know. If you are not measuring your performance on a level playing field, you don't know how you compare to those around you or rest of the world. Let's face it, if you don't know how you compare, it is easier and less costly to be complacent.

QUESTION: How big a difference, in practical terms, is there between 3 and 6 sigma?

ANSWER: Three sigma would be equivalent to one misspelled work per 15 pages of text. Six sigma would be equivalent to one misspelled word per 300,000 pages, quite a difference indeed. Now, let's put this in real world terms. Some corporations are already running at six sigma. It is self-evident they're going to perform better over the long haul. For example, several of the prestigious Japanese companies (which are doing so well in the world marketplace) are currently running at or near the 6 sigma level.

QUESTION: Many companies have been benchmarked against the 6 sigma standard, is there much difference between nations?

ANSWER: Within the US and Europe, we most often observe a 4 sigma level of operational performance, but in Japan, the attainment of 6 sigma is not uncommon.

In some areas we already have a high level of quality. The airline fatality rate is about 6.5 sigma, but airline baggage handling is about 4 sigma. Both of those areas have processes attached to them. So why is there a difference between the way your baggage is handled versus the way your life is handled? The answer is self-evident. There's a certain amount of tolerance which management has in regard to quality. If peoples' lives are at stake, you can well bet the quality will be there, but if it's just a suitcase, there is less focus. After all, a suitcase is relatively cheap and can easily be replaced -- so goes the reasoning.

When a company has its great awakening, when it realizes it is a 3 to 4 sigma organization, and has to move to six sigma, it will improve the processes by which it does its work. It all goes back to that spelling analogy. If you have to improve your quality from one misspelled word per page to one error in 300,000 pages, it won't help much to just polish up what you're doing already. You need breakthrough thinking, new paradigms, to achieve a significant improvement in process capability. In short, you must change the process. Of course, this assumes that we are first willing to change the way we think. Only then will the "do" side of things change.

THE VISION OF SIX SIGMA

σ Six Sigma Academy, Inc.   2.7   ® 1997 Sigma Consultants, L.L.C.

QUESTION: So, how does an organization put into practice the Six Sigma paradigm?

ANSWER: When an organization asks people for a 10-20 percent improvement in process capability, that's what they give. When the bar is raised to a ten-fold improvement, or even hundred-fold improvement, there are often a lot of bewildered people. Comments of, "That's impossible!" But when two or three business units achieve the quantum improvement, other managers tend to visit those facilities, study them, and transfer the beneficial practices, methods, and technology back to their own workplace.

Organizations can achieve a hundred-fold improvement and it can be done so long as they focus on the process by which they do work and maintain a never ending focus on total quality. This is the path to total customer satisfaction and business prosperity.

QUESTION: It clearly isn't enough just to urge employees to drastic levels of improvement. You have to examine the process by which you work, then involve the staff in finding out how the existing process is failing, and how it can be improved. Is this correct?

ANSWER: That's right. Empowered people (with the necessary mind tools and leadership) have the control they need to improve the way they work. Interaction, participatory management practices, the notion of empowerment, an emphasis on cycle time, and significantly higher levels of expectation in terms of process performance. These are the keys to competitiveness in the world market.

QUESTION: Can equally significant improvements be made in non-manufacturing areas?

ANSWER: Six sigma is applicable in everything we do. It can be used for such diverse tasks as cutting down on the time it takes to process a patent or decrease the cycle time of designs. In addition, Six Sigma is employed to improve the cost of those designs and concurrently enhance manufacturability.

QUESTION: What is meant by that?

ANSWER: Simple. By configuring designs to be tolerant of manufacturing and material variations, we know they can be easily manufactured when it comes time to go into production. Of course, at the same time, the products will be less costly to produce because the designs will be able to utilize less expensive components and material.

QUESTION: That's very interesting. When we talk of the quality of a product, most people assume this means higher quality components, more time spent on welding, or whatever. Does this mean an organization can make a component cheaper and please the customer more?

ANSWER: Yes. Interestingly, the first reaction most companies have when trying to increase their sigma rating is to go out and beat up on suppliers, strive for better and better components, or inspect more. Sooner or later, these companies realize that 6 sigma won't result from a sole focus on suppliers or by better inspection and sorting. They can not get there by "tightening up the tolerances." As a consequence of such revelations, they slowly begin to focus on the capability of the related processes - of all types - everything they do. When breakthrough happens, the success story spreads like a forest fire in high winds.

THE VISION OF SIX SIGMA

The Many Facets of Six Sigma

- ■ **Metric**
- ■ **Benchmark**
- ■ **Vision**
- ■ **Philosophy**
- ■ **Method**
- ■ **Tool**
- ■ **Symbol**
- ■ **Goal**
- ■ **Value**

Sigma is a letter in the Greek alphabet.

The term "sigma" is used to designate the distribution or spread about the mean (average) of any process or procedure.

For a business or manufacturing process, the sigma value is a metric that indicates how well that process is performing. The higher the sigma value, the better. Sigma measures the capability of the process to perform defect-free-work. A defect is anything that results in customer dissatisfaction.

With six sigma, the common measurement index is 'defects-per-unit," where a unit can be virtually anything -- a component, piece of material, line of code, administrative form, time frame, distance, etc.

The sigma value indicates how often defects are likely to occur. The higher the sigma value, the less likely a process will produce defects. As sigma increases, costs go down, cycle time goes down, and customer satisfaction goes up.

THE VISION OF SIX SIGMA

σ Six Sigma Academy, Inc.   2.9   ®1997 Sigma Consultants, L.L.C.

Six Sigma as a Philosophy

We are in business to make money
We make money by satisfying needs
We are able to satisfy needs by doing
Every need/do pair is an interaction
The aim of customer focus is on improving need/do interactions
Repetition of the same action constitutes a process
Improvement our business means improvement of our processes
Customers need products/services on-time, with zero defects, at the lowest cost
Suppliers create processes to generate needed products
As process capability improves, the product quality increases
As quality increases, costs and cycle-time go down
The attributes of customer satisfaction must be measured if they are to be improved
To improve means we must be able to predict and prevent, not detect and react
Prediction is correlated to certainty
Maximization of certainty is dependent upon the measurement of process capability
Process capability is best understood and reported using statistics
Statistics are dependent upon data
Data must be collected in the process according to a plan
Statistial analysis is used to convert raw data into meaningful summary information
Statistical information is used to report on, improve, and control the process
The basis of statistics is the mean and standard deviation
The mean reports on process centering
The standard deviation reports the extent of variation or "scatter" about the mean
By combining the mean and standard deviation, the "sigma" of a process can be calculated
The "sigma" of a process tells us how capable it is
The process sigma can be used to compare similar or dissimilar processes
Such comparison of processes is called benchmarking
Benchmarking is a competitive tool used to uncover what we do well and not so good
Once basic competencies and deficiencies are know, corrective action can be taken
Corrective action leads to the reduction of defects, cycle-time, and cost
The reduction of defects, cycle-time, and cost leads to improved customer satisfaction
As customer satisfaction improves, the likelihood of doing business increases
As business increases, we (as individuals) grow and prosper

THE VISION OF SIX SIGMA

The Classical View of Performance

Practical Meaning of "99% Good"

- ☛ **20,000 lost articles of mail per hour**
- ☛ **Unsafe drinking water almost 15 minutes each day**
- ☛ **5,000 incorrect surgical operations per week**
- ☛ **2 short or long landings at most major airports each day**
- ☛ **200,000 wrong drug prescriptions each year**
- ☛ **No electricity for almost 7 hours each month**

	Long-Term Yield	
3σ Capability	**93.32%**	**Historical Standard**
4σ Capability	**99.38%**	**Current Standard**
6σ Capability	**99.99966%**	**New Standard**

THE VISION OF SIX SIGMA

σ Six Sigma Academy, Inc.   2.11   ®1997 Sigma Consultants, L.L.C.

Understanding the Differences

| 3σ Capability | Historical Standard |

| 4σ Capability | Current Standard |

| 6σ Capability | New Standard |

SIGMA	AREA	SPELLING	MONEY	TIME	DISTANCE
3σ	Floor space of a small hardware store	1.5 misspelled words per page in a book	$2.7 million indebtedness per $1 billion in assets	3 1/2 months per century	Coast-to-coast trip
4σ	Floor space of a typical living room	1 misspelled word per 30 pages in a book	$63,000 indebtedness per $1 billion in assets	2 1/2 days per century	45 minutes of freeway driving (in any direction)
5σ	Size of the bottom of your telephone	1 misspelled word in a set of encyclopedias	$570 indebtedness per $1 billion in assets	30 minutes per century	A trip to the local gas station
6σ	Size of a typical diamond	1 misspelled word in all of the books contained in a small library	$2 indebtedness per $1 billion assets	6 seconds per century	4 steps in any directions

THE VISION OF SIX SIGMA

σ Six Sigma Academy, Inc.   2 . 12   ®1997 Sigma Consultants, L.L.C.

Six Sigma as a Goal

(Distribution Shifted ± 1.5σ)

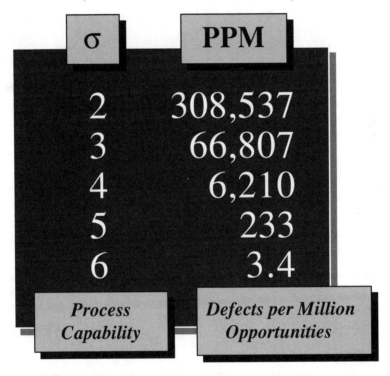

σ	PPM
2	308,537
3	66,807
4	6,210
5	233
6	3.4

Process Capability   *Defects per Million Opportunities*

Sigma is a statistical unit of measure which reflects process capability. The sigma scale of measure is perfectly correlated to such characteristics as defects-per-unit, parts-per million defective, and the probability of a failure/error

THE VISION OF SIX SIGMA

σ Six Sigma Academy, Inc.   2 . 13   ®1997 Sigma Consultants, L.L.C.

Statistical Definition of Six Sigma

Distribution Centered

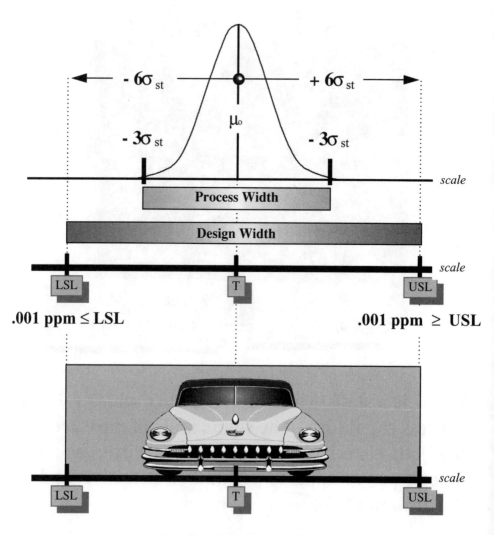

THE VISION OF SIX SIGMA

σ Six Sigma Academy, Inc.   2.14   ®1997 Sigma Consultants, L.L.C.

Statistical Definition of Six Sigma

Distribution Shifted 1.5σ

*This example shows a 1.5σshift which is positive in direction
(i.e., to the right). In practice, the shift could also be
negative; however, shift can not be both directions
simultaneously. It is one way or the other but not both.*

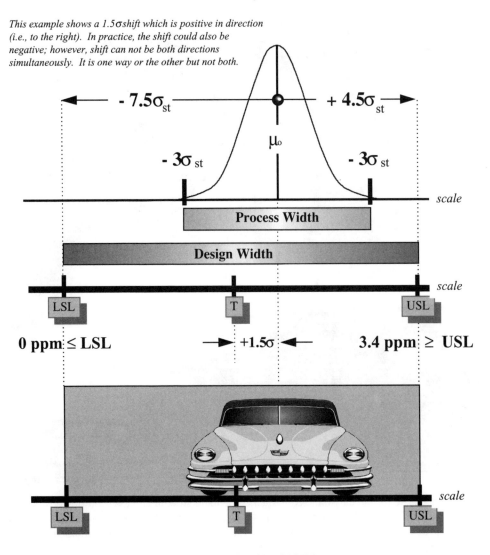

Six Sigma Academy, Inc.   2 . 15   ®1997 Sigma Consultants, L.L.C.

Understanding the Shift Factor

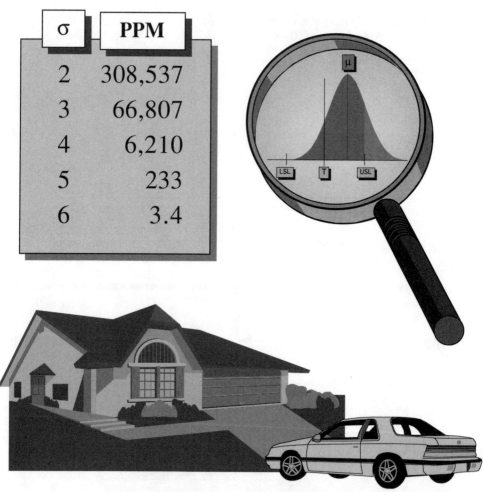

σ	PPM
2	308,537
3	66,807
4	6,210
5	233
6	3.4

To compensate for the inevitable consequences associated with process centering errors, the distribution mean is off-set by 1.5 standard deviations. This adjustment provides a more realistic idea of what the process capability will be over a many cycles of manufacturing.

 Six Sigma Academy, Inc.   2 . 16   ®1997 Sigma Consultants, L.L.C.

The Magnitude of Difference

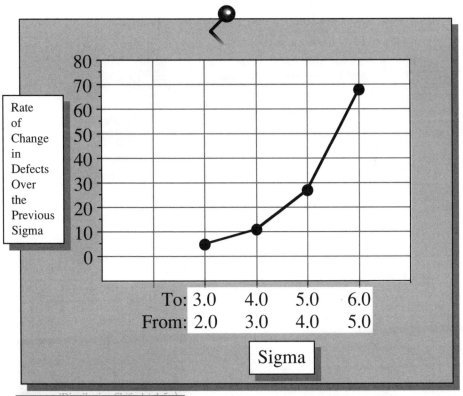

Rate of Change in Defects Over the Previous Sigma

To:	3.0	4.0	5.0	6.0
From:	2.0	3.0	4.0	5.0

Sigma

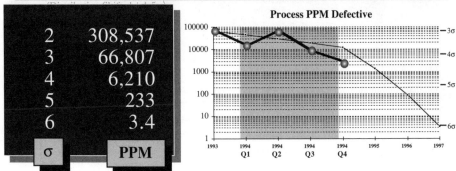

σ	PPM
2	308,537
3	66,807
4	6,210
5	233
6	3.4

Process PPM Defective

THE VISION OF SIX SIGMA

Understanding the Difference

Suppose a process produced 294,118
units of product. If the process
capability was 4σ, then the defects
produced could be represented by the
matrix of dots given below. If the
capability was 6σ, only one dot would
appear in the entire matrix. How big
would this matrix be if the process
capability was 3σ?

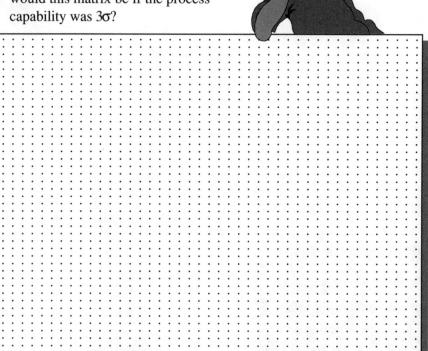

4σ Capability: Defect Dots = 1849
6σ Capability: Defect Dots =   1

Primary Sources of Variation

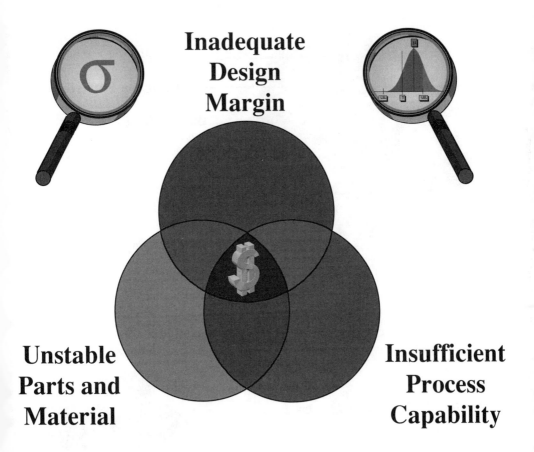

Inadequate
Design
Margin

Unstable
Parts and
Material

Insufficient
Process
Capability

Region of Six Sigma Synergy

THE VISION OF SIX SIGMA

σ Six Sigma Academy, Inc.   2 . 19   ®1997 Sigma Consultants, L.L.C.

Harvesting the Fruit of Six Sigma

Sweet Fruit
Design for Manufacturability

Process Entitlement

Bulk of Fruit
*Process Characterization
and Optimization*

Low Hanging Fruit
Seven Basic Tools

Ground Fruit
Logic and Intuition

We don't know what we don't know
We can't act on what we don't know
We won't know until we search
We won't search for what we don't question
We don't question what we don't measure
Hence, We just don't know

 Six Sigma Academy, Inc.   2 . 20

The Components of Breakthrough

Process Characterization is concerned with the identification and benchmarking of key product characteristics. By way of a gap analysis, common success factors are identified .

Process Optimization is aimed at the identification and containment of those process variables which exert undue influence over the key product characteristics.

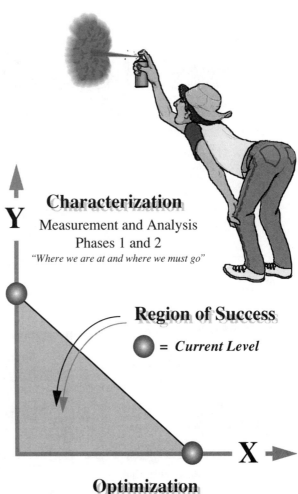

Characterization
Measurement and Analysis
Phases 1 and 2
"Where we are at and where we must go"

Region of Success

● = *Current Level*

Optimization
Improvement and Control
Phases 3 and 4
"What action we must take to get and stay there"

 Six Sigma Academy, Inc.   2.21   ®1997 Sigma Consultants, L.L.C.

The Application Roadmap

A Six Sigma Black Belt leads a Customer Focus Team through each of the breakthrough phases with respect to their "line of sight" process.

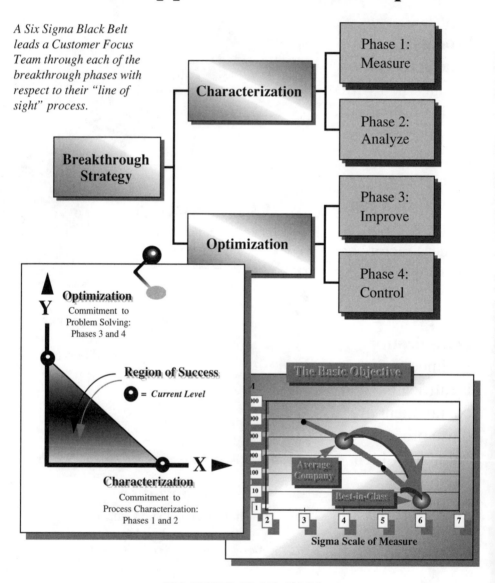

THE VISION OF SIX SIGMA

σ Six Sigma Academy, Inc.   2 . 22   ®1997 Sigma Consultants, L.L.C.

The Application Tactics

Factory XYZ	Measure	Analyze	Improve	Control
Plan				
Tools				
Procedures				
Training				
Application				
Review				

Who   Where
What   Why
When   How

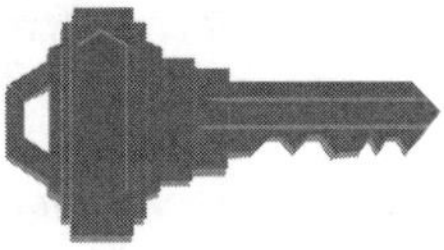

Foundation of the Tools

Data is derived from objects, situtations, or phenomena in the form of measurements.

Data is used to classify, describe, improve , or control objects, situtations, or phenomena.

Levels of Analysis:

1. We only use experience, not data.

2. We collect data, but just look at the numbers.

3. We group the data so as to form charts and graphs.

4. We use census data with descriptive statistics.

5. We use sample data with descriptive statistics.

6. We use sample data with inferential statistics.

Cost, likelihood of improvement, ability to generalize, depth of understanding, quality of knowledge and complexity increase as the level of analysis increases. So how far should we go with this stuff? "After all, I just want to lower my costs, please the customer some more . . . you know, so I can stay in business and all that stuff." Why is there such a strong emphasis on data? "I mean, I've been successful so far and we don't take a lot of measurements!" Why should I start now?

Six Sigma as a Benchmark

Which Process is Performing the Best ?

Issue	Process A Before	Process A After	Process B Before	Process B After
Yield	95%	96%	85%	87%
DPU	.0513	.0408	.1625	.1393
Steps	83	83	286	286
Step DPU	.0006	.0005	.0006	.0005
Step Yield	.9994	.9995	.9994	.9995
Sigma	4.73	4.80	4.75	4.80

Six Sigma Academy, Inc.   2 . 25   ®1997 Sigma Consultants, L.L.C.

Six Sigma as a Value

What does a Six Sigma organization look like?

Focus

Issue	Classical	Six Sigma
Analytical Perspective	Point Estimate	Variability
Management	Cost & Time	Quality & Time
Manufacturability	Trial & Error	Robust Design
Tolerancing	Worst Case	Root-Sum-of-Squares
Variable Search	One-Factor-at-a-Time	Design of Experiments
Process Adjustment	Tweeking	SPC Charts
Problems	Fixing	Preventing
Problem Solving	Expert Based	System Based
Analysis	Experience	Data
Focus	Product	Process
Behavior	Reactive	Proactive
Suppliers	Cost	Relative Capability
Reasoning	Experience Based	Statistically Based
Outlook	Short-Term	Long-Term
Decision Making	Intuition	Probability
Approach	Symptomatic	Problematic
Design	Performance	Producibility
Aim	Company	Customer
Organization	Authority	Learning
Training	Luxury	Necessity
Chain-of-Command	Heirarchy	Empowered Teams
Direction	Seat-of-Pants	Benchmarking & Metrics
Goal Setting	Realistic Perception	Reach-Out & Stretch
People	Cost	Asset
Control	Centralized	Localized
Improvement	Automation	Optimization

THE VISION OF SIX SIGMA

Periods of Implementation

Period	Motorola	Texas Instr.	ABB
1 Enlightenment	1985	1991	1993
2 Acceptance	1986	1992	1994
3 Tools	1987	1993	1995
4 Deployment	1988	1994	1996
5 Results	1989	1995	1997
6 Renewal	1990	1996	1998

The Chemistry of Six Sigma

6σ

A means to link values with actions which, in turn, sets improvement in motion.

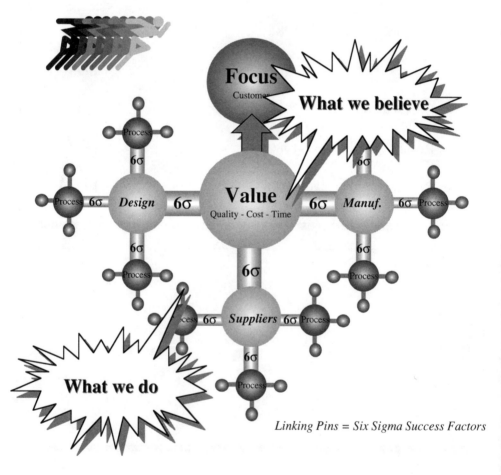

Linking Pins = Six Sigma Success Factors

THE VISION OF SIX SIGMA

σ   Six Sigma Academy, Inc.   2 . 28   ®1997 Sigma Consultants, L.L.C.

The Six Sigma Success Factors

Six Sigma Champions

Business Metrics

Common Process Metrics

Benchmarking

Stretch-Goals

Breakthrough Strategy

Six Sigma Black-Belts

Success Stories

Experiment Design & SPC

Quality and Time Focus

Design-for-Manufacturability Methods

Quality Policy and Deployment

Quality Council and Associate Membership

Empowered High-Performance Work Teams

THE VISION OF SIX SIGMA

Six Sigma and the Organization

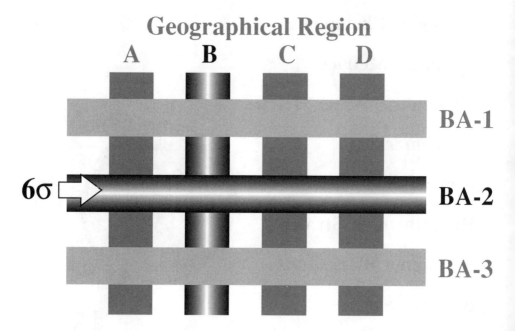

Six Sigma must be **pulled** when implementing across a Business Area, or "common product"

Six Sigma must be **pushed** when implementing in a Geographical Region.

Six Sigma should be used as a **strategy** for increasing customer focus which, in turn, drives the need for Six Sigma.

THE VISION OF SIX SIGMA

σ Six Sigma Academy, Inc.   2 . 30   ®1997 Sigma Consultants, L.L.C.

Structural Role of Six Sigma

Six Sigma is a means to realize the philosophy and values associated with Total Quality Management (TQM)

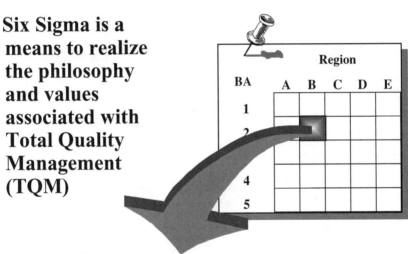

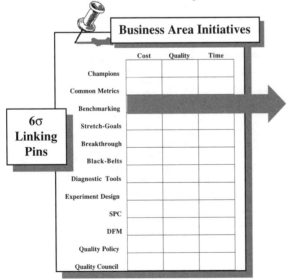

Six Sigma cuts across all of the key initiatives within any given factory. It unifies the initiatives and provides a common language which all people can understand and speak.

Six Sigma Artifacts

Six Sigma Artifacts

1	2 Level Fractional Factorial Designs	53	Multivari Charts
2	2 Level Full Factorial Designs	54	N Level Pareto Analysis
3	3 Level Fractional Factorial Designs	55	Non-Parametric Tests
4	3 Level Full Factorial Design	56	Normalized Yield
5	Advanced Control Charts	57	NP Chart
6	Analysis of Covariance	58	One Level Pareto Analysis
7	Analysis of Variance	59	OR Programming Methods
8	Attribute Sampling Plans	60	Outer Arrays
9	Autocorrelation	61	P Chart
10	B vs C Test	62	Parts-per-Million Defective
11	Bar Charts	63	Performance Metrics Manual
12	C Chart	64	Physical Models
13	Chi Square Methods	65	Pie Charts
14	Component Interchange	66	Positrol Logs
15	Continuous Sampling Plans	67	Pp
16	Control Chart Methods	68	Ppk
17	Correlation Studies	69	Precontrol
18	Cp	70	Process FMEA
19	Cpk	71	Product FMEA
20	Cross Tabulation Methods	72	R Charts
21	Cube Plots	73	Random Sampling
22	CUMSUM Charts	74	Random Strategy Designs
23	Customer Feedback Surveys	75	Realistic Tolerancing
24	Defect Probability	76	Reference Capability Data Base
25	Defects per Million Opportunities	77	Regression
26	Defects per Unit	78	Response Surface Designs
27	Distribution Goodness-of-Fit	79	Rolled Throughput Yield
28	EVOP Designs	80	RSS Analysis
29	EWMA Charts	81	S Charts
30	F Tests	82	Sequential Sampling
31	Finite Element Analysis	83	Single Factor Experiments
32	Fractional Factorials with Outer Arrays	84	Six Sigma Objective
33	Full Factorials with Outer Arrays	85	Specialized Attribute Index
34	Goals Based on Process Entitlement	86	Specialized Control Charts
35	GR&R Control Chart Method	87	Specialized Variables Index
36	GR&R Statistical DOE	88	Statistical Software Package
37	Histograms	89	t Tests
38	I-MR Charts	90	Taguchi Designs
39	Improvement Learning Curves	91	Time Series Analysis
40	Indices of Central Tendency	92	U Chart
41	Indices of Variability	93	Variable Search Techniques
42	Individual Charts	94	Xbar Charts
43	Interaction Plots	95	Yield Charts
44	Line Charts	96	Z transform
45	MA Charts	97	Z.lt
46	Main Effect Plots	98	Z.shift
47	Mathematical Models	99	Z.st
48	Mixture Designs	100	Zone Tests
49	Monte Carlo Simulation		
50	MR Charts		
51	Multi-Level Fractional Factorial Designs		
52	Multi-Level Full Factorial Designs		

THE VISION OF SIX SIGMA

The Classical Artifacts

Classical   Artifacts

1	Arbitrary Improvement Objectives	50	Process Documents
2	Arbitrary Sampling	51	Process Reengineering
3	Automated Data Acquisition	52	Process Simplification
4	Automation Controls	53	Product Tree (Denoted)
5	Calibration Certifications	54	Qualitative Interpretation
6	Cause & Effect Matrix	55	Quality Audits
7	Centralized Data Base	56	Quality Function Deployment
8	Certification	57	Quality Information Package
9	Computer Data Base	58	Quality Program Documents
10	Continuous Data	59	Routine Data Acquisition
11	Customer Documents	60	Rules of Thumb
12	Customer Surveys	61	Sporadic Data Acquisition
13	Defect Data	62	Stationary Data Base
14	Design Simplification	63	Structured Brainstorming
15	Discrete Data	64	Test Certification
16	Distributed Data Base	65	Training
17	Engineering Changes	66	Trial and Error
18	Engineering Documents	67	Vendor Feedback Surveys
19	Engineering Drawing	68	Vendor Recommendations
20	Engineering Guidelines	69	Vendor Specification Sheets
21	Engineering Specifications	70	Worst Case Analysis
22	Expert Judgment		
23	Fault Insertion Methods		
24	Fishbone Diagrams		
25	Focused Brainstorming		
26	Graphing Package		
27	Handbooks		
28	Industry Standards		
29	Inspection and Test Procedures		
30	Inspection History Files		
31	Inspector Certification		
32	Inspector Training		
33	Internal Correspondence		
34	Internally Defined		
35	Literature Reviews		
36	Machine Data Sheets		
37	Manual Data Acquisition		
38	Measurement Training		
39	Military Standards		
40	New Product Introduction Process		
41	Operator Certification		
42	Operator Training		
43	Paper Data Base		
44	Part Reduction		
45	Past Practice		
46	Poke-a-Yoke Methods		
47	Previous Drawings		
48	Procedure Documents		
49	Process Audits		

Six Sigma Executive Briefing

The Six Sigma Executive Briefing has been specifically designed for executives, managers, and supporting staff personnel. The briefing is 8 hours in duration and will provide an in-depth overview of the fundamental strategies, tactics, and tools necessary for achieving Six Sigma product designs, manufacturing processes, service quality, quality of administration. Specifically, participants of the Six Sigma Executive Briefing will discover:

The Driving Need for Six Sigma Quality

The Fundamental Objective of Six Sigma

The Basic Tenets of Six Sigma Quality

Key Business Conclusions Resulting From Global Benchmarking

Six Sigma as a Target for Total Quality Management (TQM)

The Primary Tools for Achieving Six Sigma

The Customer's Perspective of Six Sigma

The Financial Impact of Six Sigma on the Bottom Line

Strategies and Tactics for Implementing Six Sigma

Advanced Six Sigma Concepts

The Impact of Product and Process Complexity on Quality

The Impact of Six Sigma on Product Reliability

The Impact of Six Sigma on Manufacturing Cycle-Time

The Impact of Six Sigma on Inventory

Developing Six Sigma Suppliers

How to Create and Maintain Six Sigma Product Designs

How to Create and Maintain Six Sigma Manufacturing Processes

How to Create and Maintain Six Sigma Services

In addition, several "real life" case studies will be presented and thoroughly discussed. The cases are configured to clearly illustrate many of the "how to's" with respect to selected Six Sigma implementation strategies and application practices. In particular, the cases will highlight the results which were achieved and how the Six Sigma practices were embodied and institutionalized within the organization.

THE VISION OF SIX SIGMA

σ Six Sigma Academy, Inc.   2 . 34   ®1997 Sigma Consultants, L.L.C.

Customer Focus

CHAPTER THREE

Breakthrough

Breakthrough

THE VISION OF SIX SIGMA

Customer-to-Customer Circle

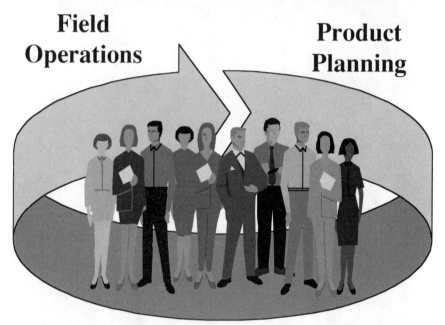

Customer Satisfaction

Field Operations

Product Planning

Manufacturing

Product Development

Quality, Cost, & Delivery

The Customer-Supplier Relationship

Deriving value from the Need - Do interaction

Customers and Suppliers
Exchange Value
through a
Need-Do Interaction.

The task for both customer and supplier is to
maximize the value derived from this interaction.

Maximizing the Interaction

Supplier   Customer

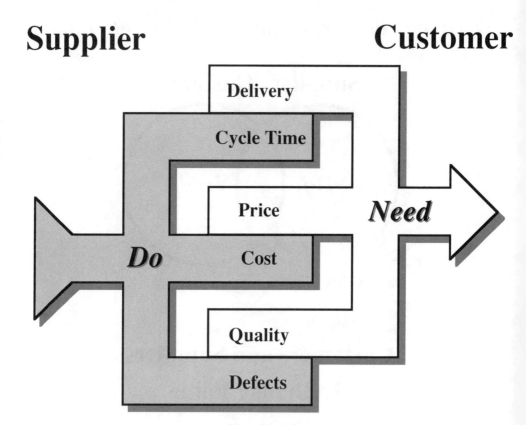

Supplier strives for performance on *Cycle Time, Cost and Defects* to meet Customers' increasing expectations on *Delivery, Price and Quality.*

σ Six Sigma Academy, Inc.   3 . 4   ®1997 Sigma Consultants, L.L.C.

Definition of Customer Satisfaction

cus'tom•er, *n* [O Fr. *coustumier*, L.L. *custumarius*, custom.]
1. a person who buys, especially one who buy regularly.
2. a person with whom one has to deal

sat•is•fac'tion, *n* [O Fr., from L. *satisfaction* (-onis), from *satisfactus*, pp. of *satisfacere*, to satisfy.]
1. to gratify fully the wants or desires of; to supply to the full extent.
2. to free from doubt, suspense, or uncertainty; to give full assurance to.
3. to comply with (rules or standards).

Embedded within these definitions are two key ideas. First, the notion that the **customer** is a person, not an organization, corporation, etc. Second, the idea that satisfaction is the extent of **certainty** a person [customer] has that the standards will be met. Naturally, this would imply that as certainty increases, the likelihood of satisfaction would likewise increase.

Establishing the Focus

Quality

Performance to the standard expected by the customer.

Customer

Anyone internal or external to the organization who comes in contact with the product or output of my work.

Anyone who's success or satisfaction depends on my actions.

Source: "Total Quality Leadership: A Path To Excellence," AlliedSignal Inc., Morristown NJ.

 Six Sigma Academy, Inc.   3.6   ®1997 Sigma Consultants, L.L.C.

The Gap in Perspectives

What Makes a Good Coffee Service?

Supplier Perspective (Hotel)	Customer Perspective (Conference Attendees)
‹ **Good Hot Coffee** ‹ **Clean China** ‹ **Clean Linen** ‹ **Attractive Display** ‹ **Extras - Snacks**	‹ **Good Hot Coffee** ‹ **Fast Line, Especially for Refills** ‹ **Close to High-Capacity Restrooms** ‹ **Close to Telephones** ‹ **Room to Chat**

. . . So why do such differences in perspective exist ?

Barry Bebb & Associates
World Class by Design Conference
November 1993
Buffalo, New York

The Role of Measurement

☞ **If we cannot express what we know in the form of numbers, we really don't know much about it.**

☞ **If we don't know much about it, we cannot control it.**

☞ **If we cannot control it, we are at the mercy of chance.**

Certainty	+	**Uncertainty**	= **100%**
Known	+	**Unknown**	= **100%**
Belief	+	**Disbelief**	= **100%**
Confidence	+	**Risk**	= **100%**
Yield	+	**Defect Rate**	= **100%**

σ Six Sigma Academy, Inc. 3.8 ®1997 Sigma Consultants, L.L.C.

The Focus of Six Sigma

To get results, should we focus our behavior on the Y or X ?

■ Y	■ $X_1 \dots X_N$
■ **Dependent**	■ **Independent**
■ **Output**	■ **Input-Process**
■ **Effect**	■ **Cause**
■ **Symptom**	■ **Problem**
■ **Monitor**	■ **Control**

If we are so good at X, why do we constantly test and inspect Y?

 Six Sigma Academy, Inc.   3.9   ®1997 Sigma Consultants, L.L.C.

Achieving Operational Excellence

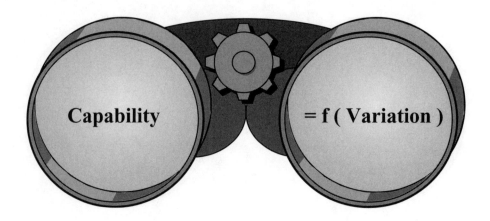

Capability   = f (Variation)

The Chain of Causation

Our survival is dependent upon growing the business.

Our business growth is largely determined by customer satisfaction.

Customer Satisfaction is governed by quality, price, and delivery.

Quality, price, and delivery are controlled by process capability.

Our process capability is greatly limited by variation.

Process variation leads to an increase in defects, cost, and cycle time.

To eliminate variation, we must apply the right knowledge.

In order to apply the right knowledge, we must first acquire it.

To acquire new knowledge means that we must have the will to survive.

THE VISION OF SIX SIGMA

Six Sigma Academy, Inc.   3 . 10   ®1997 Sigma Consultants, L.L.C.

A Model for Success

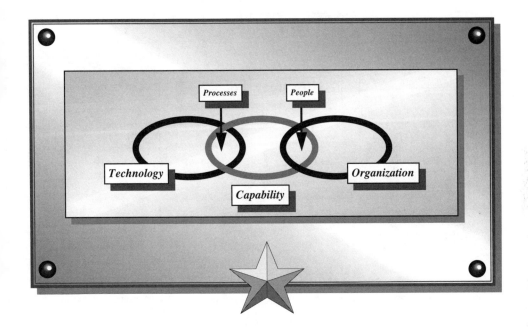

The Fundamental Logic

- Business survival is dependent upon how well we satisfy the customer
- Customer satisfaction is a function of quality, price, and delivery
- Quality, cost, and prompt delivery are dependent upon process capability
- Process capability is dependent upon the knowledge of our people
- Knowledge can be successfully organized and transferred
- The type of knowledge people pursue depends on the where they are being lead
- The direction people are being lead is established by management

. . . What implications does this hold for Customer Focus ?

The Customer Focus Initiative

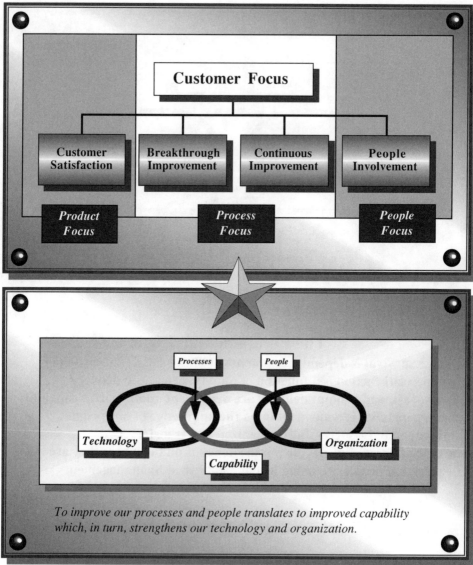

To improve our processes and people translates to improved capability which, in turn, strengthens our technology and organization.

THE VISION OF SIX SIGMA

σ Six Sigma Academy, Inc.   3 . 12   ®1997 Sigma Consultants, L.L.C.

Rotating Clevis Case Study

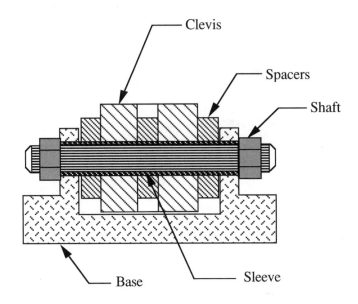

Instructions for the Case Study

1. Break into work groups, read the case study, then discuss

2. Identify a spokesperson

3. Define the strategy you would employ to the problem.

4. Define the tactics that you would use to realize the strategy.

5. Define the tools you would use to uncover key information.

6. Record results of steps 3, 4, and 5 on flipchart paper.

7. Return to classroom in [   ] minutes.

8. Present findings to class.

Rotating Clevis Case Study

Background Information and Facts

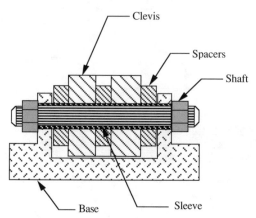

Figure 1. Rotating Clevis Assembly Manufactured by XYZ

At some point in time, XYZ Inc negotiated an extensive contract with ABC Inc to manufacture a particular clevis assembly (figure 1). This assembly was used by ABC in the manufacture of a massive piece of drilling equipment called the Widget Machine. Although XYZ was awarded the contract, there was great concern on the behalf of some senior managers within ABC. This concern was in the forefront because of certain past quality problems exhibited in similar products manufactured by XYZ. It was a known fact that XYZ would often under-bid a contract just to stop its competitors from getting the business. Through this philosophy, XYZ was able to grow at a rate of 25% annually for the last 6 years.

Interestingly, XYZ was able to design and develop the clevis assembly in only 9 months whereas the other contracted assemblies were in the development phase for roughly 14 months. After extensive management debate at XYZ, it was determined that the clevis assembly should be released for production prior to the completion of extensive   life testing. This decision was made approximately 18 months ago and was based on the belief that there was enough history to justify the decision. Shortly after this decision was made, XYZ announced a major organizational shake-up and removed 2 layers of management. In addition, the long-standing engineering manager was replaced by an engineering manager from XYZ's biggest competitor.

THE VISION OF SIX SIGMA

σ Six Sigma Academy, Inc.   3 . 14   ®1997 Sigma Consultants, L.L.C.

Rotating Clevis Case Study

Background Information and Facts

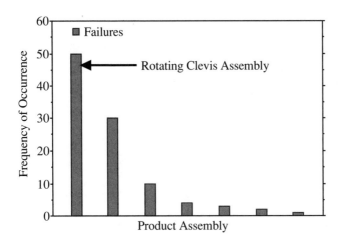

Figure 2. Graphical Display of Field Failures by Product Assembly

Since introduction of this product, things at XYZ had been running relatively smooth. Production was proceeding according to plan and all other aspects of the business were acceptable; e.g., profit, quality, cycle-time, etc. After some period of time, ABC noted an occurrence of 100 field failures across the 30,000 machines put into service thus far. Figure 2 displays a break-down of the 100 failures by product assembly. From this graph it was evident that, from ABC's point of view, the rotating clevis assembly was the most significant contributor to the Widget Machine's field performance.

However, the general manager at XYZ did not see it the way ABC did. In fact, the general manager argued that the clevis assembly was "on-track" with respect to the projected field failure rate (figure 3). It was also generally understood that ABC could expect this rate of failure given the nature of the design, manufacturing technology, and the materials used in its production processes. In fact, several meetings had been held between ABC and XYZ concerning this issue. As a consequence, XYZ believed ABC empathized with the problem and was willing to tolerate it, so long as they did not receive any nonconforming assemblies at incoming inspection.

Rotating Clevis Case Study

Background Information and Facts

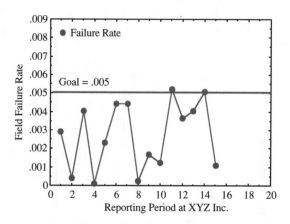

Figure 3. Field Failure Performance of the XYZ Clevis Assembly

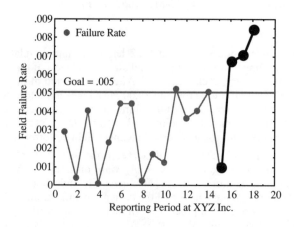

Figure 4. Field Failure Performance of the XYZ Clevis Assembly
for Reporting Periods 16 through 18

THE VISION OF SIX SIGMA

σ Six Sigma Academy, Inc.   3 . 16   ®1997 Sigma Consultants, L.L.C.

Rotating Clevis Case Study

Background Information and Facts

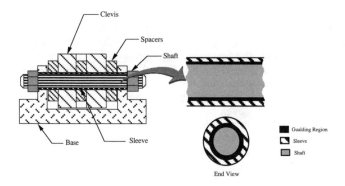

Figure 5. Exploded View of Rotating Clevis Assembly

After several more production cycles, XYZ observed that the clevis assembly was experiencing a field failure rate significantly higher that the projected goal of .005 (figure 4). Based on further conversations with ABC and a cursory engineering evaluation conducted by an outside contractor, XYZ determined that the higher-than-normal rate of failure was attributable to gaulding on the shaft/sleeve sub-assembly (figure 5). Following this, XYZ resolved itself to take corrective action and subsequently reassured ABC that the problem would be quickly remedied and quality would be returned to the goal line.

In addition, XYZ recalled a sample of the defective units for an in-depth failure analyses. The results of this analysis supported the preliminary findings -- the failures were due to excessive gaulding of the shaft/sleeve assembly. It was also noted that the problem was not due to a misapplication of the product; e.g., marginal overstress or improper service/ maintenance. Therefore, it was concluded that the problem was a design/manufacturing/ supplier issue. Subsequent analyses revealed that the failures occurred periodically and did not appear to be constrained to any specific location across the shaft/sleeve assembly. However, it was noted that the gaulding tended to appear on the those assemblies which had been inspected using the new narrow-limit gaging system. This phenomenon was true in 86% of the observed cases and only on those assemblies which had a shaft made from material purchased from JKL Inc. or FGH Inc.

During a staff meeting, the general manager of XYZ asked each of the department heads to discuss what they believed the root-cause of the problem to be and what action should be taken to correct the situation.

THE VISION OF SIX SIGMA

Six Sigma Academy, Inc.   3 . 17   ®1997 Sigma Consultants, L.L.C.

Rotating Clevis Case Study

Background Information and Facts

Design Engineering: The design manager indicated that the product configuration was sound and that the design passed a comprehensive worst-case tolerance stack analysis. To insure this, the design manager personally overviewed the calculations and was convinced that the design was free of guilt from a tolerancing perspective. However, he did indicate that one of the thermal simulations revealed a potential problem. If the assembly was subjected to operating temperatures above 250° C, excessive friction would develop as a result of lubricant break-down. In turn, this would lead to gualding in the shaft/sleeve sub-assembly. However, subsequent conversations with ABC surfaced the fact that a large number of the machines were shipped to several third world countries and, as a consequence, could have been serviced with a lubricant of less viscosity. This had been observed in several older product lines. During this conversation, ABC reminded the design manager that the initial performance specifications called for an operating temperature range of 0° to 245° C. Based on this information, the design manager stated that manufacturing, Q.A., or the suppliers were to blame.

Manufacturing: The manufacturing manager stated that the production process was state-of-the-art and that the all of employees were highly skilled at their respective jobs. As a consequence, the process could not be blamed for the problem. In fact, the manufacturing supervisors insured that the process specifications were adhered to 100% of the time. It was verified that all of the operators had received proper job training and maintained a 100% certification rate. In addition, the manufacturing department had just received the corporate award of excellence. It was also pointed out that all of the hard tooling was bought-off on the basis of first article inspection. Since the problem was periodic in nature, the tooling could not be held accountable because its influence would have a uniform impact on each production unit. Given this, the manufacturing manager indicated that the suppliers were probably guilty of providing product with a latent defect content of some type.

Supplier Quality: The supplier quality assurance manager boasted that all of the suppliers had been properly certified and used 100% inspection/test to insure that no defective product escaped their respective factories. Since all of the parts conformed to specification, the problem must be due to the design or something in the assembly process. To prove the point, the supplier quality manager made a statistical sampling of all the parts within the factory and observed a defect rate of .00002 -- obviously, this was far below the rate at which the problem was occuring. As a consequence, it was concluded that the suppliers should receive some type of quality award for providing XYZ with such a high level of quality.

THE VISION OF SIX SIGMA

Six Sigma Academy, Inc.   3 . 18   ®1997 Sigma Consultants, L.L.C.

Limitations of Inspection

CHAPTER FOUR

Breakthrough

Breakthrough

THE VISION OF SIX SIGMA

Getting to Six Sigma

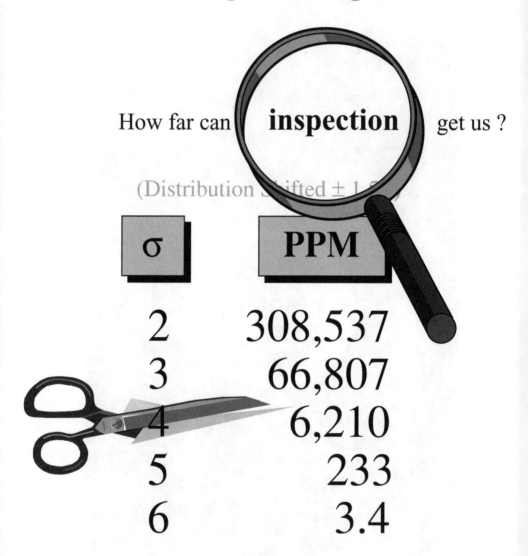

How far can **inspection** get us ?

(Distribution Shifted ± 1.5)

σ	PPM
2	308,537
3	66,807
4	6,210
5	233
6	3.4

THE VISION OF SIX SIGMA

σ Six Sigma Academy, Inc.   4 . 2   ®1997 Sigma Consultants, L.L.C.

The Inspection Exercise

Task: Count the number of times the 6th letter of the alphabet appears in the following text.

The Necessity of Training Farm Hands for First

Class Farms in the Fatherly Handling of Farm Live

Stock is Foremost in the Eyes of Farm Owners.

Since the Forefathers of the Farm Owners Trained

the Farm Hands for First Class Farms in the

Fatherly Handling of Farm Live Stock, the Farm

Owners Feel they should carry on with the Family

Tradition of Training Farm Hands of First Class

Farmers in the Fatherly Handling of Farm Live

Stock Because they Believe it is the Basis of Good

Fundamental Farm Management.

THE VISION OF SIX SIGMA

Six Sigma Academy, Inc.   4 . 3   ®1997 Sigma Consultants, L.L.C.

Results of the Exercise

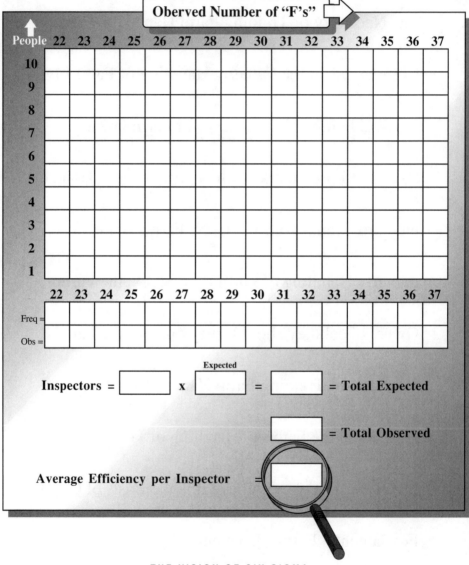

Oberved Number of "F's"

People	22	23	24	25	26	27	28	29	30	31	32	33	34	35	36	37
10																
9																
8																
7																
6																
5																
4																
3																
2																
1																
	22	23	24	25	26	27	28	29	30	31	32	33	34	35	36	37
Freq =																
Obs =																

Expected

Inspectors = [   ] x [   ] = [   ] = Total Expected

[   ] = Total Observed

Average Efficiency per Inspector = [   ]

The Impact of Added Inspection

Note: All sigma values reflect a 1.5σ shift

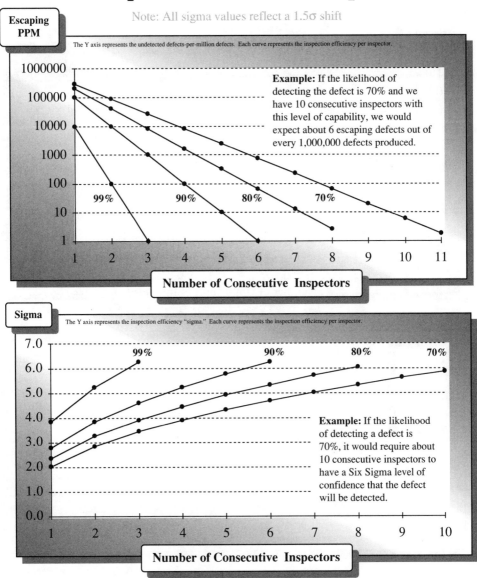

Escaping PPM

The Y axis represents the undetected defects-per-million defects. Each curve represents the inspection efficiency per inspector.

Example: If the likelihood of detecting the defect is 70% and we have 10 consecutive inspectors with this level of capability, we would expect about 6 escaping defects out of every 1,000,000 defects produced.

99% 90% 80% 70%

Number of Consecutive Inspectors

Sigma

The Y axis represents the inspection efficiency "sigma." Each curve represents the inspection efficiency per inspector.

99% 90% 80% 70%

Example: If the likelihood of detecting a defect is 70%, it would require about 10 consecutive inspectors to have a Six Sigma level of confidence that the defect will be detected.

Number of Consecutive Inspectors

THE VISION OF SIX SIGMA

Impact of Complexity on Inspection

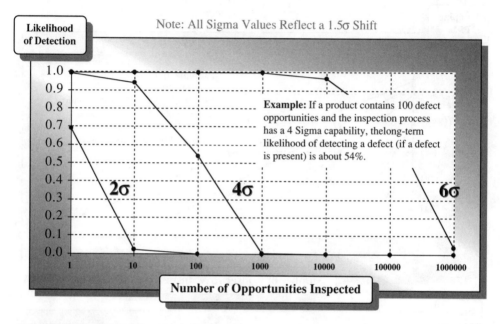

Note: All Sigma Values Reflect a 1.5σ Shift

Likelihood of Detection

Example: If a product contains 100 defect opportunities and the inspection process has a 4 Sigma capability, thelong-term likelihood of detecting a defect (if a defect is present) is about 54%.

2σ   4σ   6σ

Number of Opportunities Inspected

Six Sigma Academy, Inc.   4.6   ®1997 Sigma Consultants, L.L.C.

Probability and Capability

CHAPTER FIVE

Breakthrough

Breakthrough

THE VISION OF SIX SIGMA

The Probability Game

Since the issue of capability involves the notions of manufacturing confidence and risk, it is reasonable to assert that the concepts underlying probability should serve as the foundation of any measurement scheme. To illustrate why this is so, let us consider an analogous example.

For the moment, we shall hypothesize a pair of "manufacturing dice" and a customer requirement that only allows those combinations that yield a 3, 4, 5, ..., or 11. In this instance, a 2 or 12 represents a nonconformance to standard, or as some would say, a quality defect. Thus, we may ask the question: "To what extent will the customer be satisfied?" In the language of statistics, the question would be, "What is the probability of not rolling a 2 or 12?" In order to answer the latter question, we must apply some fundamental probability theory.

In statistical notation, the likelihood of some event A may be given by P(A). If some event A is independent of some other event, say B, the probability of both A and B occurring is P (A and B) = P(A) x P(B). In other words, the joint probability of A and B is multiplicative by nature. Since a single die has six sides, the random chance probability that any given side will be face up is 1/6 = .1667 because (a) only one side can be up at any given time, (b) there are a total of six possibilities, and (c) each of the six possibilities has the same probability of occurrence. Of course, all of this assumes the die is unbiased. Extending this reasoning to a pair of dice, we may say that the probability of rolling any given combination would be .1667 x .1667 = .0278, or 2.78 percent.

Because the occurrence of a 2 or 12 cannot happen concurrently, we say that the two outcomes are mutually exclusive of each other. This is to say that a 2 and 12 cannot occur at the same time; i.e., they are restricted from occurring together. Hence, the events of concern are mutually exclusive. Any time that two events (say, A and B) are mutually exclusive, the probability of event A or B occurring may be given by summing their individual probabilities: e.g., P (A or B) = P(A) + P(B). Since there is only one way to form a 2 and only one way to create a 12, the probability of not meeting the customer's standard, with respect to our manufacturing example, would be .0278 + .0278 = .0556, or 5.56 percent. This represents the risk of nonconformance. This may be directly verified by studying the exhaustive combinations given by a pair of dice.

Given the risk of nonconformance, with respect to our dice example, we may intuitively reason that the probability of yielding a 3, 4, 5, ..., or 11 may be calculated as 1 - .0556 = .9444. Thus, expected yield may be given by P(Y) = 1- [P(A) + P(B)]. Hence, we may now say that the likelihood of customer satisfaction is 94.44 percent. The uninformed reader is highly encouraged to gain additional knowledge concerning probability theory via almost any introductory textbook on mathematical statistics. Such knowledge is essential in order to progress beyond the elementary mathematical constructs presented in this book.

THE VISION OF SIX SIGMA

σ Six Sigma Academy, Inc.   5 . 2   ®1997 Sigma Consultants, L.L.C.

The Customer Requirements

What is the process capability?

What is the probability of meeting the requirements?

Is capability and probability related?

Suppose a certain customer permits only those combinations which yield 3, 4, 5, . . . , or 11.

 Six Sigma Academy, Inc.   5 . 3   ®1997 Sigma Consultants, L.L.C.

Computing the Risks

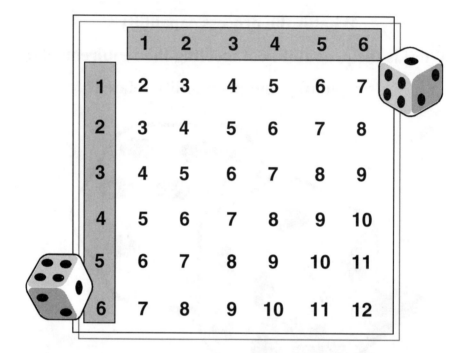

	1	2	3	4	5	6
1	2	3	4	5	6	7
2	3	4	5	6	7	8
3	4	5	6	7	8	9
4	5	6	7	8	9	10
5	6	7	8	9	10	11
6	7	8	9	10	11	12

Ways to form a "2" ☐ in ☐ = ☐

Ways to form a "12" ☐ in ☐ = ☐

Probability of Defect ➡ ☐

Six Sigma Academy, Inc.   5 . 4   ®1997 Sigma Consultants, L.L.C.

Deeper Insight Into Probability

Die 1	Die 2	Probability
1	4	.0278
2	3	.0278
3	2	.0278
4	1	.0278
	Total	.1111

What is the probability of rolling a "5" using a fair pair of dice?

	1	2	3	4	5	6
1	.0278	.0278	.0278	.0278	.0278	.0278
2	.0278	.0278	.0278	.0278	.0278	.0278
3	.0278	.0278	.0278	.0278	.0278	.0278
4	.0278	.0278	.0278	.0278	.0278	.0278
5	.0278	.0278	.0278	.0278	.0278	.0278
6	.0278	.0278	.0278	.0278	.0278	.0278

THE VISION OF SIX SIGMA

Six Sigma Academy, Inc.   5 . 5   ®1997 Sigma Consultants, L.L.C.

Establishing the Odds

Value	Combinations	Probability
2	1	.0278
3	2	.0556
4	3	.0833
5	4	.1111
6	5	.1389
7	6	.1667
8	5	.1389
9	4	.1111
10	3	.0833
11	2	.0556
12	1	.0278
Total	36	1.0000

Probability of any given value on Die 1 $\longrightarrow$ = 1/6 = .1667
Probability of any given value on Die 2 $\longrightarrow$ = 1/6 = .1667
Probability of any given combination = 1/6 x 1/6 = 1/36 = .0278

Six Sigma Academy, Inc.   5.6   ©1997 Sigma Consultants, L.L.C.

Graphing the Results

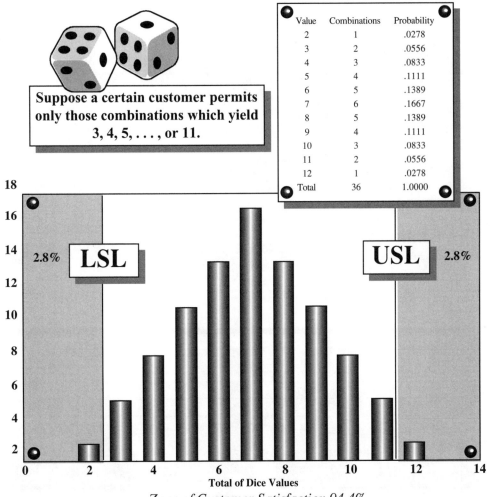

Suppose a certain customer permits only those combinations which yield 3, 4, 5, . . . , or 11.

Value	Combinations	Probability
2	1	.0278
3	2	.0556
4	3	.0833
5	4	.1111
6	5	.1389
7	6	.1667
8	5	.1389
9	4	.1111
10	3	.0833
11	2	.0556
12	1	.0278
Total	36	1.0000

2.8%   **LSL**

USL   2.8%

Total of Dice Values

Zone of Customer Satisfaction 94.4%

. . .Hence, the probability of Customer Satisfaction is 94.4 %

THE VISION OF SIX SIGMA

Six Sigma Academy, Inc.   5 . 7   ®1997 Sigma Consultants, L.L.C.

Gaining Deeper Insights

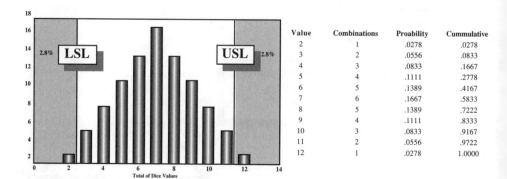

Value	Combinations	Proability	Cummulative
2	1	.0278	.0278
3	2	.0556	.0833
4	3	.0833	.1667
5	4	.1111	.2778
6	5	.1389	.4167
7	6	.1667	.5833
8	5	.1389	.7222
9	4	.1111	.8333
10	3	.0833	.9167
11	2	.0556	.9722
12	1	.0278	1.0000

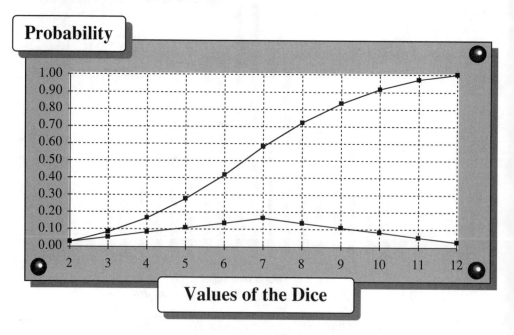

Probability

Values of the Dice

Six Sigma Academy, Inc.   5.8   ®1997 Sigma Consultants, L.L.C.

Comments on the Nature of Data

☆ Two kinds of data can be used for measuring process capability. One is data which characterizes a product or process feature in terms of its size, weight, volts. This type of data is said to be continuous by nature. In other words, the measurement scale can be meaningfully divided into finer and finer increments of precision. To apply the normal distribution, one must necessarily use continuous data.

☆ Another way to look at the data is to merely count the frequency of occurrence: e.g., the number of times something happens or fails to happen. Notice that such data is not capable of being meaningfully subdivided into more precise increments and, therefore, is said to be discrete by nature. The Poisson and binomial models are used in connection with this type of data.

☆ The validity of inferences made from discrete data are highly dependent upon the number of observations. In other words, the sample size required to characterize a discrete product or process feature is much larger than that required when continuous data is used.

THE VISION OF SIX SIGMA

Ơ Six Sigma Academy, Inc.   5.9   ®1997 Sigma Consultants, L.L.C.

Application of the Concepts

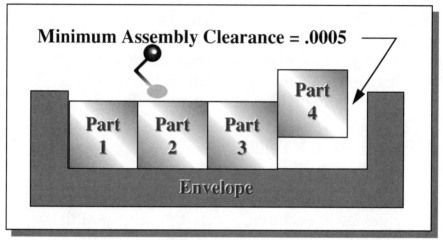

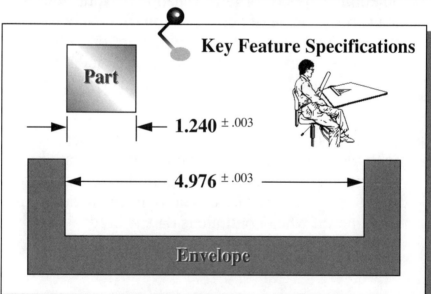

The Manufacturing Process

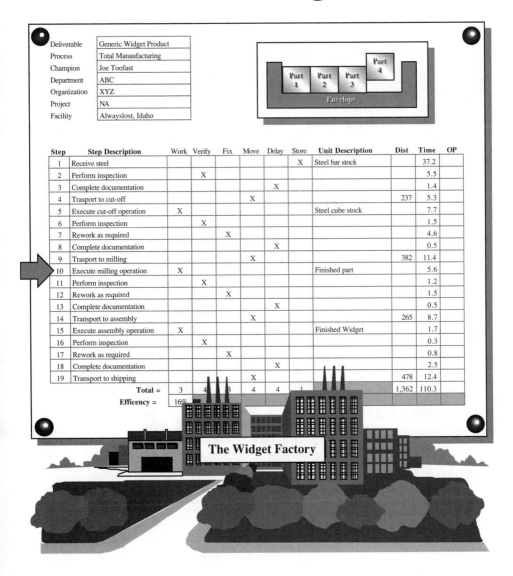

Deliverable	Generic Widget Product
Process	Total Manaufacturing
Champion	Joe Toofast
Department	ABC
Organization	XYZ
Project	NA
Facility	Alwayslost, Idaho

Step	Step Description	Work	Verify	Fix	Move	Delay	Store	Unit Description	Dist	Time	OP
1	Receive steel						X	Steel bar stock		37.2	
2	Perform inspection		X							5.5	
3	Complete documentation					X				1.4	
4	Trasport to cut-off				X				237	5.3	
5	Execute cut-off operation	X						Steel cube stock		7.7	
6	Perform inspection		X							1.5	
7	Rework as required			X						4.6	
8	Complete documentation					X				0.5	
9	Trasport to milling				X				382	11.4	
10	Execute milling operation	X						Finished part		5.6	
11	Perform inspection		X							1.2	
12	Rework as required			X						1.5	
13	Complete documentation					X				0.5	
14	Transport to assembly				X				265	8.7	
15	Execute assembly operation	X						Finished Widget		1.7	
16	Perform inspection		X							0.3	
17	Rework as required			X						0.8	
18	Complete documentation					X				2.5	
19	Transport to shipping				X				478	12.4	
	Total =	3	4	3	4	4	1		1,362	110.3	
	Efficency =	16%									

The Widget Factory

THE VISION OF SIX SIGMA

σ Six Sigma Academy, Inc.   5 . 11   ®1997 Sigma Consultants, L.L.C.

The Milling Operation

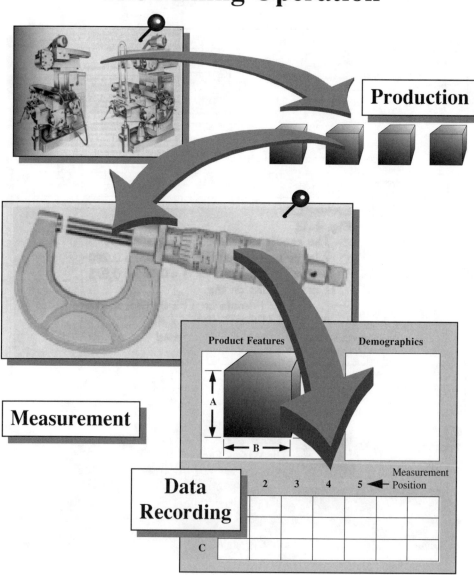

THE VISION OF SIX SIGMA

Six Sigma Academy, Inc.   5 . 12   ®1997 Sigma Consultants, L.L.C.

Establishing Process Capability

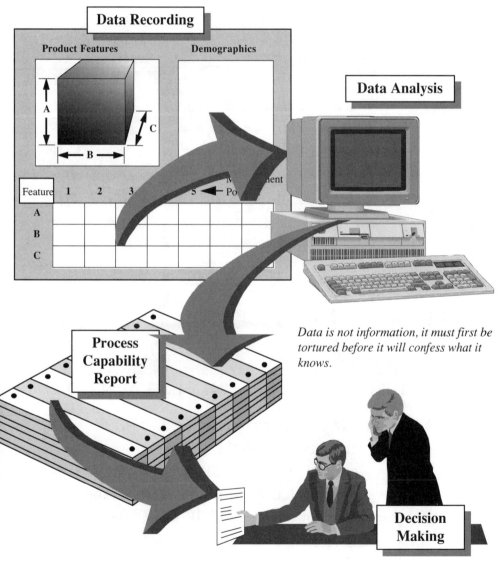

Data Recording

Product Features   Demographics

Feature | 1 | 2 | 3 | ... | ...
A | | | | |
B | | | | |
C | | | | |

Data Analysis

Process Capability Report

Data is not information, it must first be tortured before it will confess what it knows.

Decision Making

Understanding the Histogram

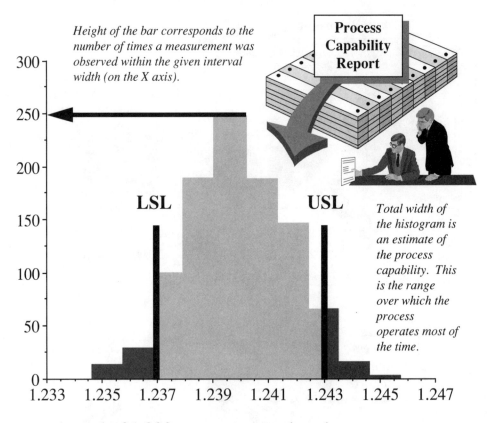

Height of the bar corresponds to the number of times a measurement was observed within the given interval width (on the X axis).

Process Capability Report

LSL   USL

Total width of the histogram is an estimate of the process capability. This is the range over which the process operates most of the time.

A total of 1,000 parts were produced.

22 parts were greater than the USL.

31 parts were less than the LSL.

53 parts were rejected of which 12 were scraped.

The probability of defect is 53/1000 =.053

The process yield is 1 -.053 = .947, or 94.7%

The Nature of Process Variation

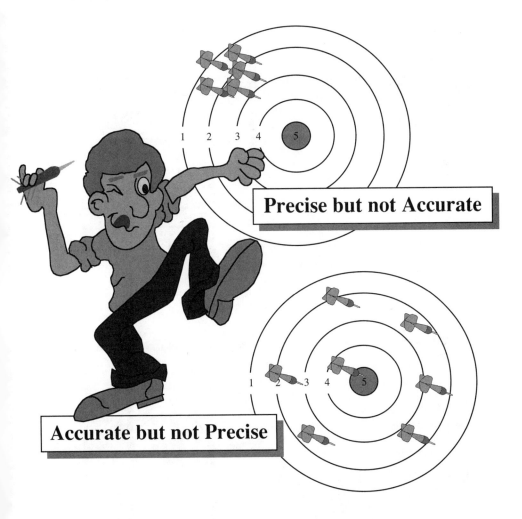

Precise but not Accurate

Accurate but not Precise

. . . So how does this principle translate into the real world?

THE VISION OF SIX SIGMA

Understanding Process Precision

Manufacturing Distribution of the Widget Part

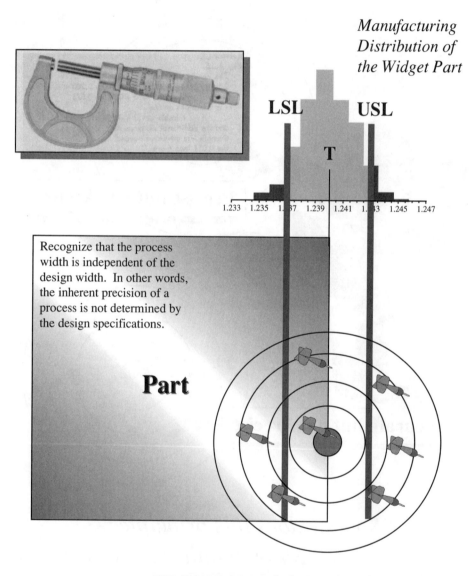

LSL   USL

T

1.233   1.235   1.237   1.239   1.241   1.243   1.245   1.247

Recognize that the process width is independent of the design width. In other words, the inherent precision of a process is not determined by the design specifications.

Part

Understanding Process Accuracy

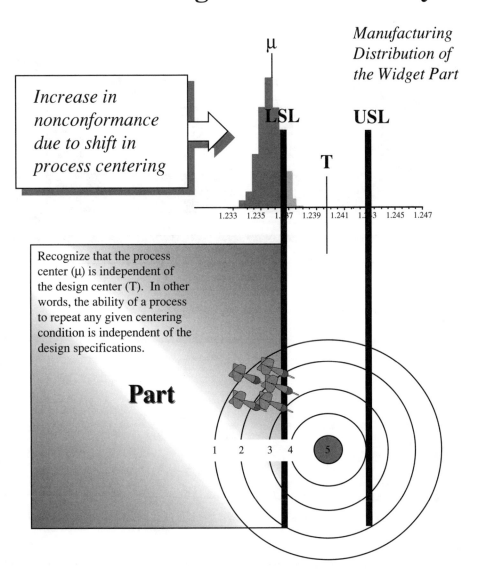

Manufacturing Distribution of the Widget Part

Increase in nonconformance due to shift in process centering

Recognize that the process center (μ) is independent of the design center (T). In other words, the ability of a process to repeat any given centering condition is independent of the design specifications.

Part

Other Histogram Applications

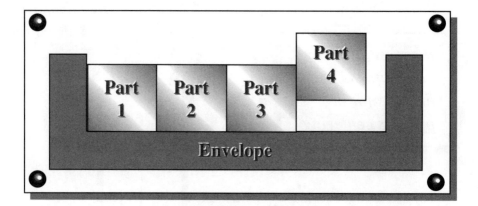

Six Sigma Academy, Inc.   5 . 18   ®1997 Sigma Consultants, L.L.C.

The Normal Curve

CHAPTER SIX

Breakthrough

Breakthrough

THE VISION OF SIX SIGMA

Forming the Normal Curve

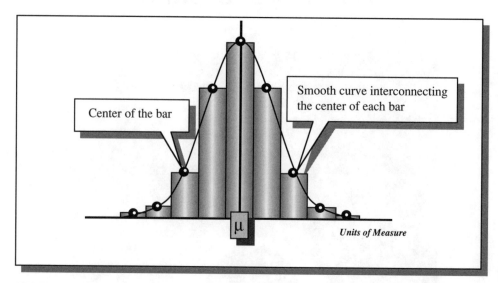

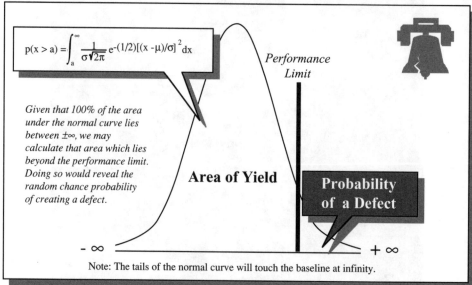

$$p(x > a) = \int_a^\infty \frac{1}{\sigma\sqrt{2\pi}}\, e^{-(1/2)[(x-\mu)/\sigma]^2} dx$$

Performance Limit

Given that 100% of the area under the normal curve lies between ±∞, we may calculate that area which lies beyond the performance limit. Doing so would reveal the random chance probability of creating a defect.

Area of Yield

Probability of a Defect

− ∞   + ∞

Note: The tails of the normal curve will touch the baseline at infinity.

THE VISION OF SIX SIGMA

Six Sigma Academy, Inc.   6 . 2   ®1997 Sigma Consultants, L.L.C.

The Normal Curve and Capability

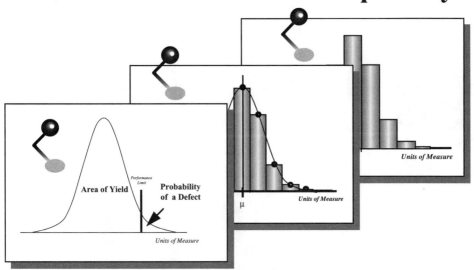

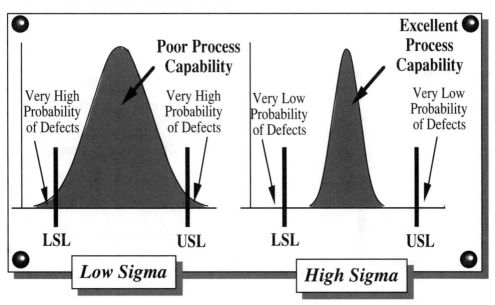

σ Six Sigma Academy, Inc.   6 . 3   ®1997 Sigma Consultants, L.L.C.

Application to the Widget Example

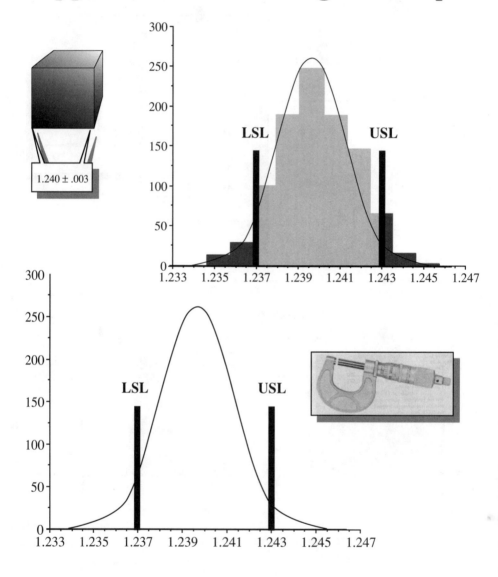

σ Six Sigma Academy, Inc.   6 . 4   ®1997 Sigma Consultants, L.L.C.

Improving Process Capability

$$Y = f (X_1 \ldots X_N)$$

The variation inherent to any dependent variable (Y) is determined by the variations inherent to each of the independent variables.

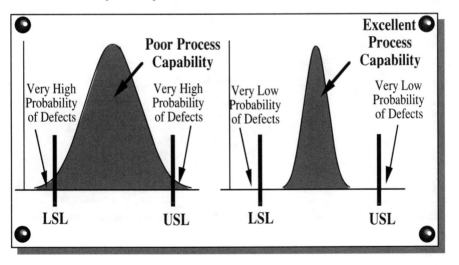

Process Capability and Defects

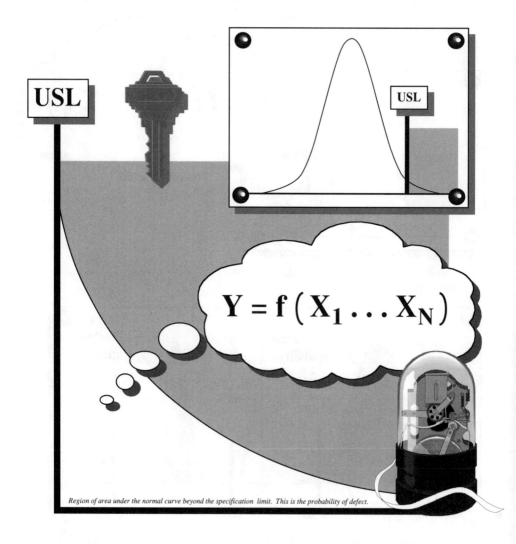

Region of area under the normal curve beyond the specification limit. This is the probability of defect.

Visualizing the Process Dynamics

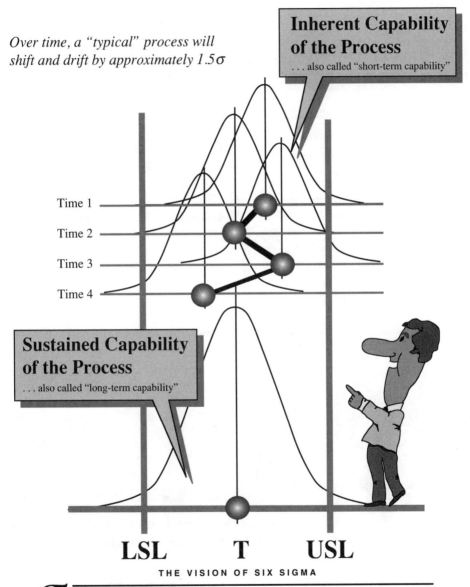

Over time, a "typical" process will shift and drift by approximately 1.5σ

Inherent Capability of the Process
. . . also called "short-term capability"

Time 1
Time 2
Time 3
Time 4

Sustained Capability of the Process
. . . also called "long-term capability"

LSL   T   USL

σ Six Sigma Academy, Inc.   6.7   ®1997 Sigma Consultants, L.L.C.

Improving Process Capability

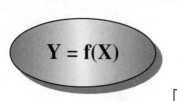

$$Y = f(X)$$

The dependent variable is sometimes refered to as the "response" variable.

The indpendent variables are often collectively refered to as the "underlying cause system" or "underlying system of causation."

- Y is the dependent variable
- X is the independent variable
- The value of Y waits upon X
- X is independent of Y

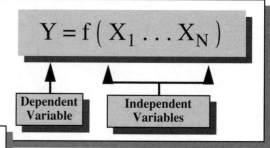

$$Y = f(X_1 \ldots X_N)$$

| Dependent Variable | Independent Variables |

$$20\% + 80\% = 100\%$$

Vital Few Variables   Trivial Many Variables

The "vital few" variables are also called "leverage" variables because they exert a disproportionately large influence on the dependent variable.

$$\Delta Y = \sqrt{X_1^2 + X_2^2}$$

$\sqrt{4^2 + 1^2} = 4.12$	$\sqrt{4^2 + 1^2} = 4.12$
$\sqrt{4^2 + 0^2} = 4.00$	$\sqrt{3^2 + 1^2} = 3.16$
$\Delta = 0.12$	$\Delta = 0.96$

Conclusion: We gain 8 times the Reduction in Y by Changing X1 versus X2; therefore, X1 has leverage.

THE VISION OF SIX SIGMA

σ Six Sigma Academy, Inc.   6 . 8   ®1997 Sigma Consultants, L.L.C.

The Focus of Improvement

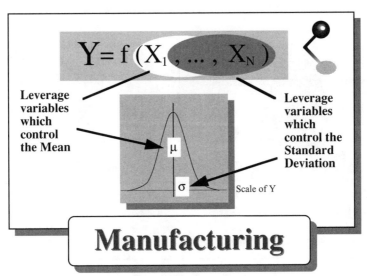

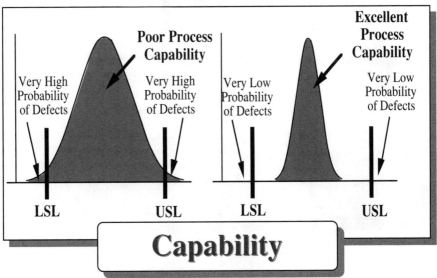

Additional Applications

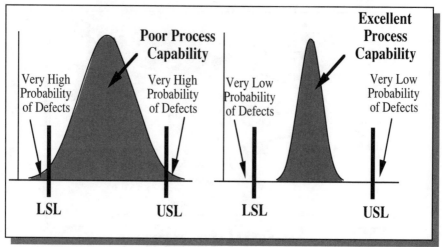

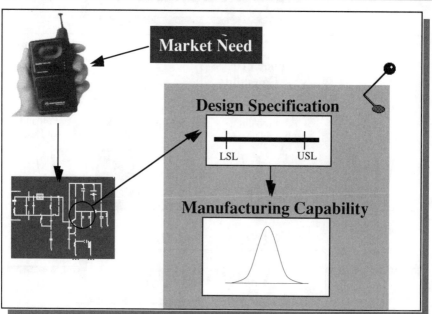

Potential Sources of Variation

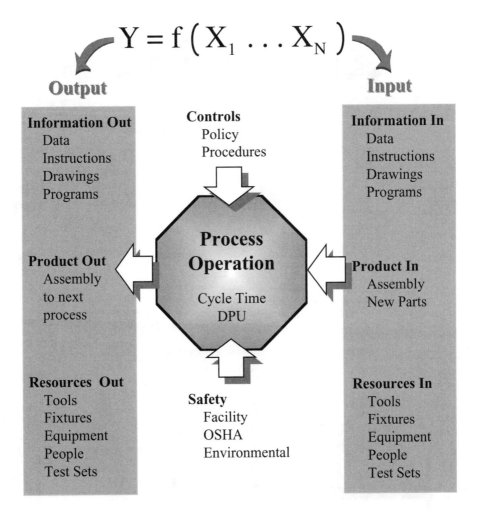

$$Y = f\left(X_1 \ldots X_N\right)$$

Output   **Input**

Information Out
Data
Instructions
Drawings
Programs

Controls
Policy
Procedures

Information In
Data
Instructions
Drawings
Programs

Process Operation

Cycle Time
DPU

Product Out
Assembly
to next
process

Product In
Assembly
New Parts

Resources Out
Tools
Fixtures
Equipment
People
Test Sets

Safety
Facility
OSHA
Environmental

Resources In
Tools
Fixtures
Equipment
People
Test Sets

Remember the "Vital Few" versus the "Trivial Many"

σ Six Sigma Academy, Inc.   6 . 11   ®1997 Sigma Consultants, L.L.C.

Implications of Variation

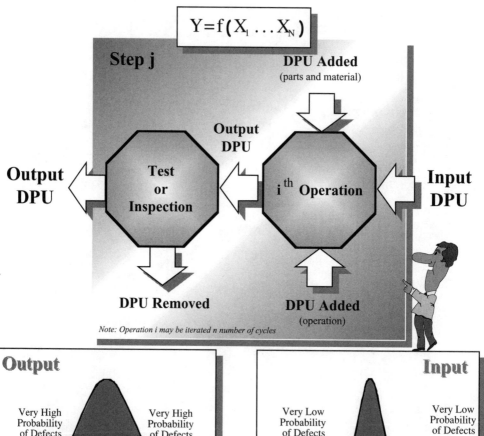

$$Y = f(X_1 \ldots X_N)$$

Step j

DPU Added
(parts and material)

Output DPU

Output DPU

Test or Inspection

i^{th} **Operation**

Input DPU

DPU Removed

DPU Added
(operation)

Note: Operation i may be iterated n number of cycles

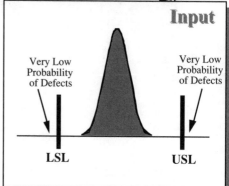

Output

Very High Probability of Defects

Very High Probability of Defects

LSL   USL

Input

Very Low Probability of Defects

Very Low Probability of Defects

LSL   USL

Six Sigma Academy, Inc.   6 . 12   ®1997 Sigma Consultants, L.L.C.

The Standard Deviation

CHAPTER SEVEN

σ
Breakthrough

Breakthrough

THE VISION OF SIX SIGMA

Purposes of the Standard Deviation

If we accept the fact that variation exists, then we must also recognize that variation in data is nothing more than some form of dispersion or scatter. Expressed differently, continuous data often disperses or spreads out relative to a particular location on some scale of measure or, as one might say, "it is scattered about the average." What this means is that the individual observations (measurements) tend to be "sprinkled" around the balance point of the data.

To illustrate, let us suppose that we were holding a funnel full of sand directly over a large piece of white paper. If we were to project a line from the center of the funnel to the paper, the point at which the line intersects the paper can be thought of as point of contact or a center point. Let us further suppose that we were to allow the sand to pour out of the funnel onto the paper while holding the funnel perfectly steady. What would happen?

As we might expect, the grains of sand would be scattered all over the piece of paper; however, the grains would tend to be most concentrated at the center point. If enough sand were to be released from the funnel, we would expect to see a pile start to form about the center point. In addition, we would also expect to see fewer grains of sand as we move farther away from the peak of the pile - assuming that the person holding the funnel did not shift it to a new center point on the paper. In this analogy, the center of the sand pile would be the arithmetic average, or balance point. But how can we describe the dispersion of the individual grains of sand? How can we express the scatter we see?

One way of expressing the degree of scatter we see would be to measure the distance between the two outermost grains of sand. This is most often called the range. One problem with using the range to express dispersion is that it does not use the additional information that all of the other individual grains of sand could give us, nor does it give us information that is relative to the center point of the pile.

In order to make the individual grains of sand relative to the total width and center point of the pile, we would need to devise an index which takes advantage of the information related to each grain of sand. As previously indicated, one such index is called the standard deviation. This particular index is a summary number that conveys to us the relative distance any particular observation is from the arithmetic balance point of its distribution.

THE VISION OF SIX SIGMA

σ   Six Sigma Academy, Inc.   7 . 2   ®1997 Sigma Consultants, L.L.C.

Properties of the Mean

Let us now consider several statistical properties of the mean. First, the mean is very responsive to every value in the data set from which it was computed. When we say that it is "responsive," we are saying that its numerical value is sensitive to the values of the other numbers. That is, if any of the other numbers were to change in magnitude, then the mean would also be affected to some degree. The larger the change, the more the mean will change.

Along these same lines is the second property of the mean - its sensitivity to extreme values. For instance, if we had two small numbers (say, 2 and 4), it is readily apparent that the mean would be 3. Now, let us add a third number (say, 6). Given this, the new average would be 4. This would represent a location change of 1 unit in the mean (from 3 to 4). However, if that third number had been 21, the mean would now be 9. As you can see, this would represent a location change of 6 units. In the first set of three numbers (2, 4, and 6) there was only a 1.33-fold change in the average; however, in the second set of three numbers (2, 4, and 21), there was a 3-fold change in the location. This would tend to tell us that the arithmetic mean is very sensitive to any unbalanced change in the data, as well as extreme values.

In the instance of our widget example, if more were to be produced, say three more, it is possible that the mean (μ) would change in value. Should this happen, we could say the mean shifted to some higher or lower level. In other words, if the cause system (X1...XN) underlying Y were to change, we would see some degree of change in the population or "universe" average (μ). In short, if the cause system were to be suddenly altered, μ would "shift" its location.

Yet another property of the mean would be its ability to resist the influence of sampling fluctuations. This particular property is extremely important whenever random sampling is performed and the assumption of normality is reasonable. For example, let us suppose that we were randomly to draw 100 samples of size 5 from a normally distributed population. If we were to determine the mean, median, and mode for each of the 100 samples and then compare how much each measure of central tendency changed from sample to sample, we would find that the arithmetic average (mean) would be the most resilient to fluctuation.

In general, this holds true for most of the different types of distributions that are commonly used in statistical work. Given these, as well as other properties, the mean is perhaps the most useful measure of central tendency - hence its wide application, reputation, and use in the 6σ quality philosophy.

THE VISION OF SIX SIGMA

σ Six Sigma Academy, Inc.   7.3   ®1997 Sigma Consultants, L.L.C.

Properties of the Standard Deviation

Yet another way to describe the nature of the standard deviation is by its unique properties. First, much like the mean, it is very sensitive or responsive to the position of every value in a distribution. If a single value out of a reasonably large distribution of values is shifted to an extreme position, the standard deviation will change noticeably. Expressed differently, the standard deviation is not robust against extreme values. As a result of this property, the standard deviation may not be the best choice among measures of variability when the distribution is markedly skewed or extreme values are present. Of course, mathematical transformations can sometimes be employed to rectify the undesirable situations.[5]

When the deviations are calculated from the arithmetic average, the sum of squares (SS) is smaller than if another measure of central tendency had been used (e.g., mode, median, etc.). Given this, we have yet another way to describe the arithmetic average (mean): that point which minimizes the sum of squares. Another property of the standard deviation would be its resistance to sampling fluctuations. That is to say, the standard deviation does not change a whole lot, as compared to other measures of variability, given normal fluctuations in repeated random samples.

Still another characteristic would be its similarity to the mean in that it is "kind of like" the average of all of the squared deviations. In this respect, it is highly sensitive to extreme values and location. Like the mean, it is used in many descriptive and inferential statistics. In addition, it is probably the most used measure of variability (indicator of dispersion or"scatter").

THE VISION OF SIX SIGMA

The Range Method

Because this particular method of computing the sample standard deviation is based on the sample ranges, it is sometimes referred to as the "range method." In general, the range method should be used when rational subgrouping serves as the basis of the sampling scheme. In general, the deviation method should be employed when it is not possible to define rational subgroups. The notion of a "rational subgroup" will be presented in great detail later in the discussion. For the moment, we need only recognize that it is related to a sampling technique designed to limit systematic variations within the sample.

Computing the sample standard deviation via the range method is a relatively easy task. First, the range (R) of each subgroup (G1, ..., G6) must be determined. This may be done by subtracting the minimum value (Xmin) in a particular subgroup - say, Gj - from the maximum value (Xmax) contained within Gj. This may be expressed as

$$Rj = Xmax - Xmin$$

Eq. (1)

Next, we need to find the average range $(\overline{R})$. In the context of Eq. (1), the average range may be given by

$$\overline{R} = \sum_{j=1}^{N} R_j/N$$

Eq. (2)

where Rj is the range of the jth subgroup (Gj) and N is the total number of subgroups. Once the average range $(\overline{R})$ has been computed, the sample standard deviation may be calculated by dividing the average range $(\overline{R})$ by the appropriate constant (d2*) listed in table 1. This operation may be expressed as

$$S = \overline{R}/d2*$$

Eq. (3)

where d2* = 2.353 for the case when there are N = 6 subgroups, under the special condition n = 5. Obviously, if there were more or less subgroups, the value of d2* would be differen

Table 1. Tabulated Values of d2* for a Selected
Number of Subgroups (N) of Size n = 5

N	d2*	N	d2*
1	2.474	8	2.346
2	2.405	10	2.342
3	2.379	11	2.339
5	2.358	20	2.334
6	2.353	∞	2.326

The Standard Deviation

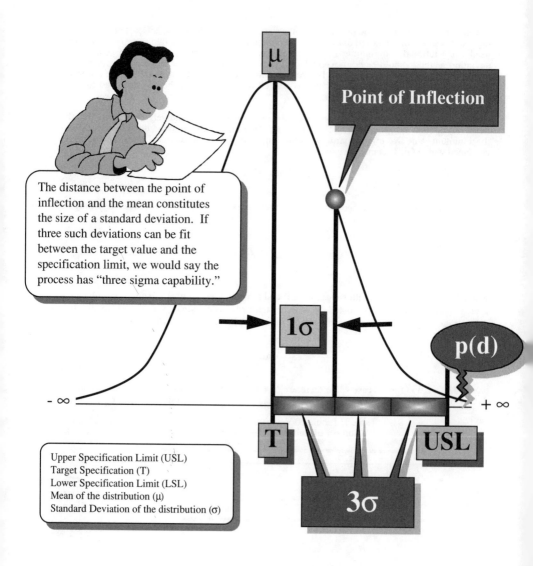

μ

Point of Inflection

The distance between the point of inflection and the mean constitutes the size of a standard deviation. If three such deviations can be fit between the target value and the specification limit, we would say the process has "three sigma capability."

1σ

p(d)

- ∞

+ ∞

T

USL

3σ

Upper Specification Limit (USL)
Target Specification (T)
Lower Specification Limit (LSL)
Mean of the distribution (μ)
Standard Deviation of the distribution (σ)

The Computational Equations

Population Mean

$$\mu = \frac{\sum\limits_{i=1}^{N} X_i}{N}$$

Population Standard Deviation

$$\sigma = S = \sqrt{\frac{\sum\limits_{i=1}^{N} (X_i - \mu)^2}{N}}$$

Sample Mean

$$\hat{\mu} = \overline{X} = \frac{\sum\limits_{i=1}^{n} X_i}{n}$$

Sample Standard Deviation

$$\hat{\sigma} = s = \sqrt{\frac{\sum\limits_{i=1}^{n} (X_i - \overline{X})^2}{n-1}}$$

THE VISION OF SIX SIGMA

σ Six Sigma Academy, Inc.   7.7   ®1997 Sigma Consultants, L.L.C.

Exercise 1: Standard Deviation

	X	X - $\overline{X}$	$(X - \overline{X})^2$
1			
2			
3			
4			
5			
6			
7			
8			
9			
10			
Σ			
$\overline{X}$			
$\hat{\sigma}^2$			
$\hat{\sigma}$			

$$\overline{X} = \frac{\sum\limits_{i=1}^{n} X_i}{n} \qquad \widehat{\sigma} = \sqrt{\frac{\sum\limits_{i=1}^{n}(X_i - \overline{X})^2}{n-1}}$$

THE VISION OF SIX SIGMA

σ Six Sigma Academy, Inc.   7 . 8   ®1997 Sigma Consultants, L.L.C.

The Quadratic Deviation

Squaring is a means to weight extreme deviations from the natural center of the data.

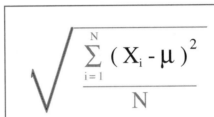

$$\sqrt{\dfrac{\sum\limits_{i=1}^{N}(X_i - \mu)^2}{N}}$$

Scale of $(X - \mu)^2$

The influence of squaring is nonlinear.

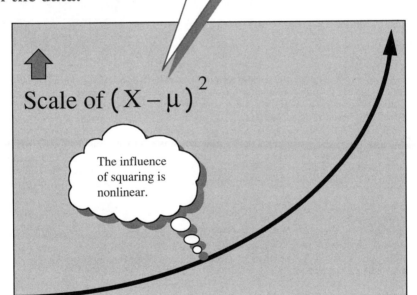

0

Scale of $(X - \mu)$

THE VISION OF SIX SIGMA

σ Six Sigma Academy, Inc.   7.9   ®1997 Sigma Consultants, L.L.C.

Degrees of Freedom

$$\widehat{\sigma} = s = \sqrt{\dfrac{\sum\limits_{i=1}^{n}(X_i - \overline{X})^2}{n-1}}$$

The use of n–1 is a mathematical device employed for the purposes of deriving an unbiased estimator of the population standard deviation. In the given context, n–1 is referred to as "degrees of freedom." When the total sums-of-squared deviations is given and the pair-wise deviation contrasts are made for n observations, the last contrast is fixed; hence, there are n–1 degrees of freedom from which to accumulate the total. More specifically, degrees of freedom may be defined as (n–1) independent contrasts out of n observations. For example, in a sample with n = 5, measurements X1, X2, X3, X4, and X5, are made. The independent contrasts are X1, - X2, X2 - X3, X3 - X4, and X4 - X5. The additional contrast, X1 - X5, is not independent since its value is known from

$$(X1 - X2) + (X2 - X3) + (X3 - X4) + (X4 - X5) = X1 - X5$$

Therefore, for a sample of n = 5, there are four (n–1) independent contrasts or "degrees of freedom." In this instance, all but one of the contrasts are free to vary in magnitude, given that the total is fixed. Thus, when n is large, the degree of bias is small; therefore, there is little need for such a corrective device.

THE VISION OF SIX SIGMA

Six Sigma Academy, Inc.   7 . 10   ®1997 Sigma Consultants, L.L.C.

Influence of Sample Size

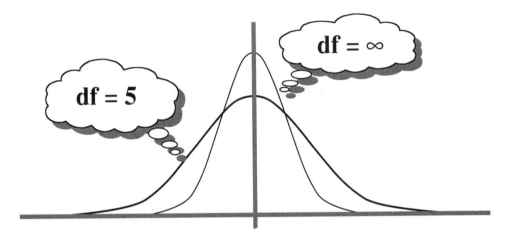

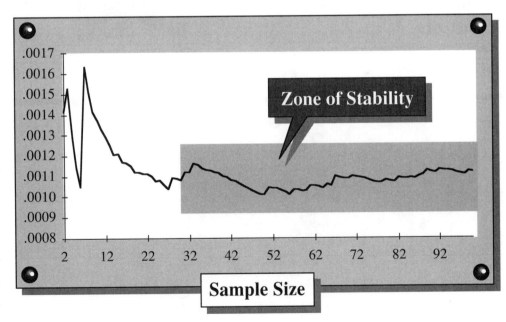

Illustration 1a

A certain engineer made some measurements on the product characteristic called "Y." A single measurement was taken every hour on the hour. Using the measurements gathered between 8:00 AM and 12:00 PM, the engineer prepared to compute the standard deviation.

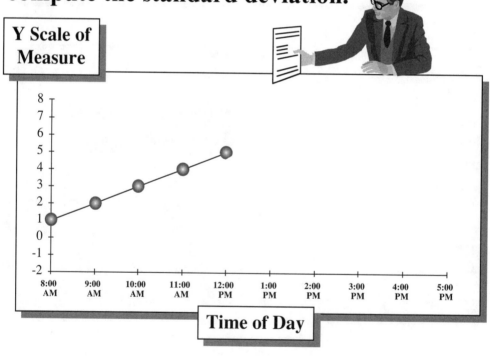

THE VISION OF SIX SIGMA

Six Sigma Academy, Inc.   7 . 12   ®1997 Sigma Consultants, L.L.C.

Illustration 1b

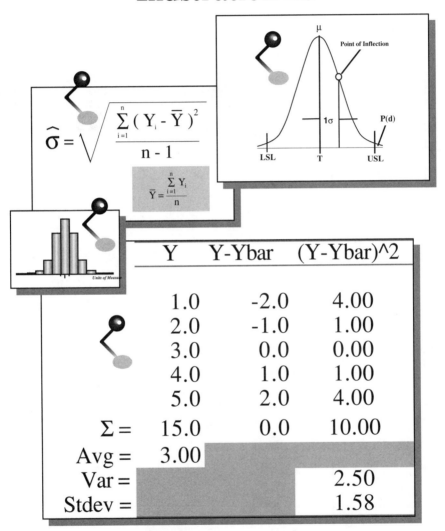

$$\widehat{\sigma} = \sqrt{\frac{\sum_{i=1}^{n}(Y_i - \overline{Y})^2}{n-1}}$$

$$\overline{Y} = \frac{\sum_{i=1}^{n} Y_i}{n}$$

Y	Y-Ybar	(Y-Ybar)^2
1.0	-2.0	4.00
2.0	-1.0	1.00
3.0	0.0	0.00
4.0	1.0	1.00
5.0	2.0	4.00
Σ = 15.0	0.0	10.00
Avg = 3.00		
Var =		2.50
Stdev =		1.58

. . . So what does 1.58 mean?

THE VISION OF SIX SIGMA

Illustration 1c

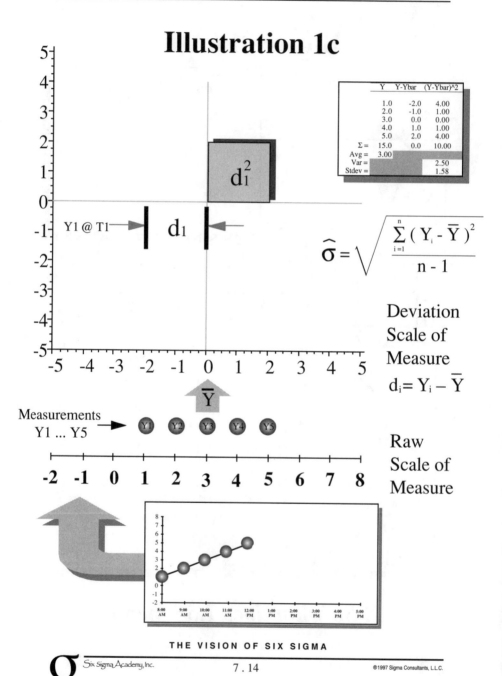

	Y	Y-Ybar	(Y-Ybar)^2
	1.0	-2.0	4.00
	2.0	-1.0	1.00
	3.0	0.0	0.00
	4.0	1.0	1.00
	5.0	2.0	4.00
Σ =	15.0	0.0	10.00
Avg =	3.00		
Var =			2.50
Stdev =			1.58

$$\hat{\sigma} = \sqrt{\dfrac{\sum\limits_{i=1}^{n}\left(Y_i - \overline{Y}\right)^2}{n-1}}$$

Deviation
Scale of
Measure
$$d_i = Y_i - \overline{Y}$$

Measurements
Y1 ... Y5

Raw
Scale of
Measure

THE VISION OF SIX SIGMA

σ Six Sigma Academy, Inc.   7.14   ®1997 Sigma Consultants, L.L.C.

Illustration 1d

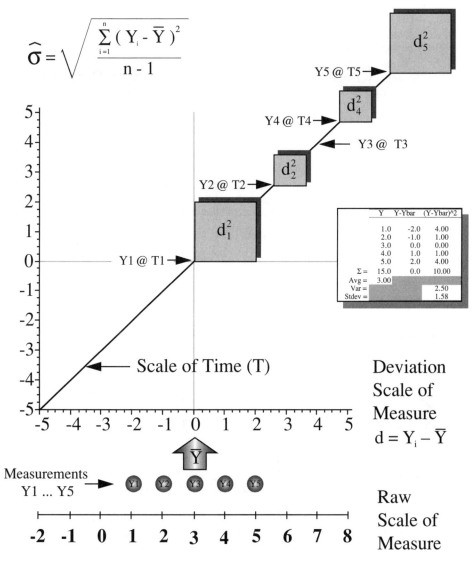

$$\hat{\sigma} = \sqrt{\frac{\sum_{i=1}^{n}(Y_i - \overline{Y})^2}{n-1}}$$

Y	Y-Ybar	(Y-Ybar)^2
1.0	-2.0	4.00
2.0	-1.0	1.00
3.0	0.0	0.00
4.0	1.0	1.00
5.0	2.0	4.00
Σ = 15.0	0.0	10.00
Avg = 3.00		
Var =		2.50
Stdev =		1.58

Deviation Scale of Measure
$d = Y_i - \overline{Y}$

Raw Scale of Measure

THE VISION OF SIX SIGMA

σ Six Sigma Academy, Inc.   7 . 15   ®1997 Sigma Consultants, L.L.C.

Illustration 1e

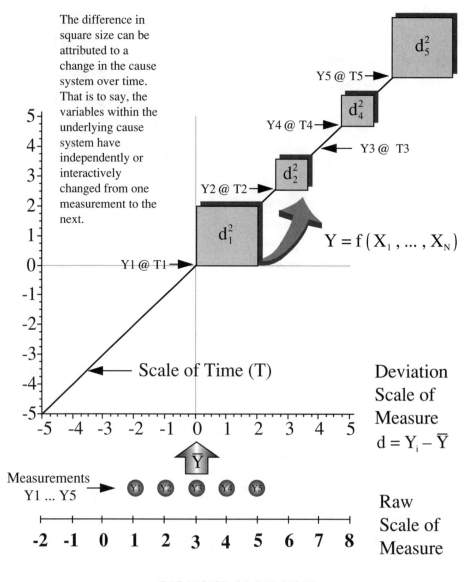

The difference in square size can be attributed to a change in the cause system over time. That is to say, the variables within the underlying cause system have independently or interactively changed from one measurement to the next.

d_5^2

Y5 @ T5 →

d_4^2

Y4 @ T4 →

← Y3 @ T3

d_2^2

Y2 @ T2 →

d_1^2

$Y = f(X_1, ..., X_N)$

Y1 @ T1 →

← Scale of Time (T)

Deviation Scale of Measure

$d = Y_i - \overline{Y}$

$\overline{Y}$

Measurements Y1 ... Y5 → (Y1) (Y2) (Y3) (Y4) (Y5)

Raw Scale of Measure

THE VISION OF SIX SIGMA

σ Six Sigma Academy, Inc.   7 . 16   ®1997 Sigma Consultants, L.L.C.

Illustration 1f

$$\hat{\sigma} = \sqrt{\frac{\sum\limits_{i=1}^{n}(Y_i - \overline{Y})^2}{n-1}}$$

Sum-of-Squares
SS

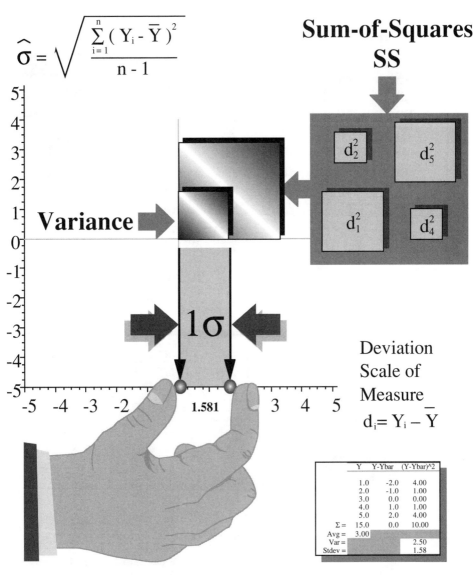

Variance

d_2^2 d_5^2 d_1^2 d_4^2

1σ

1.581

Deviation
Scale of
Measure
$d_i = Y_i - \overline{Y}$

	Y	Y-Ybar	(Y-Ybar)^2
	1.0	-2.0	4.00
	2.0	-1.0	1.00
	3.0	0.0	0.00
	4.0	1.0	1.00
	5.0	2.0	4.00
Σ =	15.0	0.0	10.00
Avg =	3.00		
Var =			2.50
Stdev =			1.58

THE VISION OF SIX SIGMA

σ Six Sigma Academy, Inc.   7 . 17   ®1997 Sigma Consultants, L.L.C.

Calculating By Hand

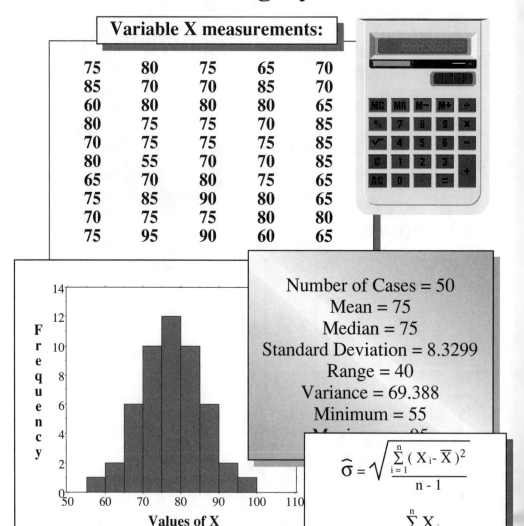

Variable X measurements:

75	80	75	65	70
85	70	70	85	70
60	80	80	80	65
80	75	75	70	85
70	75	75	75	85
80	55	70	70	85
65	70	80	75	65
75	85	90	80	65
70	75	75	80	80
75	95	90	60	65

Number of Cases = 50
Mean = 75
Median = 75
Standard Deviation = 8.3299
Range = 40
Variance = 69.388
Minimum = 55

$$\widehat{\sigma} = \sqrt{\frac{\sum_{i=1}^{n}(X_i - \overline{X})^2}{n-1}}$$

$$\overline{X} = \frac{\sum_{i=1}^{n} X_i}{n}$$

THE VISION OF SIX SIGMA

Six Sigma Academy, Inc.   7.18   ®1997 Sigma Consultants, L.L.C.

Calculating By Computer - 1a

General Rule: Always graph the data prior to performing a statistical analysis.

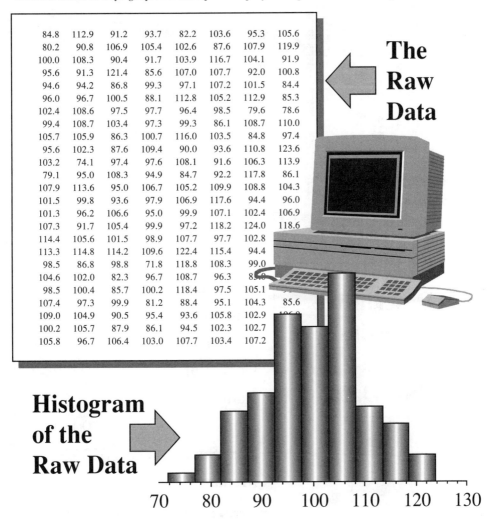

84.8	112.9	91.2	93.7	82.2	103.6	95.3	105.6
80.2	90.8	106.9	105.4	102.6	87.6	107.9	119.9
100.0	108.3	90.4	91.7	103.9	116.7	104.1	91.9
95.6	91.3	121.4	85.6	107.0	107.7	92.0	100.8
94.6	94.2	86.8	99.3	97.1	107.2	101.5	84.4
96.0	96.7	100.5	88.1	112.8	105.2	112.9	85.3
102.4	108.6	97.5	97.7	96.4	98.5	79.6	78.6
99.4	108.7	103.4	97.3	99.3	86.1	108.7	110.0
105.7	105.9	86.3	100.7	116.0	103.5	84.8	97.4
95.6	102.3	87.6	109.4	90.0	93.6	110.8	123.6
103.2	74.1	97.4	97.6	108.1	91.6	106.3	113.9
79.1	95.0	108.3	94.9	84.7	92.2	117.8	86.1
107.9	113.6	95.0	106.7	105.2	109.9	108.8	104.3
101.5	99.8	93.6	97.9	106.9	117.6	94.4	96.0
101.3	96.2	106.6	95.0	99.9	107.1	102.4	106.9
107.3	91.7	105.4	99.9	97.2	118.2	124.0	118.6
114.4	105.6	101.5	98.9	107.7	97.7	102.8	
113.3	114.8	114.2	109.6	122.4	115.4	94.4	
98.5	86.8	98.8	71.8	118.8	108.3	99.0	
104.6	102.0	82.3	96.7	108.7	96.3	85.6	
98.5	100.4	85.7	100.2	118.4	97.5	105.1	
107.4	97.3	99.9	81.2	88.4	95.1	104.3	85.6
109.0	104.9	90.5	95.4	93.6	105.8	102.9	106.0
100.2	105.7	87.9	86.1	94.5	102.3	102.7	
105.8	96.7	106.4	103.0	107.7	103.4	107.2	

The
Raw
Data

Histogram
of the
Raw Data

70   80   90   100   110   120   130

THE VISION OF SIX SIGMA

σ Six Sigma Academy, Inc.   7 . 19   ® 1997 Sigma Consultants, L.L.C.

Calculating By Computer - 1b

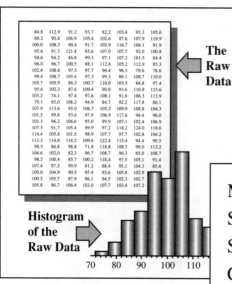

$$\hat{\sigma} = \sqrt{\dfrac{\sum\limits_{i=1}^{n} (X_i - \overline{X})^2}{n - 1}}$$

The
Raw
Data

$$\overline{X} = \dfrac{\sum\limits_{i=1}^{n} X_i}{n}$$

Histogram
of the
Raw Data

70   80   90   100   110

Descriptive Statistics for the Raw Data

Mean	100.30
Std. Dev.	10.01
Std. Error	.71
Count	200
Minimum	71.75
Maximum	123.99
Variance	100.18
Coef. Var.	9.98E-2
Range	52.23
Sum	20060.33
Sum Squares	2032020.74
Median	100.45

The Widget Example Data

g	X1	X2	X3	X4	X5
1	1.242	1.239	1.239	1.242	1.240
2	1.240	1.241	1.240	1.239	1.242
3	1.239	1.239	1.239	1.239	1.240
4	1.241	1.240	1.240	1.240	1.241
5	1.240	1.241	1.240	1.238	1.241
6	1.241	1.240	1.240	1.240	1.239
7	1.237	1.240	1.240	1.237	1.238
8	1.240	1.242	1.240	1.240	1.238
9	1.240	1.239	1.240	1.239	1.242
10	1.239	1.239	1.241	1.239	1.240
11	1.239	1.238	1.242	1.238	1.240
12	1.239	1.241	1.239	1.239	1.242
13	1.239	1.242	1.239	1.239	
14	1.240	1.239	1.240	1.239	
15	1.241	1.240	1.240	1.240	
16	1.240	1.239	1.240	1.240	
17	1.241	1.239	1.238	1.240	
18	1.239	1.239	1.241	1.241	1.239
19	1.240	1.239	1.240	1.238	1.242
20	1.241	1.240	1.241	1.239	1.240

1.240 ± .003

Dimension
"B"

Sampling Strategy: 5 consecutive parts were selected every hour. Each group (g) of parts was labeled and set aside for careful measurement of dimension "B." The location of each measurement was arbitrarily chosen by the inspector.

THE VISION OF SIX SIGMA

Six Sigma Academy, Inc.   7 . 21   ®1997 Sigma Consultants, L.L.C.

The Widget Part Analysis

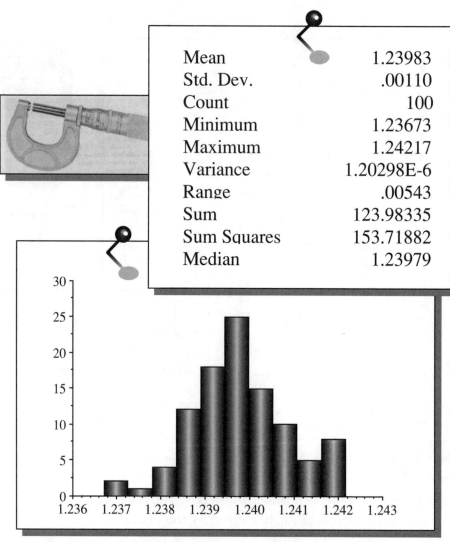

Mean	1.23983
Std. Dev.	.00110
Count	100
Minimum	1.23673
Maximum	1.24217
Variance	1.20298E-6
Range	.00543
Sum	123.98335
Sum Squares	153.71882
Median	1.23979

General Rule: Always graph the data prior to any form of analysis.

THE VISION OF SIX SIGMA

Six Sigma Academy, Inc.   7 . 22   ®1997 Sigma Consultants, L.L.C.

The Range and Standard Deviation

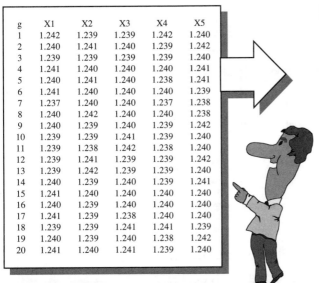

g	X1	X2	X3	X4	X5
1	1.242	1.239	1.239	1.242	1.240
2	1.240	1.241	1.240	1.239	1.242
3	1.239	1.239	1.239	1.239	1.240
4	1.241	1.240	1.240	1.240	1.241
5	1.240	1.241	1.240	1.238	1.241
6	1.241	1.240	1.240	1.240	1.239
7	1.237	1.240	1.240	1.237	1.238
8	1.240	1.242	1.240	1.240	1.238
9	1.240	1.239	1.240	1.239	1.242
10	1.239	1.239	1.241	1.239	1.240
11	1.239	1.238	1.242	1.238	1.240
12	1.239	1.241	1.239	1.239	1.242
13	1.239	1.242	1.239	1.239	1.240
14	1.240	1.239	1.240	1.239	1.241
15	1.241	1.240	1.240	1.240	1.240
16	1.240	1.239	1.240	1.240	1.240
17	1.241	1.239	1.238	1.240	1.240
18	1.239	1.239	1.241	1.241	1.239
19	1.240	1.239	1.240	1.238	1.242
20	1.241	1.240	1.241	1.239	1.240

Range	Stdev
.0030	.0015
.0030	.0011
.0010	.0004
.0010	.0005
.0030	.0012
.0020	.0007
.0030	.0015
.0040	.0014
.0030	.0012
.0020	.0009
.0040	.0017
.0030	.0014
.0030	.0013
.0020	.0008
.0010	.0004
.0010	.0004
.0030	.0011
.0020	.0011
.0040	.0015
.0020	.0008

Standard Deviation

$Y = 7.789E-5 + .387 * X; R^2 = .88$

Range

The Dynamic Range Exercise

Range   ## Stdev

					Row Range
1	2	3	4	5	4
1	2	3	4	5	4
1	2	3	4	5	4
1	2	3	4	5	4
1	2	3	4	5	4
		Overall Range =			4

					Row Stdev
1	2	3	4	5	1.58
1	2	3	4	5	1.58
1	2	3	4	5	1.58
1	2	3	4	5	1.58
1	2	3	4	5	1.58
		Overall Stdev =			1.44

So what is causing the difference between the upper and lower graphs?

					Row Range
1	2	3	4	5	4
2	3	4	5	6	4
3	4	5	6	7	4
4	5	6	7	8	4
5	6	7	8	9	4
		Overall Range =			8

					Row Stdev
1	2	3	4	5	1.58
2	3	4	5	6	1.58
3	4	5	6	7	1.58
4	5	6	7	8	1.58
5	6	7	8	9	1.58
		Overall Stdev =			2.04

. . . What Conclusions Can We Draw?

Visualizing the Process Dynamics

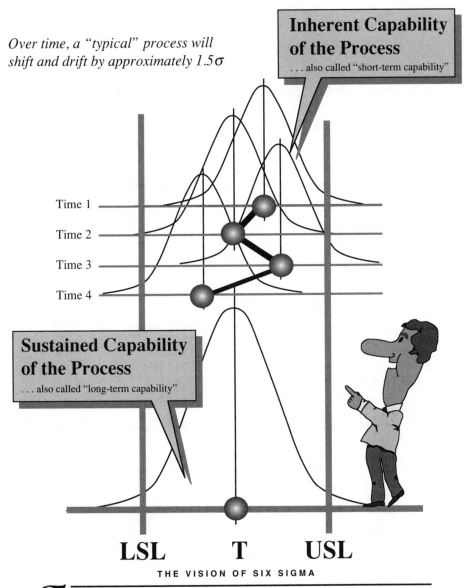

Over time, a "typical" process will shift and drift by approximately 1.5σ

Inherent Capability of the Process
. . . also called "short-term capability"

Time 1
Time 2
Time 3
Time 4

Sustained Capability of the Process
. . . also called "long-term capability"

LSL   T   USL

THE VISION OF SIX SIGMA

The Idea of Rational Subgroups

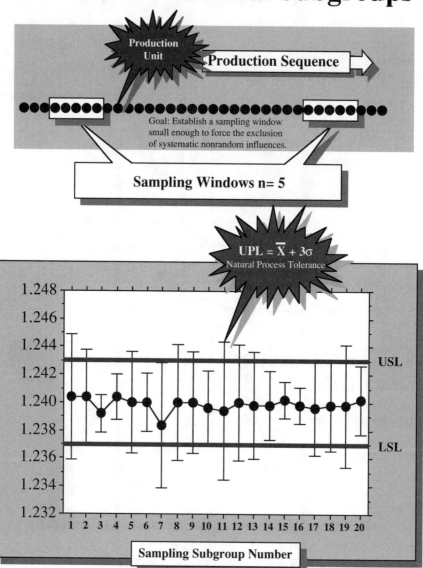

Production Unit

Production Sequence →

Goal: Establish a sampling window small enough to force the exclusion of systematic nonrandom influences.

Sampling Windows n= 5

$$UPL = \overline{X} + 3\sigma$$
Natural Process Tolerance

Sampling Subgroup Number

THE VISION OF SIX SIGMA

σ Six Sigma Academy, Inc.   7 . 26   ®1997 Sigma Consultants, L.L.C.

The Components of Variation

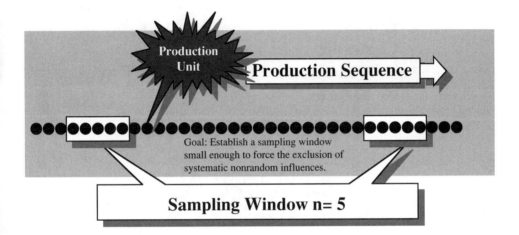

Production Unit

Production Sequence →

Goal: Establish a sampling window small enough to force the exclusion of systematic nonrandom influences.

Sampling Window n= 5

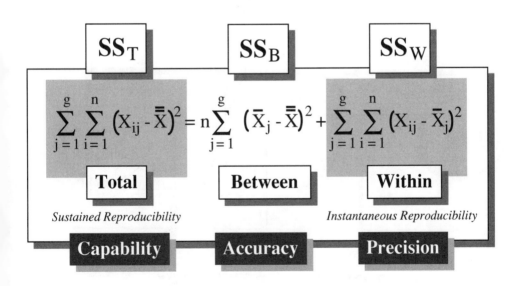

SS_T SS_B SS_W

$$\sum_{j=1}^{g} \sum_{i=1}^{n} (X_{ij} - \bar{\bar{X}})^2 = n\sum_{j=1}^{g} (\bar{X}_j - \bar{\bar{X}})^2 + \sum_{j=1}^{g} \sum_{i=1}^{n} (X_{ij} - \bar{X}_j)^2$$

Total   **Between**   **Within**

Sustained Reproducibility   *Instantaneous Reproducibility*

Capability   **Accuracy**   **Precision**

Visualizing the Components

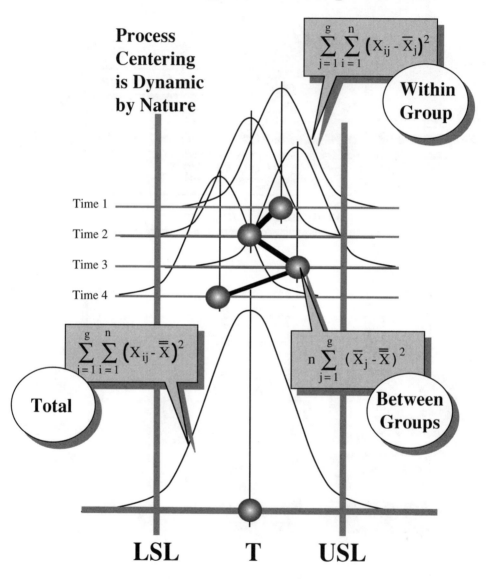

Process Centering is Dynamic by Nature

$$\sum_{j=1}^{g} \sum_{i=1}^{n} (X_{ij} - \overline{X}_j)^2$$

Within Group

Time 1
Time 2
Time 3
Time 4

$$\sum_{j=1}^{g} \sum_{i=1}^{n} (X_{ij} - \overline{\overline{X}})^2$$

$$n \sum_{j=1}^{g} (\overline{X}_j - \overline{\overline{X}})^2$$

Total

Between Groups

LSL   T   USL

THE VISION OF SIX SIGMA

Widget Characterization - 1a

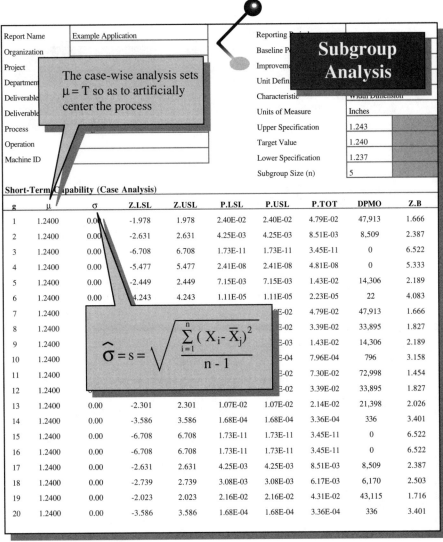

Report Name	Example Application
Organization	
Project	
Department	
Deliverable	
Deliverable	
Process	
Operation	
Machine ID	

The case-wise analysis sets $\mu = T$ so as to artificially center the process

Subgroup Analysis

Reporting Period	
Baseline Period	
Improvement	
Unit Definition	
Characteristic	Width Dimension
Units of Measure	Inches
Upper Specification	1.243
Target Value	1.240
Lower Specification	1.237
Subgroup Size (n)	5

Short-Term Capability (Case Analysis)

g	μ	σ	Z.LSL	Z.USL	P.LSL	P.USL	P.TOT	DPMO	Z.B
1	1.2400	0.00	-1.978	1.978	2.40E-02	2.40E-02	4.79E-02	47,913	1.666
2	1.2400	0.00	-2.631	2.631	4.25E-03	4.25E-03	8.51E-03	8,509	2.387
3	1.2400	0.00	-6.708	6.708	1.73E-11	1.73E-11	3.45E-11	0	6.522
4	1.2400	0.00	-5.477	5.477	2.41E-08	2.41E-08	4.81E-08	0	5.333
5	1.2400	0.00	-2.449	2.449	7.15E-03	7.15E-03	1.43E-02	14,306	2.189
6	1.2400	0.00	4.243	4.243	1.11E-05	1.11E-05	2.23E-05	22	4.083
7	1.2400						4.79E-02	47,913	1.666
8	1.2400						3.39E-02	33,895	1.827
9	1.2400						1.43E-02	14,306	2.189
10	1.2400						7.96E-04	796	3.158
11	1.2400						7.30E-02	72,998	1.454
12	1.2400						3.39E-02	33,895	1.827
13	1.2400	0.00	-2.301	2.301	1.07E-02	1.07E-02	2.14E-02	21,398	2.026
14	1.2400	0.00	-3.586	3.586	1.68E-04	1.68E-04	3.36E-04	336	3.401
15	1.2400	0.00	-6.708	6.708	1.73E-11	1.73E-11	3.45E-11	0	6.522
16	1.2400	0.00	-6.708	6.708	1.73E-11	1.73E-11	3.45E-11	0	6.522
17	1.2400	0.00	-2.631	2.631	4.25E-03	4.25E-03	8.51E-03	8,509	2.387
18	1.2400	0.00	-2.739	2.739	3.08E-03	3.08E-03	6.17E-03	6,170	2.503
19	1.2400	0.00	-2.023	2.023	2.16E-02	2.16E-02	4.31E-02	43,115	1.716
20	1.2400	0.00	-3.586	3.586	1.68E-04	1.68E-04	3.36E-04	336	3.401

$$\hat{\sigma} = s = \sqrt{\frac{\sum_{i=1}^{n}(X_i - \overline{X}_j)^2}{n-1}}$$

Format L2

THE VISION OF SIX SIGMA

Six Sigma Academy, Inc.   7 . 29   ®1997 Sigma Consultants, L.L.C.

Widget Characterization - 1b

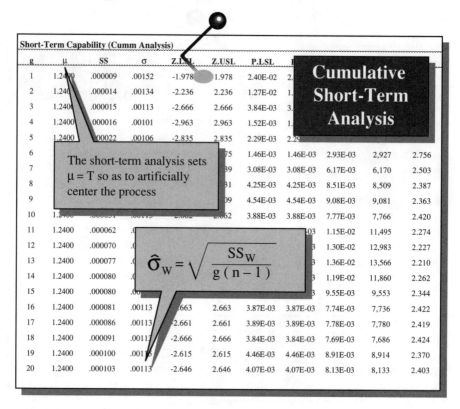

Short-Term Capability (Cumm Analysis)

g	μ	SS	σ	Z.LSL	Z.USL	P.LSL				
1	1.2400	.000009	.00152	-1.978	1.978	2.40E-02	2.			
2	1.2400	.000014	.00134	-2.236	2.236	1.27E-02	1.			
3	1.2400	.000015	.00113	-2.666	2.666	3.84E-03	3.			
4	1.2400	.000016	.00101	-2.963	2.963	1.52E-03	1.			
5	1.2400	.00022	.00106	-2.835	2.835	2.29E-03	2.29			
6					75	1.46E-03	1.46E-03	2.93E-03	2,927	2.756
7					39	3.08E-03	3.08E-03	6.17E-03	6,170	2.503
8					31	4.25E-03	4.25E-03	8.51E-03	8,509	2.387
9					09	4.54E-03	4.54E-03	9.08E-03	9,081	2.363
10	1.2400	.000051	.00115	-2.662	2.662	3.88E-03	3.88E-03	7.77E-03	7,766	2.420
11	1.2400	.000062						1.15E-02	11,495	2.274
12	1.2400	.000070						1.30E-02	12,983	2.227
13	1.2400	.000077						1.36E-02	13,566	2.210
14	1.2400	.000080						1.19E-02	11,860	2.262
15	1.2400	.000080						9.55E-03	9,553	2.344
16	1.2400	.000081	.00113	2.663	2.663	3.87E-03	3.87E-03	7.74E-03	7,736	2.422
17	1.2400	.000086	.00113	-2.661	2.661	3.89E-03	3.89E-03	7.78E-03	7,780	2.419
18	1.2400	.000091	.00113	-2.666	2.666	3.84E-03	3.84E-03	7.69E-03	7,686	2.424
19	1.2400	.000100	.00113	-2.615	2.615	4.46E-03	4.46E-03	8.91E-03	8,914	2.370
20	1.2400	.000103	.00113	-2.646	2.646	4.07E-03	4.07E-03	8.13E-03	8,133	2.403

Cumulative Short-Term Analysis

The short-term analysis sets $\mu = T$ so as to artificially center the process

$$\hat{\sigma}_W = \sqrt{\frac{SS_W}{g\,(n-1)}}$$

Widget Characterization - 1c

Long-Term Capability (Cumm Analysis)

g	μ	SS	σ	Z.LSL	Z.USL	P.LSL	P.USL				ift
1	1.2404	.000009	.00152	-2.242	1.71	1.25E-02	4.32E-02				4
2	1.2404	.000014	.00126	-2.688	2.055	3.59E-03	1.99E-02				2
3	1.2400	.000020	.00120	-2.510	2.510	6.04E-03	6.04E-03				9
4	1.2401	.0022	.00107	-2.894	2.707	1.90E-03	3.39E-03				7
5	1.2401	.028	.00108	-2.860	2.711	2.12E-03	3.35E-03				1
6	1.						1.26E-03	1.92E-03	3.18E-03	3,179	2.729	0.027
7	1.						1.04E-02	4.80E-03	1.52E-02	15,236	2.164	0.338
8	1.						1.03E-02	5.25E-03	1.56E-02	15,552	2.156	0.231
9	1.						9.26E-03	5.03E-03	1.43E-02	14,289	2.190	0.173
10	1.2398	.000069	.00116	-2.598	2.000	8.24E-03	3.81E-03	1.21E-02	12,050	2.256	0.164
11	1.2398	.000081	.00122	-2.280	2.616	1.10E-02	4.45E-03	1.55E-02	15,487	2.158	0.116
12	1.2398	.000089							1.57E-02	15,678	2.153	0.074
13	1.2398	.000096							1.53E-02	15,305	2.163	0.048
14	1.2398	.000099							1.31E-02	13,123	2.223	0.039
15	1.2398	.000100							1.06E-02	10,593	2.305	0.039
16	1.2398	.000101	.00113	1	2.799	6.02E-03	2.57E-03	8.59E-03	8,588	2.383	0.038
17	1.2398	.000106	.00113	509	2.823	6.05E-03	2.38E-03	8.43E-03	8,427	2.390	0.029
18	1.2398	.000111	.00112	2.525	2.843	5.78E-03	2.23E-03	8.01E-03	8,010	2.409	0.015
19	1.2398	.000120	.00112	-2.497	2.814	6.26E-03	2.45E-03	8.70E-03	8,704	2.378	-0.009
20	1.2398	.000123	.00112	-2.543	2.830	5.49E-03	2.33E-03	7.82E-03	7,817	2.418	-0.014

Cumulative Long-Term Analysis

$$\bar{\bar{X}} = \frac{\displaystyle\sum_{j=1}^{g} \sum_{i=1}^{n} X_{ij}}{ng}$$

$$\hat{\sigma}_T = \sqrt{\frac{SS_T}{ng - 1}}$$

Widget Characterization - 1d

Analyzing the Sum-of-Squares . . .

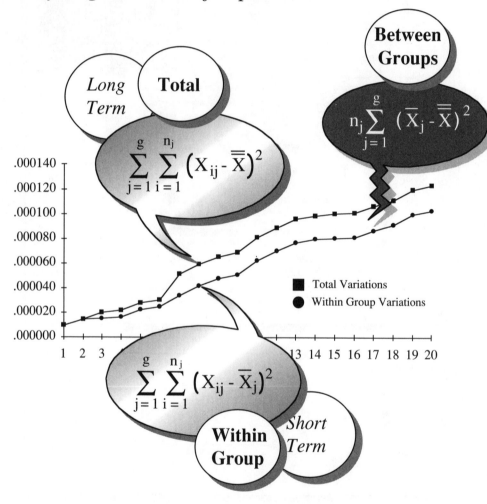

THE VISION OF SIX SIGMA

Six Sigma Academy, Inc.   7 . 32   ®1997 Sigma Consultants, L.L.C.

Widget Characterization - 1e

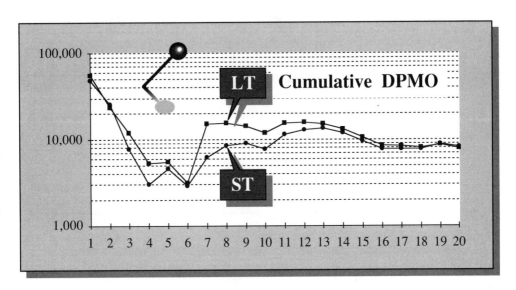

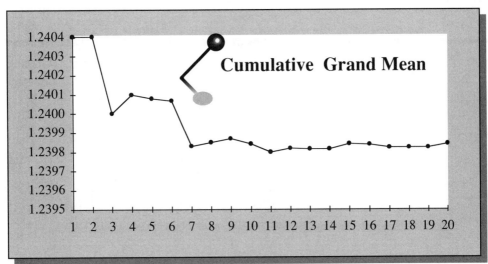

σ Six Sigma Academy, Inc.   7 . 33   ®1997 Sigma Consultants, L.L.C.

Widget Characterization - 1f

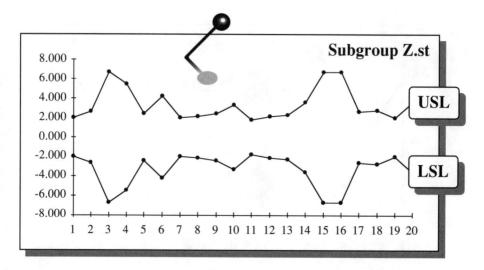

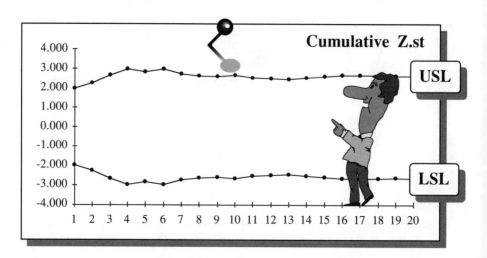

The Standard Transform

CHAPTER EIGHT

Breakthrough

Breakthrough

THE VISION OF SIX SIGMA

The Standard Transform

In many instances, we need to be able to compute the probability of exceeding a given design constraint without the aid of an illustration, or the complexity of mathematical integration. In such instances, we need only employ what is known as the "standard Z transform." Notice that it is also referred to as the "standard normal deviate." The reader should be aware that both usages will be employed in subsequent discussions and illustrations.

Essentially, the standard transform, or "Z" scale of measure, transforms a set of data such that the mean is always equal to zero ($\mu = 0$) and the standard deviation is always equal to one ($\sigma = 1.0$). Of course, the use of such a transformation assumes that the underlying distribution is normal. Statistically speaking, this would be to say $Z \sim \text{NID}$ (0, 1). In addition, the raw units of measure (e.g., inches as related to our widget example) are eliminated, or lost, by virtue of the transformation process. That is to say, the Z measurement scale is without units.

To illustrate how the standard transform is used, let's suppose we wanted to know how many σ are equivalent to 1.242 inches. To get the answer, we must transform the measurement of interest into a Z value by applying the following equation:

$$Z = \frac{(X - \mu)}{\sigma}$$

Eq. (1)

This particular equation is for population values. If a sample is used, then substitute $\overline{x}$ for μ and s for σ. Substituting the values of our known population parameters into the equation, we would have:

$$Z = \frac{1.242 - 1.240}{.001}$$

Eq. (2)

Making the necessary calculations reveals $Z = 2.000$. This tells us that the length measurement of 1.242 lies 2σ to the right of μ. It would be to the right because the Z equivalent of 1.242 in. is positive. If Z were a negative number, say -2.000, then the corresponding product measurement value would lie to the left of μ. We shall see later why the standard transform is so important, but for now, let's just recognize that it's an invaluable tool.

Using Z as a Measure of Capability

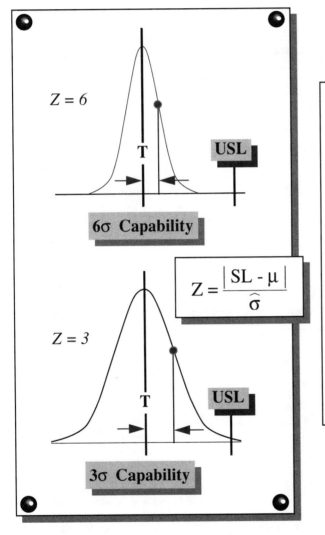

$$Z = \frac{|SL - \mu|}{\widehat{\sigma}}$$

As variation decreases, capability increases and, as a consequence, the standard deviation (σ) gets smaller which, in turn, decreases the probability of a defect.

The Standard Normal Deviate

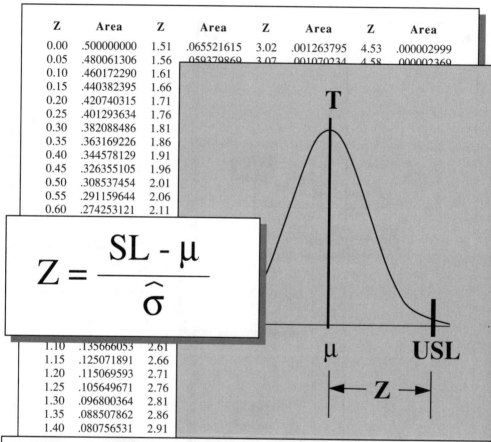

Z	Area	Z	Area	Z	Area	Z	Area
0.00	.500000000	1.51	.065521615	3.02	.001263795	4.53	.000002999
0.05	.480061306	1.56	.059379869	3.07	.001070234	4.58	.000002369
0.10	.460172290	1.61					
0.15	.440382395	1.66					
0.20	.420740315	1.71					
0.25	.401293634	1.76					
0.30	.382088486	1.81					
0.35	.363169226	1.86					
0.40	.344578129	1.91					
0.45	.326355105	1.96					
0.50	.308537454	2.01					
0.55	.291159644	2.06					
0.60	.274253121	2.11					
1.10	.135666053	2.61					
1.15	.125071891	2.66					
1.20	.115069593	2.71					
1.25	.105649671	2.76					
1.30	.096800364	2.81					
1.35	.088507862	2.86					
1.40	.080756531	2.91					

$$Z = \frac{SL - \mu}{\hat{\sigma}}$$

Of course, this entire discussion assumes that the underlying distribution is normal. We must always remain cognizant of the fact that whenever a table of normal area is used to establish a rate of nonconformance, and the actual distribution is markedly skewed (i.e., non-normal), the likelihood of grossly distorted estimates is quite high. To avoid such distortion, it is often possible to mathematically transform the raw data. If the transformation is done correctly, the data are artificially forced to a state of normality. Only then can reliable estimates of nonconformance be rendered. Even then, one must always check to be sure that the transformed data retains correlation to the raw data. If not, resultant estimates could be highly misleading.

THE VISION OF SIX SIGMA

σ Six Sigma Academy, Inc.   8 . 4   ®1997 Sigma Consultants, L.L.C.

The Standard Normal Deviate

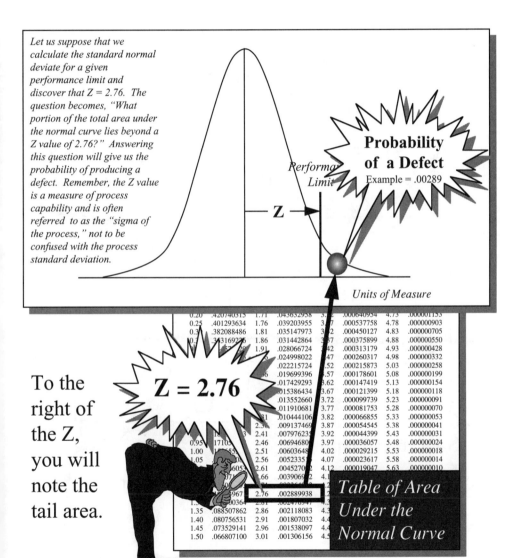

Let us suppose that we calculate the standard normal deviate for a given performance limit and discover that Z = 2.76. The question becomes, "What portion of the total area under the normal curve lies beyond a Z value of 2.76?" Answering this question will give us the probability of producing a defect. Remember, the Z value is a measure of process capability and is often referred to as the "sigma of the process," not to be confused with the process standard deviation.

Probability of a Defect
Example = .00289

Performance Limit

Z

Units of Measure

To the right of the Z, you will note the tail area.

Z = 2.76

0.20	.420740315	1.71	.043632958	3.?	.000640954	4.73	.000001153
0.25	.401293634	1.76	.039203955	3.?7	.000537758	4.78	.000000903
0.3?	.382088486	1.81	.035147973	3.?2	.000450127	4.83	.000000705
0.?	.?43169??	1.86	.031442864	?.?7	.000375899	4.88	.000000550
	.????	1.91	.028066724	?.42	.000313179	4.93	.000000428
			.024998022	?.47	.000260317	4.98	.000000332
		?	.022215724	?.52	.000215873	5.03	.000000258
		?.?	.019699396	?.57	.000178601	5.08	.000000199
			.017429293	?.62	.000147419	5.13	.000000154
			.015386434	3.67	.000121399	5.18	.000000118
			.013552660	3.72	.000099739	5.23	.000000091
			.011910681	3.77	.000081753	5.28	.000000070
		?.?1	.010444106	3.82	.000066855	5.33	.000000053
		2.??	.009137469	3.87	.000054545	5.38	.000000041
		2.41	.00797623?	3.92	.000044399	5.43	.000000031
0.95	.17105?	2.46	.0069468??	3.97	.000036057	5.48	.000000024
1.00	.1?755?	2.51	.00603648	4.02	.000029215	5.53	.000000018
1.05	.????	2.56	.0052335?	4.07	.000023617	5.58	.000000014
	.?605?	2.61	.0045270??	4.12	.000019047	5.63	.000000010
	.?7??	1.66	.0039069??	4.1?			
	.?967	2.76	.002889938				
	.?0364	2.?1	.0024?894?	4.?			
1.35	.088507862	2.86	.002118083	4.?			
1.40	.080756531	2.91	.001807032	4.4			
1.45	.073529141	2.96	.001538097	4.4			
1.50	.066807100	3.01	.001306156	4.5			

2.76   .002889938

Table of Area Under the Normal Curve

THE VISION OF SIX SIGMA

Six Sigma Academy, Inc.   8 . 5   ®1997 Sigma Consultants, L.L.C.

The Universal Equation for Z

$$Z = \frac{SL - \lambda}{\sigma}$$

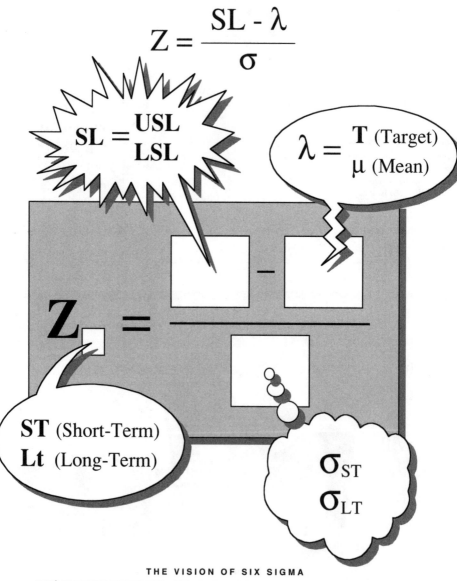

$$SL = \frac{USL}{LSL}$$

$$\lambda = \frac{T \text{ (Target)}}{\mu \text{ (Mean)}}$$

$$Z_\square =$$

ST (Short-Term)
Lt (Long-Term)

$$\sigma_{ST}$$
$$\sigma_{LT}$$

THE VISION OF SIX SIGMA

σ Six Sigma Academy, Inc.   8.6   ®1997 Sigma Consultants, L.L.C.

Selecting an Appropriate Z

 Eq. 8.1 $Z = \dfrac{SL - T}{\hat{\sigma}_{st}}$

This Z value is designated as Z.st. It describes how precise the process is at any given moment in time. For this reason, it is referred to as "instantaneous capability." It is also called "short-term capability." In context of the Six Sigma Program, it is the value used when referring to the "SIGMA" of a process. It represents the true potential of the process technology to meet the given performance specification(s); i.e., what the process can do if everything is controlled to such an extent that only background (white) noise is present. It reflects the process capability under the assumption of random variation and does not give consideration to the process center. This metric assumes the data were gathered in accordance to the principals and spirit of a "rational sampling" plan. For a unilateral tolerance with no target Eq. 2 should be used.

Eq. 8.3 $Z = \dfrac{SL - T}{\hat{\sigma}_{lt}}$

This Z value is designated as Z.lt.d. It is a measure of long-term process capability. It reflects the influence of white noise, as well as the dynamic variations due to nonrandom process centering error; i.e., shifts and drifts in the process mean across sampling subgroups. It assumes that the errors in process centering are dynamic and will eventually average out (over a great many cycles) to the target specification. In context of the Six Sigma Program, it is not often used, except in some design engineering applications. This metric assumes the data were gathered in accordance to the principals and spirit of a "rational sampling" plan. For a unilateral tolerance with no target value, this equation can not be used. In such an event, Eq. 4 should be employed to estimate long-term process capability.

Eq. 8.2 $Z = \dfrac{SL - \hat{\mu}}{\hat{\sigma}_{st}}$

This Z value is designated as Z.lt. It is a measure of long-term capability and, when used properly, reflects process accuracy when compared to Z.st; e.g., Z.st - Z.lt = Z.shift. Expressed differently, it reflects how well the process remains centered over time. Of course, it ignores any nonrandom process centering errors which may occur between sampling intervals. This metric assumes the data were gathered in accordance to the principals and spirit of a "rational sampling" plan. However, in the instance of a unilateral tolerance with no target specification, the given Z value will reflect only short-term capability. In this circumstance, the mean becomes the target. Consequently, it will produce the same result as Eq. 1; therefore, it should be designated as Z.st and so interpreted.

⭐ **Eq. 8.4** $Z = \dfrac{SL - \hat{\mu}}{\hat{\sigma}_{lt}}$

This Z value is designated as Z.lt.s. It describes the sustained reproducibility of a process. Because of this, it is also called "long-term capability." In context of the Six Sigma Program, it is the value used to estimate the long-term process "PPM." It reflects the influence of white noise, dynamic nonrandom process centering error, and any static off-set present in the process mean. From this perspective, it considers all of the "vital few" sources of manufacturing error. It is a measure of how well the process is controlled (over many cycles) when compared to Z.st. This metric assumes the data were gathered in accordance to the principals and spirit of a "rational sampling" plan. This equation is applicable to all types of tolerances.

THE VISION OF SIX SIGMA

σ Six Sigma Academy, Inc.   8 . 7   ®1997 Sigma Consultants, L.L.C.

Statistical Definition of Six Sigma

Distribution Centered

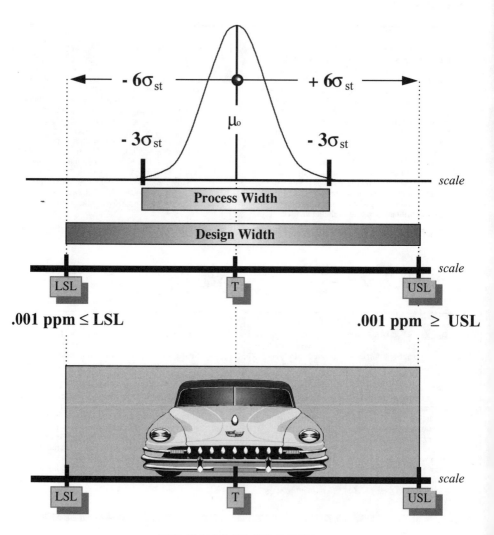

.001 ppm ≤ LSL

.001 ppm ≥ USL

THE VISION OF SIX SIGMA

Statistical Definition of Six Sigma

Distribution Shifted 1.5σ

*This example shows a 1.5σ shift which is positive in direction
(i.e., to the right). In practice, the shift could also be
negative; however, shift can not be both directions
simultaneously. It is one way or the other but not both.*

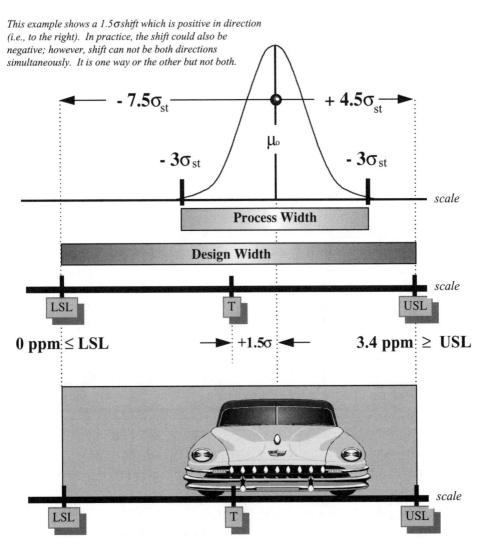

THE VISION OF SIX SIGMA

σ Six Sigma Academy, Inc.   8.9   ®1997 Sigma Consultants, L.L.C.

The Widget Example Data

g	X1	X2	X3	X4	X5
1	1.242	1.239	1.239	1.242	1.240
2	1.240	1.241	1.240	1.239	1.242
3	1.239	1.239	1.239	1.239	1.240
4	1.241	1.240	1.240	1.240	1.241
5	1.240	1.241	1.240	1.238	1.241
6	1.241	1.240	1.240	1.240	1.239
7	1.237	1.240	1.240	1.237	1.238
8	1.240	1.242	1.240	1.240	1.238
9	1.240	1.239	1.240	1.239	1.242
10	1.239	1.239	1.241	1.239	1.240
11	1.239	1.238	1.242	1.238	1.240
12	1.239	1.241	1.239	1.239	1.242
13	1.239	1.242	1.239	1.239	1.240
14	1.240	1.239	1.240	1.239	1.241
15	1.241	1.240	1.240	1.240	1.240
16	1.240	1.239	1.240	1.240	1.240
17	1.241	1.239	1.238	1.240	1.240
18	1.239	1.239	1.241	1.241	1.239
19	1.240	1.239	1.240	1.238	1.242
20	1.241	1.240	1.241	1.239	1.240

Sampling Strategy: 5 consecutive parts were selected every hour $(X_1, \dots, X_N)$. Each group (g) of parts was labeled and set aside for careful measurement of dimension "B." The location of measurement was arbitrarily chosen by the inspector.

Widget Characterization - 2a

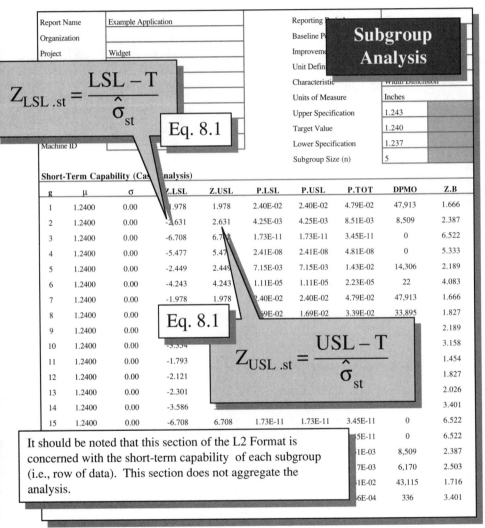

Report Name	Example Application
Organization	
Project	Widget

Subgroup Analysis

Reporting P...	
Baseline P...	
Improveme...	
Unit Defini...	
Characteristic	Width Dimension
Units of Measure	Inches
Upper Specification	1.243
Target Value	1.240
Lower Specification	1.237
Subgroup Size (n)	5

$$Z_{LSL\,.st} = \frac{LSL - T}{\hat{\sigma}_{st}}$$

Eq. 8.1

Machine ID

Short-Term Capability (Ca... nalysis)

g	μ	σ	Z.LSL	Z.USL	P.LSL	P.USL	P.TOT	DPMO	Z.B
1	1.2400	0.00	.978	1.978	2.40E-02	2.40E-02	4.79E-02	47,913	1.666
2	1.2400	0.00	-2.631	2.631	4.25E-03	4.25E-03	8.51E-03	8,509	2.387
3	1.2400	0.00	-6.708	6.7..	1.73E-11	1.73E-11	3.45E-11	0	6.522
4	1.2400	0.00	-5.477	5.47	2.41E-08	2.41E-08	4.81E-08	0	5.333
5	1.2400	0.00	-2.449	2.449	7.15E-03	7.15E-03	1.43E-02	14,306	2.189
6	1.2400	0.00	-4.243	4.243	1.11E-05	1.11E-05	2.23E-05	22	4.083
7	1.2400	0.00	-1.978	1.978	2.40E-02	2.40E-02	4.79E-02	47,913	1.666
8	1.2400	0.00			9E-02	1.69E-02	3.39E-02	33,895	1.827
9	1.2400	0.00							2.189
10	1.2400	0.00	-3.334						3.158
11	1.2400	0.00	-1.793						1.454
12	1.2400	0.00	-2.121						1.827
13	1.2400	0.00	-2.301						2.026
14	1.2400	0.00	-3.586						3.401
15	1.2400	0.00	-6.708	6.708	1.73E-11	1.73E-11	3.45E-11	0	6.522

Eq. 8.1

$$Z_{USL\,.st} = \frac{USL - T}{\hat{\sigma}_{st}}$$

It should be noted that this section of the L2 Format is concerned with the short-term capability of each subgroup (i.e., row of data). This section does not aggregate the analysis.

...5E-11	0	6.522
...1E-03	8,509	2.387
...7E-03	6,170	2.503
...1E-02	43,115	1.716
...6E-04	336	3.401

Format L2

THE VISION OF SIX SIGMA

σ Six Sigma Academy, Inc.   8.11   ®1997 Sigma Consultants, L.L.C.

Widget Characterization - 2b

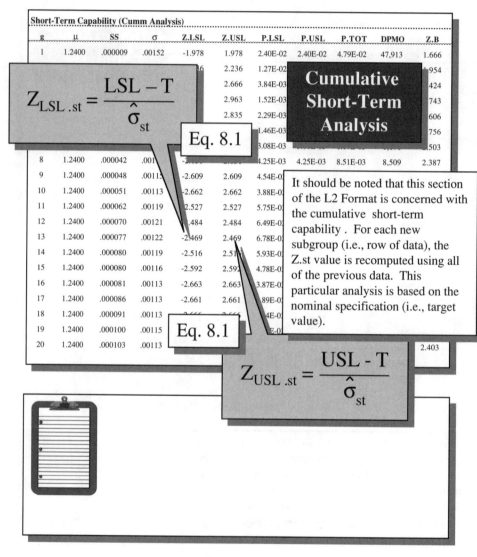

Short-Term Capability (Cumm Analysis)

g	μ	SS	σ	Z.LSL	Z.USL	P.LSL	P.USL	P.TOT	DPMO	Z.B
1	1.2400	.000009	.00152	-1.978	1.978	2.40E-02	2.40E-02	4.79E-02	47,913	1.666
					2.236	1.27E-02				.954
					2.666	3.84E-03				.424
					2.963	1.52E-03				.743
					2.835	2.29E-03				.606
						1.46E-03				.756
						3.08E-03				.503
8	1.2400	.000042	.001			4.25E-03	4.25E-03	8.51E-03	8,509	2.387
9	1.2400	.000048	.0011	-2.609	2.609	4.54E-0				
10	1.2400	.000051	.00113	-2.662	2.662	3.88E-0				
11	1.2400	.000062	.00119	2.527	2.527	5.75E-0				
12	1.2400	.000070	.00121	.484	2.484	6.49E-0				
13	1.2400	.000077	.00122	-2.469	2.469	6.78E-0				
14	1.2400	.000080	.00119	-2.516	2.51	5.93E-0				
15	1.2400	.000080	.00116	-2.592	2.59	4.78E-0				
16	1.2400	.000081	.00113	-2.663	2.663	3.87E-0				
17	1.2400	.000086	.00113	-2.661	2.661	89E-0				
18	1.2400	.000091	.00113			4E-0				
19	1.2400	.000100	.00115			E-0				
20	1.2400	.000103	.00113							2.403

$$Z_{LSL.st} = \frac{LSL - T}{\hat{\sigma}_{st}}$$

Eq. 8.1

Cumulative Short-Term Analysis

It should be noted that this section of the L2 Format is concerned with the cumulative short-term capability. For each new subgroup (i.e., row of data), the Z.st value is recomputed using all of the previous data. This particular analysis is based on the nominal specification (i.e., target value).

Eq. 8.1

$$Z_{USL.st} = \frac{USL - T}{\hat{\sigma}_{st}}$$

Widget Characterization - 2c

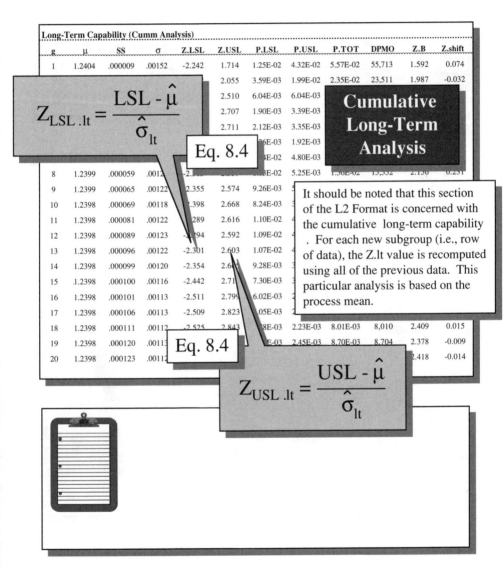

Long-Term Capability (Cumm Analysis)

g	μ	SS	σ	Z.LSL	Z.USL	P.LSL	P.USL	P.TOT	DPMO	Z.B	Z.shift
1	1.2404	.000009	.00152	-2.242	1.714	1.25E-02	4.32E-02	5.57E-02	55,713	1.592	0.074
					2.055	3.59E-03	1.99E-02	2.35E-02	23,511	1.987	-0.032
					2.510	6.04E-03	6.04E-03				
					2.707	1.90E-03	3.39E-03				
					2.711	2.12E-03	3.35E-03				
						6E-03	1.92E-03				
						E-02	4.80E-03				
8	1.2399	.000059	.0012	-2.		8E-02	5.25E-03	1.56E-02	15,552	2.156	0.231
9	1.2399	.000065	.00122	2.355	2.574	9.26E-03					
10	1.2398	.000069	.00118	.398	2.668	8.24E-03					
11	1.2398	.000081	.00122	289	2.616	1.10E-02					
12	1.2398	.000089	.00123	94	2.592	1.09E-02					
13	1.2398	.000096	.00122	-2.301	2.603	1.07E-02					
14	1.2398	.000099	.00120	-2.354	2.6	9.28E-03					
15	1.2398	.000100	.00116	-2.442	2.71	7.30E-03					
16	1.2398	.000101	.00113	-2.511	2.799	6.02E-03					
17	1.2398	.000106	.00113	-2.509	2.823	05E-03					
18	1.2398	.000111	.00112	-2.525	2.843	8E-03	2.23E-03	8.01E-03	8,010	2.409	0.015
19	1.2398	.000120	.0011			E-03	2.45E-03	8.70E-03	8,704	2.378	-0.009
20	1.2398	.000123	.0011							2.418	-0.014

$$Z_{LSL\,.lt} = \frac{LSL - \hat{\mu}}{\hat{\sigma}_{lt}}$$

Eq. 8.4

Cumulative Long-Term Analysis

It should be noted that this section of the L2 Format is concerned with the cumulative long-term capability. For each new subgroup (i.e., row of data), the Z.lt value is recomputed using all of the previous data. This particular analysis is based on the process mean.

Eq. 8.4

$$Z_{USL\,.lt} = \frac{USL - \hat{\mu}}{\hat{\sigma}_{lt}}$$

Widget Characterization - 2d

Eq. 8.1 - Case-wise

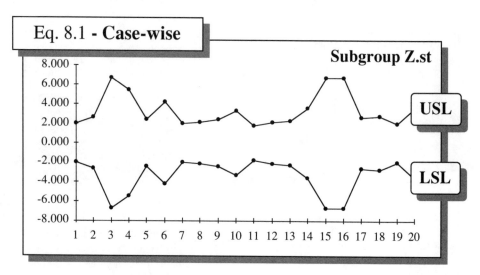

Eq. 8.1 - Cumulative

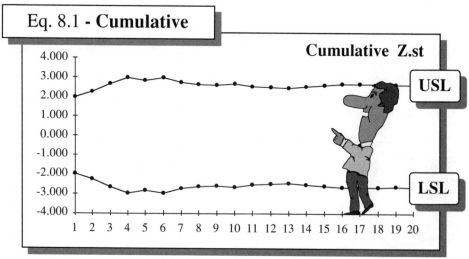

THE VISION OF SIX SIGMA

σ Six Sigma Academy, Inc.   8 . 14   ®1997 Sigma Consultants, L.L.C.

Widget Characterization - 2e

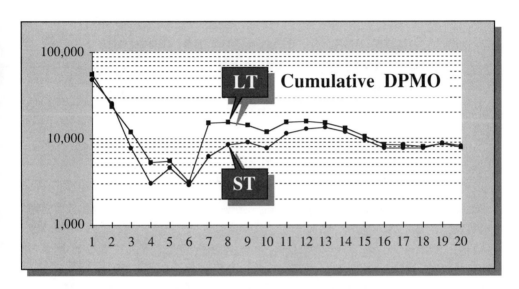

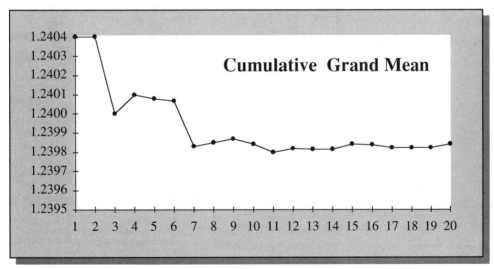

THE VISION OF SIX SIGMA

Six Sigma Academy, Inc.   8 . 15   ®1997 Sigma Consultants, L.L.C.

Process Capability Ratios: Cp

> ➢ The greater the design margin, the lower the Total Defects Per Unit (TDU).
> ➢ Design margin is measured by the Process Capability Index (Cp)

$$Cp = \frac{(\text{Maximum Allowable Range of Characteristic})}{(\text{Normal Variation of Process -- Short Term})}$$

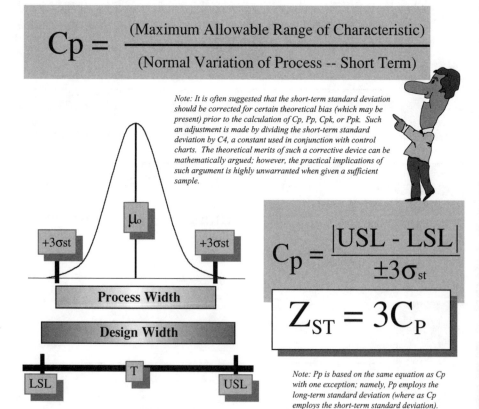

Note: It is often suggested that the short-term standard deviation should be corrected for certain theoretical bias (which may be present) prior to the calculation of Cp, Pp, Cpk, or Ppk. Such an adjustment is made by dividing the short-term standard deviation by C4, a constant used in conjunction with control charts. The theoretical merits of such a corrective device can be mathematically argued; however, the practical implications of such argument is highly unwarranted when given a sufficient sample.

$+3\sigma st$ $+3\sigma st$

Process Width

Design Width

μ_o

LSL   T   USL

$$C_p = \frac{|USL - LSL|}{\pm 3\sigma_{st}}$$

$$Z_{ST} = 3C_P$$

Note: Pp is based on the same equation as Cp with one exception; namely, Pp employs the long-term standard deviation (where as Cp employs the short-term standard deviation).

THE VISION OF SIX SIGMA

Process Capability Ratios: Cpk

$$Cpk = Cp (1 - k)$$

Note: Ppk is based on the same equation as Cpk with one exception; namely, Pp employs the long-term standard deviation (where as Cp employs the short-term standard deviation).

Where k1 is the proportion of the tolerance zone consumed by the static mean shift

$$k = \frac{|T - \mu|}{(USL - LSL)/2}$$

Example: Cp = 2 , k = .25

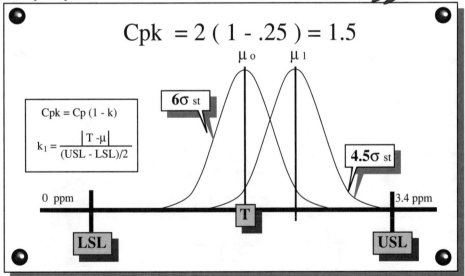

$$Cpk = 2 (1 - .25) = 1.5$$

μ_0 μ_1

6σ st

Cpk = Cp (1 - k)

$$k_1 = \frac{|T - \mu|}{(USL - LSL)/2}$$

4.5σ st

0 ppm   3.4 ppm

T

LSL   USL

THE VISION OF SIX SIGMA

σ Six Sigma Academy, Inc.   8 . 17   ®1997 Sigma Consultants, L.L.C.

Process Capability Ratios: Pp

Note: Pp is based on the same equation as Cp with one exception; namely, Pp employs the long-term standard deviation (where as Cp employs the short-term standard deviation).

$$P_p = \frac{|USL - LSL|}{\pm 3\sigma_{lt}}$$

$$Z_{LT} = 3P_P$$

$$P_p = \frac{(\text{Maximum Allowable Range of Characteristic})}{(\text{Normal Variation of Process -- Long Term})}$$

Short-term distribution displays only pure error, i.e., white noise only. Mean is artifically centered on the target value (by virtue of the equation).

Long-term distribution displays white and black noise. In this instance, black noise are the nonrandom variations in the process mean which tends to expand the standard deviation. In the instance of Pp, the mean is artifically centered on the target value (by virtue of the equation).

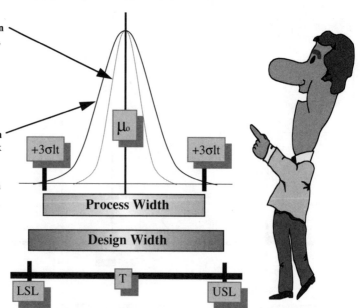

μ_o

$+3\sigma lt$ $+3\sigma lt$

Process Width

Design Width

LSL   T   USL

THE VISION OF SIX SIGMA

Process Capability Ratios: Ppk

$$Ppk = Pp \, (1 - k)$$

Note: Ppk is based on the same equation as Cpk with one exception; namely, Pp employs the long-term standard deviation (where as Cp employs the short-term standard deviation).

Where k1 is the proportion of the tolerance zone consumed by the static mean shift

Note: The k value is computed the same way as in the Cpk metric. Again, the only difference is that Cpk utilizes the short-term standard deviation whereas Ppk employs the long-term standard deviation.

$$k = \frac{|T - \mu|}{(USL - LSL)/2}$$

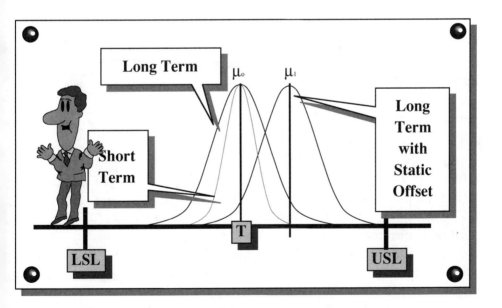

Six Sigma Academy, Inc.   8 . 19   ®1997 Sigma Consultants, L.L.C.

Impact of Process Capability

- If the process mean stays centered on the targeted nominal, then k = 0 (because the numerator of the equation equals 0) and Cpk = Cp.

$$C_p = \frac{USL - LSL}{6\sigma}$$

- For individual parts, the design ideal is Cp = 2; in other words, the design specification is twice as "wide" as the true capability of the process. This is where the phrase "Six Sigma Quality" originated; since the process capability is ±3σ, a design specification twice as wide would be ±6σ.

- However, as indicated by the existence of the Cpk measure, processes rarely stay centered on their targeted nominals. Shifts of 1.5σ to either side of the mean are common, even in well-controlled processes.

$$C_{pk} = C_p (1 - k)$$

- Therefore, in practice, an ultimate Z-value of 4.5 is considered Six Sigma Quality. Consulting the Z-table, we find the probability associated with a Z-value of 4.5 to be .0000034. If this value is obtained, then only 3.4 out of every million parts manufactured will be defective.

$$k = \frac{|\text{nominal} - \mu|}{(USL - LSL)/2}$$

Note: Cpk does not take into account long-term dynamic variations in the mean; however, it does consider static offset in the mean.

THE VISION OF SIX SIGMA

Indices of Process Capability

Eq. 8.1

Short-Term Capability

Cp	Z.st	DPO	PPM
0.50	1.5	.0668072	66,807
0.67	2.0	.0227501	22,750
0.83	2.5	.0062097	6,210
1.00	3.0	.0013500	1,350
1.17	3.5	.0002327	233
1.33	4.0	.0000317	32
1.50	4.5	.0000034	3.4
1.67	5.0	.0000003	.3
1.83	5.5	.0000000	.02
2.00	6.0	.0000000	.001

Note: The short-term capability assumes the process mean is centered on the target specification.

Eq. 8.2

Long-Term Capability

Cpk	Z.lt	DPO	PPM
0.00	0.0	.5000000	500,000
0.17	0.5	.3085375	308,538
0.33	1.0	.1586553	158,655
0.50	1.5	.0668072	66,807
0.67	2.0	.0227501	22,750
0.83	2.5	.0062097	6,210
1.00	3.0	.0013500	1,350
1.17	3.5	.0002327	233
1.33	4.0	.0000317	32
1.50	4.5	.0000034	3.4

Note: The long-term capability assumes the process mean is shifted from the target specification by 1.5σ, without dynamic mean variation.

THE VISION OF SIX SIGMA

MiniTab: Six Sigma Reports

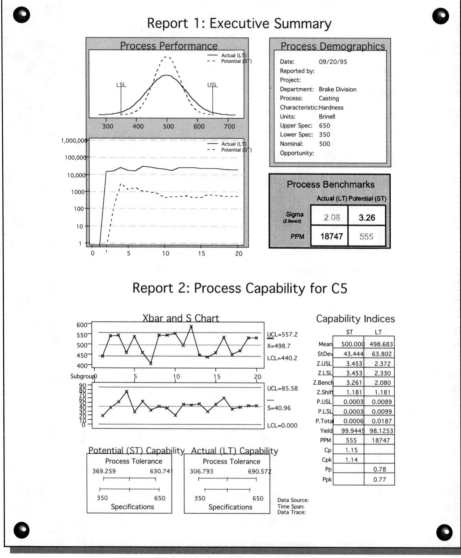

Report 1: Executive Summary

Process Performance

Process Demographics

Date:	09/20/95
Reported by:	
Project:	
Department:	Brake Division
Process:	Casting
Characteristic:	Hardness
Units:	Brinell
Upper Spec:	650
Lower Spec:	350
Nominal:	500
Opportunity:	

Process Benchmarks

	Actual (LT)	Potential (ST)
Sigma (Z.Bench)	2.08	3.26
PPM	18747	555

Report 2: Process Capability for C5

Xbar and S Chart

UCL=557.2
X=498.7
LCL=440.2

UCL=85.58
S=40.96
LCL=0.000

Capability Indices

	ST	LT
Mean	500.000	498.683
StDev	43.444	63.802
Z.USL	3.453	2.372
Z.LSL	3.453	2.330
Z.Bench	3.261	2.080
Z.Shift	1.181	1.181
P.USL	0.0003	0.0089
P.LSL	0.0003	0.0099
P.Total	0.0006	0.0187
Yield	99.9445	98.1253
PPM	555	18747
Cp	1.15	
Cpk	1.14	
Pp		0.78
Ppk		0.77

Potential (ST) Capability

Process Tolerance
369.259   630.741

350   650
Specifications

Actual (LT) Capability

Process Tolerance
306.793   690.572

350   650
Specifications

Data Source:
Time Span:
Data Trace:

MiniTab: Six Sigma Reports

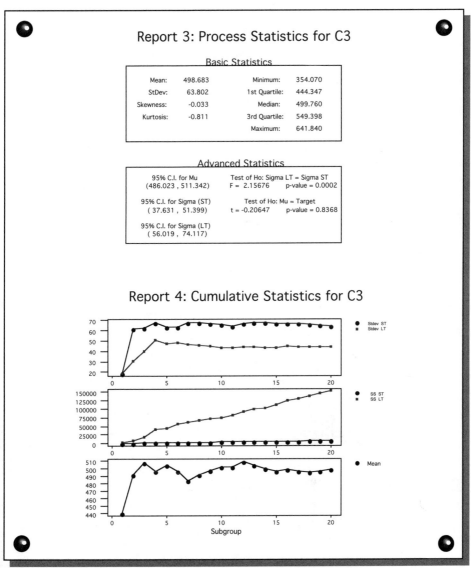

Report 3: Process Statistics for C3

Basic Statistics

Mean:	498.683	Minimum:	354.070
StDev:	63.802	1st Quartile:	444.347
Skewness:	-0.033	Median:	499.760
Kurtosis:	-0.811	3rd Quartile:	549.398
		Maximum:	641.840

Advanced Statistics

95% C.I. for Mu	Test of Ho: Sigma LT = Sigma ST
(486.023 , 511.342)	F = 2.15676 p-value = 0.0002
95% C.I. for Sigma (ST)	Test of Ho: Mu = Target
(37.631 , 51.399)	t = -0.20647 p-value = 0.8368
95% C.I. for Sigma (LT)	
(56.019 , 74.117)	

Report 4: Cumulative Statistics for C3

Six Sigma Academy, Inc.   8 . 23   ®1997 Sigma Consultants, L.L.C.

MiniTab: Six Sigma Reports

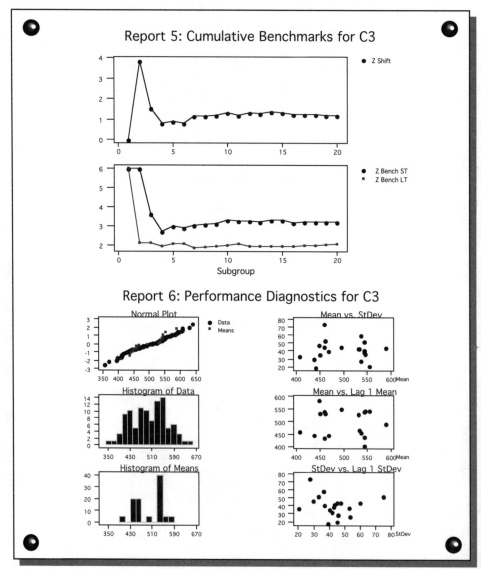

Report 5: Cumulative Benchmarks for C3

Report 6: Performance Diagnostics for C3

THE VISION OF SIX SIGMA

Six Sigma Academy, Inc.   8 . 24   ®1997 Sigma Consultants, L.L.C.

Area Under the Normal Curve

Z	Area	Z	Area	Z	Area	Z	Area
0.00	.500000000	0.31	.378280378	0.62	.267628915	0.93	.176185648
0.01	.496010676	0.32	.374484058	0.63	.264347322	0.94	.173608881
0.02	.492021745	0.33	.370699868	0.64	.261086339	0.95	.171056222
0.03	.488033608	0.34	.366928146	0.65	.257846158	0.96	.168527698
0.04	.484046662	0.35	.363169226	0.66	.254626970	0.97	.166023330
0.05	.480061306	0.36	.359423441	0.67	.251428959	0.98	.163543138
0.06	.476077938	0.37	.355691117	0.68	.248252302	0.99	.161087131
0.07	.472096957	0.38	.351972578	0.69	.245097172	1.00	.158655319
0.08	.468118758	0.39	.348268143	0.70	.241963737	1.01	.156247703
0.09	.464143737	0.40	.344578129	0.71	.238852160	1.02	.153864282
0.10	.460172290	0.41	.340902845	0.72	.235762595	1.03	.151505047
0.11	.456204810	0.42	.337242600	0.73	.232695195	1.04	.149169987
0.12	.452241690	0.43	.333597697	0.74	.229650105	1.05	.146859086
0.13	.448283321	0.44	.329968434	0.75	.226627465	1.06	.144572322
0.14	.444330093	0.45	.326355105	0.76	.223627409	1.07	.142309669
0.15	.440382395	0.46	.322758000	0.77	.220650066	1.08	.140071097
0.16	.436440613	0.47	.319177404	0.78	.217695561	1.09	.137856572
0.17	.432505132	0.48	.315613598	0.79	.214764010	1.10	.135666053
0.18	.428576335	0.49	.312066857	0.80	.211855526	1.11	.133499498
0.19	.424654603	0.50	.308537454	0.81	.208970217	1.12	.131356858
0.20	.420740315	0.51	.305025654	0.82	.206108183	1.13	.129238082
0.21	.416833847	0.52	.301531718	0.83	.203269522	1.14	.127143113
0.22	.412935575	0.53	.298055905	0.84	.200454323	1.15	.125071891
0.23	.409045869	0.54	.294598464	0.85	.197662672	1.16	.123024352
0.24	.405165100	0.55	.291159644	0.86	.194894649	1.17	.121000426
0.25	.401293634	0.56	.287739685	0.87	.192150328	1.18	.119000043
0.26	.397431834	0.57	.284338824	0.88	.189429778	1.19	.117023125
0.27	.393580063	0.58	.280957293	0.89	.186733064	1.20	.115069593
0.28	.389738679	0.59	.277595318	0.90	.184060243	1.21	.113139364
0.29	.385908035	0.60	.274253121	0.91	.181411369	1.22	.111232349
0.30	.382088486	0.61	.270930916	0.92	.178786490	1.23	.109348459

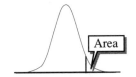

Area

THE VISION OF SIX SIGMA

Area Under the Normal Curve

Z	Area	Z	Area	Z	Area	Z	Area
1.24	.107487599	1.55	.060570681	1.86	.031442864	2.17	.015003519
1.25	.105649671	1.56	.059379869	1.87	.030742014	2.18	.014628823
1.26	.103834574	1.57	.058207490	1.88	.030054147	2.19	.014262206
1.27	.102042204	1.58	.057053373	1.89	.029379092	2.20	.013903531
1.28	.100272453	1.59	.055917348	1.90	.028716674	2.21	.013552660
1.29	.098525211	1.60	.054799243	1.91	.028066724	2.22	.013209458
1.30	.096800364	1.61	.053698886	1.92	.027429070	2.23	.012873791
1.31	.095097795	1.62	.052616103	1.93	.026803541	2.24	.012545527
1.32	.093417384	1.63	.051550719	1.94	.026189969	2.25	.012224533
1.33	.091759009	1.64	.050502560	1.95	.025588185	2.26	.011910681
1.34	.090122544	1.65	.049471451	1.96	.024998022	2.27	.011603842
1.35	.088507862	1.66	.048457216	1.97	.024419313	2.28	.011303889
1.36	.086914832	1.67	.047459678	1.98	.023851893	2.29	.011010698
1.37	.085343321	1.68	.046478660	1.99	.023295597	2.30	.010724144
1.38	.083793192	1.69	.045513986	2.00	.022750262	2.31	.010444106
1.39	.082264309	1.70	.044565478	2.01	.022215724	2.32	.010170462
1.40	.080756531	1.71	.043632958	2.02	.021691823	2.33	.009903094
1.41	.079269714	1.72	.042716249	2.03	.021178399	2.34	.009641883
1.42	.077803715	1.73	.041815172	2.04	.020675291	2.35	.009386713
1.43	.076358386	1.74	.040929549	2.05	.020182343	2.36	.009137469
1.44	.074933578	1.75	.040059203	2.06	.019699396	2.37	.008894039
1.45	.073529141	1.76	.039203955	2.07	.019226296	2.38	.008656310
1.46	.072144921	1.77	.038363628	2.08	.018762889	2.39	.008424172
1.47	.070780764	1.78	.037538044	2.09	.018309020	2.40	.008197516
1.48	.069436514	1.79	.036727024	2.10	.017864539	2.41	.007976235
1.49	.068112013	1.80	.035930393	2.11	.017429293	2.42	.007760223
1.50	.066807100	1.81	.035147973	2.12	.017003135	2.43	.007549376
1.51	.065521615	1.82	.034379586	2.13	.016585916	2.44	.007343590
1.52	.064255396	1.83	.033625058	2.14	.016177490	2.45	.007142765
1.53	.063008277	1.84	.032884212	2.15	.015777711	2.46	.006946800
1.54	.061780094	1.85	.032156872	2.16	.015386434	2.47	.006755597

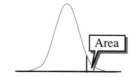

THE VISION OF SIX SIGMA

Area Under the Normal Curve

Z	Area	Z	Area	Z	Area	Z	Area
2.48	.006569059	2.79	.002635273	3.10	.000967555	3.41	.000324885
2.49	.006387090	2.80	.002555001	3.11	.000935392	3.42	.000313179
2.50	.006209596	2.81	.002476947	3.12	.000904215	3.43	.000301867
2.51	.006036485	2.82	.002401055	3.13	.000873995	3.44	.000290937
2.52	.005867664	2.83	.002327274	3.14	.000844707	3.45	.000280376
2.53	.005703044	2.84	.002255552	3.15	.000816324	3.46	.000270173
2.54	.005542538	2.85	.002185838	3.16	.000788822	3.47	.000260317
2.55	.005386056	2.86	.002118083	3.17	.000762175	3.48	.000250797
2.56	.005233515	2.87	.002052239	3.18	.000736360	3.49	.000241603
2.57	.005084829	2.88	.001988258	3.19	.000711352	3.50	.000232725
2.58	.004939916	2.89	.001926093	3.20	.000687130	3.51	.000224151
2.59	.004798693	2.90	.001865699	3.21	.000663671	3.52	.000215873
2.60	.004661082	2.91	.001807032	3.22	.000640954	3.53	.000207882
2.61	.004527002	2.92	.001750048	3.23	.000618956	3.54	.000200168
2.62	.004396376	2.93	.001694703	3.24	.000597657	3.55	.000192722
2.63	.004269129	2.94	.001640957	3.25	.000577038	3.56	.000185536
2.64	.004145185	2.95	.001588769	3.26	.000557078	3.57	.000178601
2.65	.004024470	2.96	.001538097	3.27	.000537758	3.58	.000171909
2.66	.003906912	2.97	.001488904	3.28	.000519060	3.59	.000165452
2.67	.003792440	2.98	.001441150	3.29	.000500965	3.60	.000159224
2.68	.003680984	2.99	.001394798	3.30	.000483456	3.61	.000153215
2.69	.003572475	3.00	.001349813	3.31	.000466516	3.62	.000147419
2.70	.003466847	3.01	.001306156	3.32	.000450127	3.63	.000141830
2.71	.003364033	3.02	.001263795	3.33	.000434273	3.64	.000136440
2.72	.003263967	3.03	.001222694	3.34	.000418939	3.65	.000131242
2.73	.003166587	3.04	.001182819	3.35	.000404108	3.66	.000126230
2.74	.003071829	3.05	.001144139	3.36	.000389767	3.67	.000121399
2.75	.002979633	3.06	.001106621	3.37	.000375899	3.68	.000116742
2.76	.002889938	3.07	.001070234	3.38	.000362490	3.69	.000112252
2.77	.002802684	3.08	.001034947	3.39	.000349527	3.70	.000107926
2.78	.002717815	3.09	.001000730	3.40	.000336997	3.71	.000103756

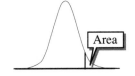

Area

THE VISION OF SIX SIGMA

Area Under the Normal Curve

Z	Area	Z	Area	Z	Area	Z	Area
3.72	.000099739	4.03	.000028003	4.34	.000007198	4.65	.000001697
3.73	.000095868	4.04	.000026839	4.35	.000006879	4.66	.000001617
3.74	.000092138	4.05	.000025721	4.36	.000006574	4.67	.000001541
3.75	.000088546	4.06	.000024648	4.37	.000006282	4.68	.000001469
3.76	.000085086	4.07	.000023617	4.38	.000006002	4.69	.000001399
3.77	.000081753	4.08	.000022627	4.39	.000005734	4.70	.000001333
3.78	.000078543	4.09	.000021676	4.40	.000005478	4.71	.000001270
3.79	.000075453	4.10	.000020764	4.41	.000005233	4.72	.000001210
3.80	.000072477	4.11	.000019888	4.42	.000004998	4.73	.000001153
3.81	.000069613	4.12	.000019047	4.43	.000004773	4.74	.000001098
3.82	.000066855	4.13	.000018241	4.44	.000004558	4.75	.000001046
3.83	.000064201	4.14	.000017466	4.45	.000004353	4.76	.000000996
3.84	.000061646	4.15	.000016723	4.46	.000004156	4.77	.000000948
3.85	.000059187	4.16	.000016011	4.47	.000003968	4.78	.000000903
3.86	.000056822	4.17	.000015327	4.48	.000003787	4.79	.000000859
3.87	.000054545	4.18	.000014671	4.49	.000003615	4.80	.000000818
3.88	.000052355	4.19	.000014042	4.50	.000003451	4.81	.000000779
3.89	.000050249	4.20	.000013439	4.51	.000003293	4.82	.000000741
3.90	.000048222	4.21	.000012860	4.52	.000003143	4.83	.000000705
3.91	.000046273	4.22	.000012305	4.53	.000002999	4.84	.000000671
3.92	.000044399	4.23	.000011773	4.54	.000002861	4.85	.000000639
3.93	.000042597	4.24	.000011263	4.55	.000002730	4.86	.000000608
3.94	.000040864	4.25	.000010774	4.56	.000002604	4.87	.000000578
3.95	.000039198	4.26	.000010306	4.57	.000002484	4.88	.000000550
3.96	.000037596	4.27	.000009857	4.58	.000002369	4.89	.000000523
3.97	.000036057	4.28	.000009426	4.59	.000002259	4.90	.000000498
3.98	.000034577	4.29	.000009014	4.60	.000002154	4.91	.000000473
3.99	.000033155	4.30	.000008619	4.61	.000002054	4.92	.000000450
4.00	.000031789	4.31	.000008240	4.62	.000001959	4.93	.000000428
4.01	.000030476	4.32	.000007878	4.63	.000001867	4.94	.000000407
4.02	.000029215	4.33	.000007530	4.64	.000001780	4.95	.000000387

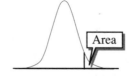

THE VISION OF SIX SIGMA

Area Under the Normal Curve

Z	Area	Z	Area	Z	Area	Z	Area
4.96	.000000368	5.27	.000000074	5.58	.000000014	5.89	.0000000024
4.97	.000000350	5.28	.000000070	5.59	.000000013	5.90	.0000000022
4.98	.000000332	5.29	.000000066	5.60	.000000012	5.91	.0000000021
4.99	.000000316	5.30	.000000063	5.61	.000000012	5.92	.0000000020
5.00	.000000300	5.31	.000000059	5.62	.000000011	5.93	.0000000019
5.01	.000000285	5.32	.000000056	5.63	.000000010	5.94	.0000000018
5.02	.000000271	5.33	.000000053	5.64	.0000000098	5.95	.0000000017
5.03	.000000258	5.34	.000000051	5.65	.0000000092	5.96	.0000000016
5.04	.000000245	5.35	.000000048	5.66	.0000000087	5.97	.0000000015
5.05	.000000232	5.36	.000000045	5.67	.0000000083	5.98	.0000000014
5.06	.000000221	5.37	.000000043	5.68	.0000000078	5.99	.0000000013
5.07	.000000210	5.38	.000000041	5.69	.0000000074	6.00	.0000000012
5.08	.000000199	5.39	.000000039	5.70	.0000000070		
5.09	.000000189	5.40	.000000037	5.71	.0000000066		
5.10	.000000180	5.41	.000000035	5.72	.0000000062		
5.11	.000000171	5.42	.000000033	5.73	.0000000059		
5.12	.000000162	5.43	.000000031	5.74	.0000000056		
5.13	.000000154	5.44	.000000029	5.75	.0000000053		
5.14	.000000146	5.45	.000000028	5.76	.0000000050		
5.15	.000000138	5.46	.000000026	5.77	.0000000047		
5.16	.000000131	5.47	.000000025	5.78	.0000000044		
5.17	.000000125	5.48	.000000024	5.79	.0000000042		
5.18	.000000118	5.49	.000000022	5.80	.0000000040		
5.19	.000000112	5.50	.000000021	5.81	.0000000037		
5.20	.000000107	5.51	.000000020	5.82	.0000000035		
5.21	.000000101	5.52	.000000019	5.83	.0000000033		
5.22	.000000096	5.53	.000000018	5.84	.0000000031		
5.23	.000000091	5.54	.000000017	5.85	.0000000030		
5.24	.000000086	5.55	.000000016	5.86	.0000000028		
5.25	.000000082	5.56	.000000015	5.87	.0000000027		
5.26	.000000078	5.57	.000000014	5.88	.0000000025		

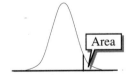

Area

THE VISION OF SIX SIGMA

Impact of Process Centering

CHAPTER NINE

Breakthrough

Breakthrough

THE VISION OF SIX SIGMA

The Nature of Statistical Problems

Problem with Spread

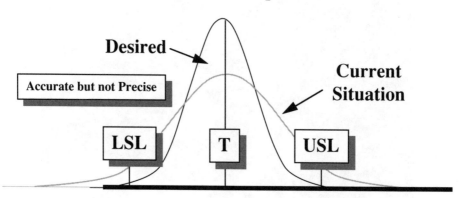

Problem with Centering

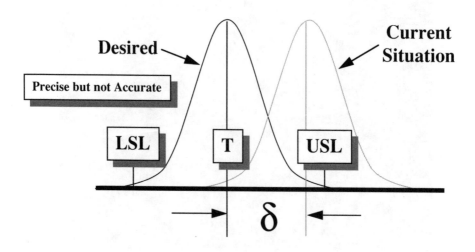

Process Centering and Capability

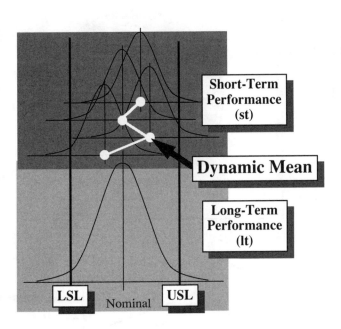

The long-term distribution is larger than the short-term as a result of dynamic variations in the process mean over time

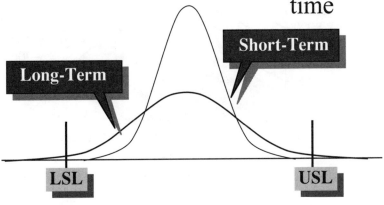

THE VISION OF SIX SIGMA

σ Six Sigma Academy, Inc.   9 . 3   ®1997 Sigma Consultants, L.L.C.

Deeper Insight Into Shifts and Drifts

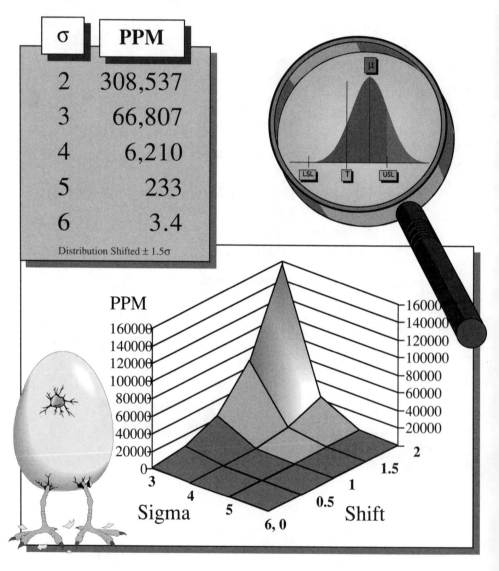

σ	PPM
2	308,537
3	66,807
4	6,210
5	233
6	3.4

Distribution Shifted ± 1.5σ

Influence of the 1.5σ Shift

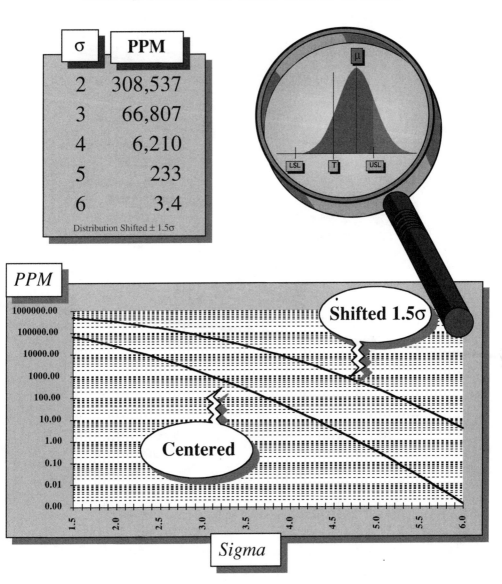

σ	PPM
2	308,537
3	66,807
4	6,210
5	233
6	3.4

Distribution Shifted ± 1.5σ

Shifted 1.5σ

Centered

Sigma

THE VISION OF SIX SIGMA

Types of Centering Behavior

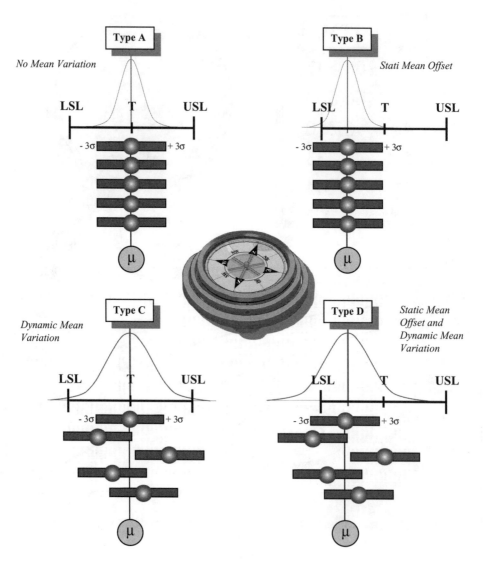

Type A

No Mean Variation

LSL   T   USL

-3σ $+3\sigma$

μ

Type B

Stati Mean Offset

LSL   T   USL

-3σ $+3\sigma$

μ

Type C

Dynamic Mean Variation

LSL   T   USL

-3σ $+3\sigma$

μ

Type D

Static Mean Offset and Dynamic Mean Variation

LSL   T   USL

-3σ $+3\sigma$

μ

Six Sigma Academy, Inc.   9 . 6   ®1997 Sigma Consultants, L.L.C.

The Components of Variation

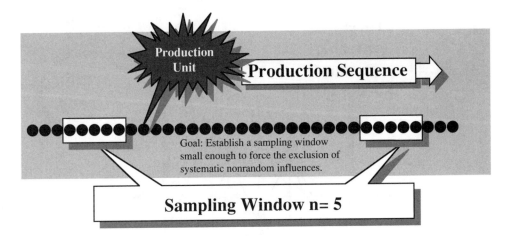

Goal: Establish a sampling window small enough to force the exclusion of systematic nonrandom influences.

Sampling Window n= 5

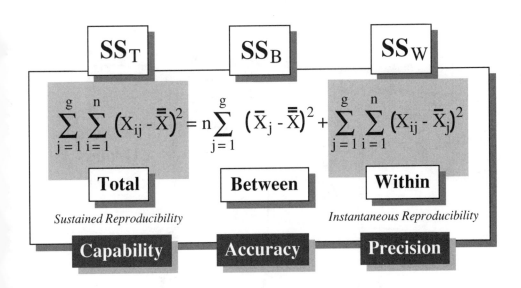

$$\sum_{j=1}^{g} \sum_{i=1}^{n} \left(X_{ij} - \bar{\bar{X}}\right)^2 = n\sum_{j=1}^{g} \left(\bar{X}_j - \bar{\bar{X}}\right)^2 + \sum_{j=1}^{g} \sum_{i=1}^{n} \left(X_{ij} - \bar{X}_j\right)^2$$

SS_T	SS_B	SS_W
Total	**Between**	**Within**
Sustained Reproducibility		*Instantaneous Reproducibility*
Capability	**Accuracy**	**Precision**

Visualizing the Components

Type C Process Centering Condition

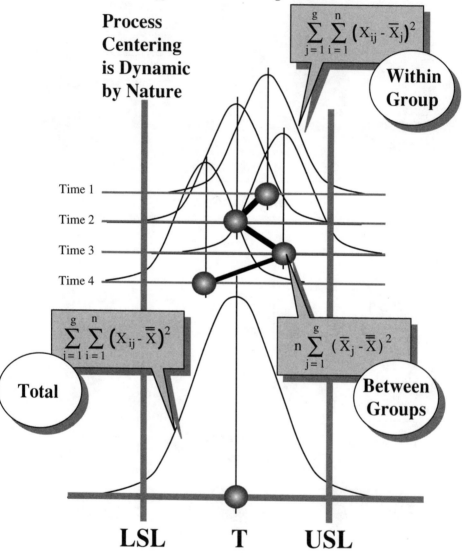

Process Centering is Dynamic by Nature

$$\sum_{j=1}^{g} \sum_{i=1}^{n} (X_{ij} - \overline{X}_j)^2$$

Within Group

Time 1

Time 2

Time 3

Time 4

$$\sum_{j=1}^{g} \sum_{i=1}^{n} (X_{ij} - \overline{\overline{X}})^2$$

Total

$$n \sum_{j=1}^{g} (\overline{X}_j - \overline{\overline{X}})^2$$

Between Groups

LSL   T   USL

THE VISION OF SIX SIGMA

The Basis for Research

At this point in the discussion we must turn our attention to the research of Bender (1975), Gilson (1951), and Evans (1975). In essence, their work focused on the problems associated with establishing engineering tolerances in light of nonrandom manufacturing variations which assume the form of mean shifts and drifts. In synopsis, Evans pointed out that

> *... shifts and drifts in the mean of the distribution of a component occur for a number of reasons ... for example, tool wear is one source of a gradual [nonrandom] drift... which can cause [nonrandom] shifts in the distribution. Except in special cases, it is almost impossible to predict quantitatively the changes in the distribution of a component value which will occur, but the knowledge that they will occur enables us to cope with the difficulty. A solution proposed by Bender ... allows for [nonrandom] shifts and drifts. Bender suggests that one should use*

$$V = 1.5 \ \sqrt{VAR\ (X)}$$

> *as the standard deviation of the response ... [so as] to relate the component tolerances and the response tolerance.*

In view of this research, we may generalize to the case

$$\sigma_T^2 = (c\sigma_W)^2$$

or

$$c = \frac{\sigma_T}{\sigma_W}$$

where c is the magnitude of inflation imposed upon the instantaneous reproducibility. In short, it may be said that c is a compensatory constant used to correct the sustained reproduciblity for the effect of nonrandom manufacturing errors which perturbs the process center. Again, calling upon the previously mentioned research, we would discover that the general range of c, for "typical manufacturing processes," may be given as

$$1.4 \leq c \leq 1.8 \ .$$

Six Sigma Academy, Inc.   9 . 9   ®1997 Sigma Consultants, L.L.C.

Analysis of Shifts and Drifts

If σ^2_T and σ^2_W can be estimated using a rational sampling strategy we may express c as

$$\hat{c} = \frac{\sqrt{\dfrac{SS_T}{ng-1}}}{\sqrt{\dfrac{SS_W}{g(n-1)}}}$$

By virtue of the additive properties of independent variances, it can be shown that

$$\hat{c}^2 = \frac{\dfrac{SS_B + SS_W}{ng-1}}{\dfrac{SS_W}{g(n-1)}} = \frac{SS_B + SS_W}{SS_W} \cdot \frac{g(n-1)}{ng-1}$$

By simple rearrangement, the average quadratic mean deviation is given as

$$\frac{\sum_{j=1}^{g} \left(\overline{X}_j - \overline{\overline{X}}\right)^2}{g} = \hat{\sigma}^2_W \frac{\hat{c}^2(ng-1) - g(n-1)}{ng}$$

So the "typical" dynamic mean shift which can be expressed as

$$\delta\sigma_W = \sqrt{\frac{\sum_{j=1}^{g} \left(\overline{X}_j - \overline{\overline{X}}\right)^2}{g}} = \hat{\sigma}_W \sqrt{\left[\frac{\hat{c}^2(ng-1) - g(n-1)}{ng}\right]}$$

By standardizing, we observe that

$$Z_{Shift.Typ} = \sqrt{\left[\frac{\hat{c}^2(ng-1) - g(n-1)}{ng}\right]}$$

THE VISION OF SIX SIGMA

Six Sigma Academy, Inc.   9 . 10   ®1997 Sigma Consultants, L.L.C.

Results for Typical Sampling Plans

In the spirit of establishing a standard mean shift correction, let us consider the general range of conventional rational sampling practices given by the combinations

$$4 \leq n \leq 6$$

and

$$25 \leq g \leq 100.$$

Perhaps the most commonly employed combination is that of n=5 and g=50. Under this combination, the total sample size is ng=250. Such a sample size has been recommended by other authors writing on the topic of process capability studies.

For the case c=1.8 and a common rational sampling strategy (n=5 and g=50), we compute $Z_{Shift}=1.49$. Hence, the establishment of $\delta=1.5\sigma$ as the typical mean shift correction for Motorola's Six Sigma initiative is justified.

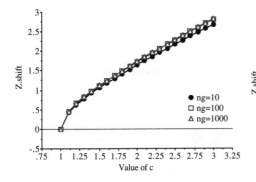

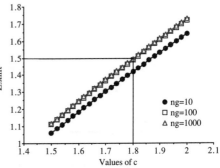

THE VISION OF SIX SIGMA

Six Sigma Academy, Inc.   9.11   ®1997 Sigma Consultants, L.L.C.

Generalizing the Correction

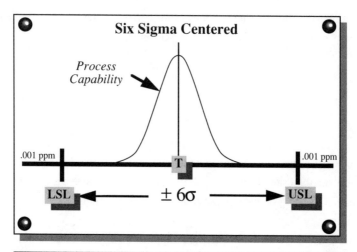

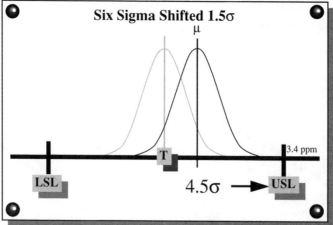

The 1.5σ shift is used as a compensatory off-set in the mean to generally account for dynamic nonrandom variations in process centering. It represents the average amount of change in a typical process over many cycles of that process.

Creating a Truth Table

FROM

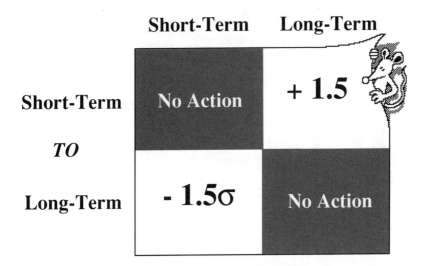

Short-term data is free of assignable causes, thus it represents the effect of random causes only.

Long-term data reflects the influence of random causes as well as assignable phenomena.

If the yield or defect data were gathered over many intervals of production, consider the situation to be long-term; otherwise, assume it to be short-term.

Applying the Truth Table

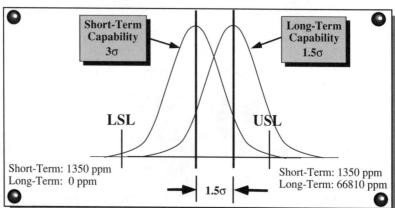

Short-Term Capability 3σ

Long-Term Capability 1.5σ

LSL   USL

Short-Term: 1350 ppm
Long-Term: 0 ppm

Short-Term: 1350 ppm
Long-Term: 66810 ppm

1.5σ

If the initial data was given as 3 σ short-term, the conversion to long-term would be

$$3\sigma - 1.5\sigma = 1.5\sigma$$

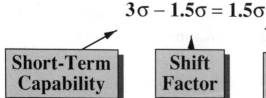

Short-Term Capability

Shift Factor

Long-Term Capability

The resultant describes the long-term performance of the process, inclusive of assignable causes which impact process centering. The outcome constitutes the sustained reproducibility of the process.

Guidelines for the Correction

Guideline 1:   If a metric is computed on the basis of data gathered over many cycles or time intervals, the resultant value should be regarded as a long-term measure of performance. Naturally, the long-term metric must be converted to a probability. Once expressed as a probability, Z.lt value may be established by way of a table of area-under-the-normal-curve, or any acceptable computational device. If we seek to forecast short-term performance (Z.st), we must add a shift factor (Z.shift) to Z.lt so as to remove time related sources of error which tend to upset process centering. Recognize that the actual value of Z.shift is seldom known in practice; therefore, it may be necessary to apply the accepted convention and set Z.shift = 1.50; otherwise, use the actual value. As a consequence of this linear transformation, the final Z value should reflect only random sources of error and, therefore, serve as a projection of short-term performance. Thus, we are able to artificially remove the effect of nonrandom influences (i.e., normal process centering errors) from the analysis via the transform Z.st = Z.lt + Z.shift.

Guideline 2:   If a metric is computed on the basis of data gathered over a very limited number of cycles or time intervals, the resultant value should be regarded as a short-term measure of performance.   Naturally, the short-term metric must be converted to a probability. Once expressed as a probability, Z.st may be established by way of a table of area-under-the-normal-curve, or any acceptable computational device. If we seek to forecast long-term performance, we must subtract Z.shift from Z.st so as to approximate the long-term capability. Recognize that the actual value of Z.shift is seldom known in practice; therefore, it may be necessary to apply the accepted convention and set Z.shift = 1.50. If the actual value is known, use it. As a consequence of this linear transformation, the final Z value reflects both random and nonrandom sources of error and, therefore, is a projection of long-term performance. Thus, we are able to artificially induce the effect of nonrandom influences (i.e., normal process centering errors) into the analysis by way of Z.st - Z.shift = Z.lt.

Guideline 3:   In general, if the originating data is discrete by nature, the resulting Z transform should be regarded as long-term. The logic of this guideline is simple; a fairly large number of cycles or time intervals is often required to generate enough nonconformities from which to generate a relatively stable estimate of Z. Hence, it is reasonable to conclude that both random and nonrandom influences are reflected in such data. In this instance, guideline 1 would be applied.

Guideline 4:   In general, if the originating data is continuous by nature and was gathered under the constraint of sequential or random sampling across a very limited number of cycles or time intervals, the resulting Z value should be regarded as short-term. The logic of this guideline is simple; data gathered over a very limited number cycles or time intervals only reflects random influences (white noise) and, as a consequence, tends to exclude nonrandom sources of variation, such as process centering errors.

Guideline 5:   Whenever it is desirable to report the corresponding "sigma" of a given performance metric, the short-term Z must be used. For example, let us suppose that we find 6210 ppm defective. In this instance, we must translate 6210 ppm into its corresponding "sigma" value. Doing so reveals Z.lt = 2.50. Since the originating data was long-term by nature, guidelines 1 and 3 apply. In this case, Z.lt + Z.shift = 2.5 + 1.5 = 4.0. Since no other estimate of Z.shift was available, the convention of 1.5 was employed.

THE VISION OF SIX SIGMA

Insight into the Correction

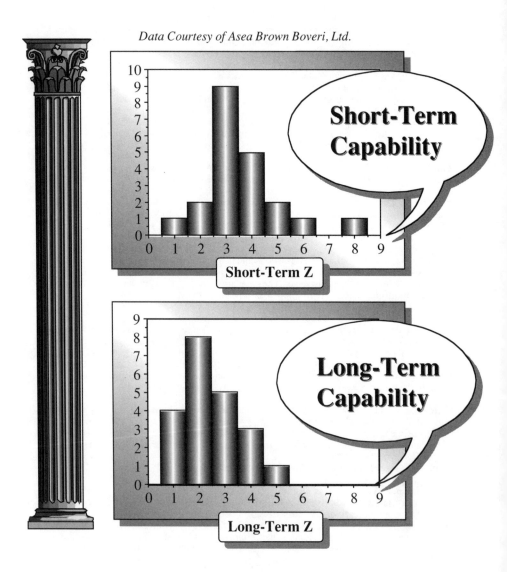

Data Courtesy of Asea Brown Boveri, Ltd.

Studying the Emperical Evidence

Data Courtesy of Asea Brown Boveri, Ltd.

. . . So what does this
scattergram have to
tell us about mean shifts?

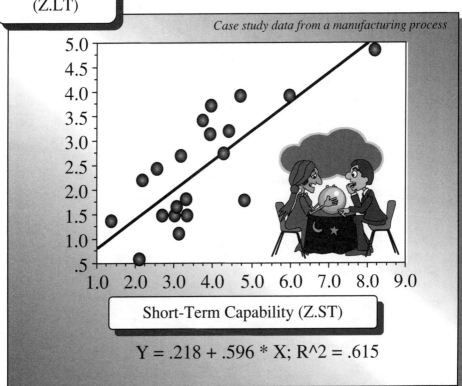

Long-Term Capability (Z.LT)

Case study data from a manufacturing process

Short-Term Capability (Z.ST)

$$Y = .218 + .596 * X; R^2 = .615$$

THE VISION OF SIX SIGMA

Six Sigma Academy, Inc.   9 . 17   ®1997 Sigma Consultants, L.L.C.

Some Major Conclusions

Data Courtesy of Asea Brown Boveri, Ltd.

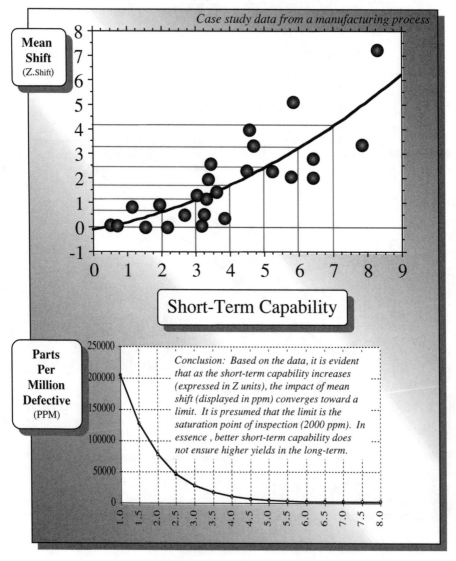

Case study data from a manufacturing process

Mean Shift (Z.Shift)

Short-Term Capability

Parts Per Million Defective (PPM)

Conclusion: Based on the data, it is evident that as the short-term capability increases (expressed in Z units), the impact of mean shift (displayed in ppm) converges toward a limit. It is presumed that the limit is the saturation point of inspection (2000 ppm). In essence, better short-term capability does not ensure higher yields in the long-term.

σ Six Sigma Academy, Inc.   9 . 18   ®1997 Sigma Consultants, L.L.C.

Practical Implications: Part A

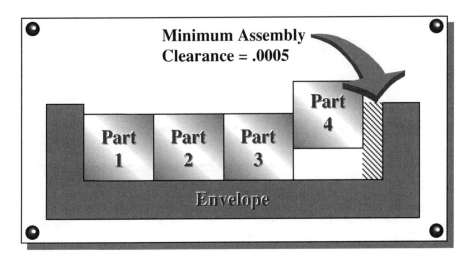

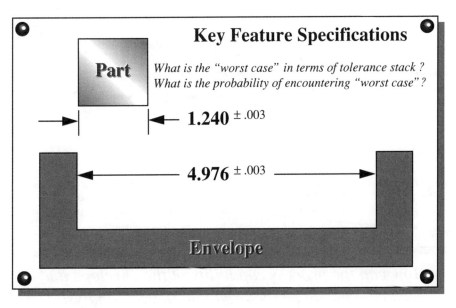

THE VISION OF SIX SIGMA

Six Sigma Academy, Inc.   9 . 19   ®1997 Sigma Consultants, L.L.C.

Practical Implications: Part A

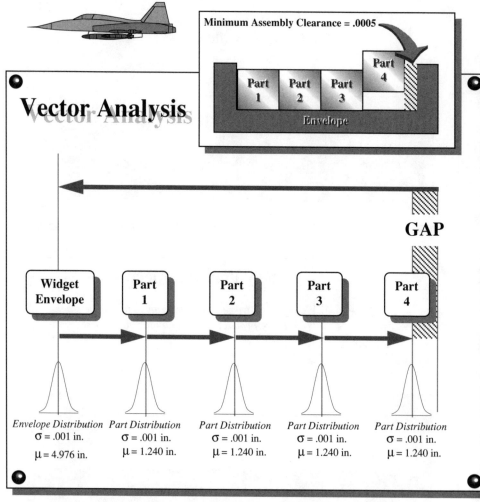

Minimum Assembly Clearance = .0005

| Part 1 | Part 2 | Part 3 | Part 4 |

Envelope

Vector Analysis

GAP

| Widget Envelope | Part 1 | Part 2 | Part 3 | Part 4 |

Envelope Distribution	Part Distribution	Part Distribution	Part Distribution	Part Distribution
$\sigma = .001$ in.	$\sigma = .001$ in.	$\sigma = .001$ in.	$\sigma = .001$ in.	$\sigma = .001$ in.
$\mu = 4.976$ in.	$\mu = 1.240$ in.	$\mu = 1.240$ in.	$\mu = 1.240$ in.	$\mu = 1.240$ in.

*How can the process capability of the envelope and
each component be factored into the gap analysis?*

THE VISION OF SIX SIGMA

Practical Implications: Part B

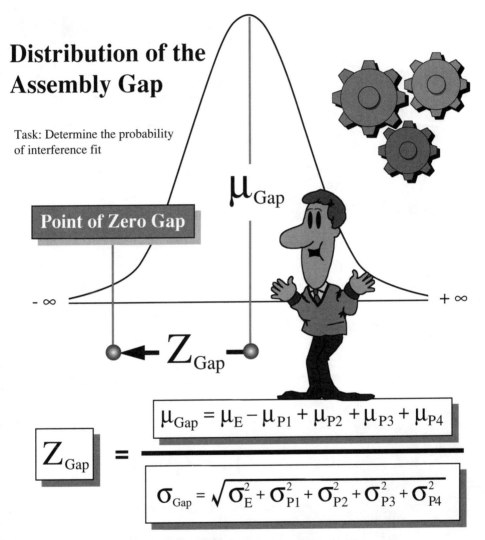

Distribution of the Assembly Gap

Task: Determine the probability of interference fit

Point of Zero Gap

μ_{Gap}

$-\infty$ $+\infty$

Z_{Gap}

$$Z_{Gap} = \frac{\mu_{Gap} = \mu_E - \mu_{P1} + \mu_{P2} + \mu_{P3} + \mu_{P4}}{\sigma_{Gap} = \sqrt{\sigma_E^2 + \sigma_{P1}^2 + \sigma_{P2}^2 + \sigma_{P3}^2 + \sigma_{P4}^2}}$$

If we know the "typical" mean off-set for the envelope and each of the parts, how could this knowledge be used to make the design robust against such shifts and drifts?

THE VISION OF SIX SIGMA

σ Six Sigma Academy, Inc.   9 . 21   ®1997 Sigma Consultants, L.L.C.

Design for Manufacturability

$$Z_{Gap} = \frac{\mu_{Gap} = \mu_E - \mu_{P1} + \mu_{P2} + \mu_{P3} + \mu_{P4}}{\sigma_{Gap} = \sqrt{\sigma_E^2 + \sigma_{P1}^2 + \sigma_{P2}^2 + \sigma_{P3}^2 + \sigma_{P4}^2}}$$

$$V_{Pool} = \sigma_{Gap} \left(Z_{Gap\,;\,Actual} - Z_{Gap\,;\,Need} \right)$$

$$\mu_{Adjusted} = \mu_i + \lambda_i V_{Pool}$$

THE VISION OF SIX SIGMA

σ Six Sigma Academy, Inc.   9 . 22   ®1997 Sigma Consultants, L.L.C.

Defects-Per-Unit

CHAPTER TEN

Breakthrough

Breakthrough

THE VISION OF SIX SIGMA

The Defects-Per-Unit Metric

For the sake of discussion, let us suppose that a certain product design may be represented by the area of a rectangle. We shall also postulate that each rectangle contains 10 equal areas of opportunity for nonconformance to standard. Figure 1 illustrates this particular product concept.

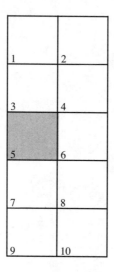

Figure 1. Abstract Unit of Product Consisting of 10 Equal
Areas of Opportunity for Nonconformance

Let us now suppose the quality records related to our example product indicate that, out of the last 1000 units manufactured, 1000 nonconformities were detected. For our example, we would compute

$$dpu = \frac{d}{u}$$

Eq. (1)

where dpu is the defects per unit, d is the frequency or "number" of observed defects, and u is the number of units produced. In this instance, we would determine that dpu = 1000/1000= 1.0. This means that, on the average, each unit of manufactured product will contain 1 such defect. Of course, this assumes the defects are randomly distributed. We must also recognize, however, that within each unit of product there are 10 equal areas of opportunity for nonconformance to standard. Because of this, we may now calculate

THE VISION OF SIX SIGMA

 Six Sigma Academy, Inc.   10 . 2   ®1997 Sigma Consultants, L.L.C.

$$dpm = \frac{dpu}{m}$$

Eq. (2)

where dpm defines the defects-per-unit opportunity, and m is the number of independent opportunities for nonconformance per unit. In the instance of our abstract product, m= 10. Because m = 10 is given as a design constant, we may easily demonstrate that the probability of a nonconformance per-unit area of opportunity is (1000/1000)/10 = .10, or 10 percent. Inversely, we may argue that there is a 100(1.00 - 0.10) = 90 percent chance of not encountering a nonconformance with respect to any given unit area of opportunity.

It is very interesting to note that the probability of zero defects, for any given unit of product, would be $.90^{10}$ = .348678, or 34.87 percent. Now, if we increase the number of opportunities for nonconformance such that m = 100, it should be apparent that the probability of nonconformance-per-unit area of opportunity would be 1/100 = .01, or 1 percent. Consequently, the likelihood that any given unit of product will be defect free would be $(1-.01)^{100}$ = $.99^{100}$ = .366032, or 36.60 percent.

At this point, we should consider Table 1. Notice that the table displays the effect of m on the likelihood of zero defects for any given unit of product, given dpu = 1.0. The reader should also notice that as m approaches infinity, the probability that any given unit of product will be defect free approaches e^{dpu}. Further study shows that the probability that any given unit of product will be defect free is approximated by e^{-dpu}. In this case, the probability of zero defects would be e^{-dpu} = e^{-1} = .367879441, or roughly 36.79 percent.

This point will be of immense importance to us in the following discussion concerning the Poisson distribution. As we shall see, this particular distribution is an invaluable tool when assessing process capability.

Table 1. Probability of Zero Defects as m Increases Under the Constraint dpu = 1.0

Number of Areas of Opportunity Per Unit of Product (m)	Confidence That Any Given Area Will Not Contain a Defect* (y)	Probability That Any Given Unit of Product Will Not Contain a Defect y^m
10	.9	.348678440
100	.99	.36603234 1
1000	.999	.367695425
10000	.9999	.367861050
100000	.99999	.367877601
1000000	.999999	.367879625
10000000	.9999999	.367879459

*Observed dpu = 1.0

Keying off the latter arguments, we may now ask the question, "What is the probability that any given unit of manufactured product will contain two, three, or even more defects?" Well, when the probability of nonconformance per opportunity is less than 10 percent, but the overall likelihood of observing a defect is high, the Poisson distribution can be employed to answer such questions. As may be apparent, these criteria seem applicable to our abstract product example. Given reasonable compliance to the underlying assumptions, we may calculate the probability (Y) by virtue of the Poisson relation. This particular relation is most often expressed as

$$Y = \frac{(np)^r e^{-np}}{r!}$$

Eq. (3)

where n is the total number of independent trials, p is the probability of occurrence, and r is the number of occurrences. Throughout the remainder of this bookl, the term "occurrences" can be used interchangeably with the word "defects." In most instances, the Poisson equation will allow us to avoid the burdensome calculations often associated with the binomial model, as will be discussed in greater detail later on. Such an approximation of the binomial is called "Poisson's Exponential Binomial Limit" or simply, "Poisson's Law." To better relate the Poisson relation to our example, we may rewrite Eq. (3) as

$$Y = \frac{(d/u)^r e^{-d/u}}{r!}$$

Eq. (4)

where d is the number of nonconformities or "defects," and u is the number of units produced. At this point in our discussion, the reader should recognize that d = np. Obviously, normalizing per unit of product reveals that d/u = np/u. Hence, a substitution of terms may be made for the normalized case where u = 1. For the special case of r = 0, Eq. (4) reduces to

$$Y = e^{-d/u}$$

Eq. (5)

Thus, the relation described in Eq. (5) reflects first-time yield (Y_{FT}) for a specified d/u. Obviously, if Y_{FT} is known, or may be rationally postulated, we may solve for d/u by calculating

$$d/u = -\ln (Y_{FT})$$

Eq. (6)

where ln is the natural log. As we shall see, this is also a very useful tool when conducting a producibility analysis. Through the application of Eq. (4), we may create a window from which to view the expected distribution of defects across u number of production units. It would reveal the theoretical number of production units expected to have 0, 1, 2, 3, ..., or more defects. For example, if we were to manufacture, say 1,000 units of product and subsequently discover d/u = 1.0, then we would expect the frequency distribution given in Table 2.

THE VISION OF SIX SIGMA

Table 2. Poisson Distribution of Defects Under the Constraint
that m is Large and dpu = 1.0

Number of Defects (r)	Probability of Exactly r Defects* p(r)	Number of Units With Exactly r Defects (u)	Total Number of Defects Contained Within u Units (d)	Expected Number of Escaping Defects** d(I -E)
0	.3679	368	0	0
1	.3679	368	368	4
2	.1839	184	368	4
3	.0613	61	183	2
4	.0153	15	60	0
5	.0031	3	15	0
6	.0005	1	6	0
7	.0001	0	0	0
8	.0000	0	0	0
TOTAL	1.0000	1000	1000	10

* Theoretically, r assumes values to infinity, but beyond r = 8, the resultant probability is so small it is negligible for the case dpu =1.0.
** Assumed test/inspection efficiency (E) = 99%

Should the assumptions surrounding the Poisson model prove to be unreasonable, we may turn to the binomial model. This particular model may be given by

$$Y = \frac{m!}{r!(m-r)!} \, p^r q^{m-r}$$

Eq. (7)

where p is the constant probability of an event and q = 1 - p. Interestingly, for the special case of r = 0, the binomial model reduces to

$$Y = (1-p)^m$$

Eq. (8)

Because of this special case (i.e., r = 0), we conclude that the probability of zero defects, subject only to the assumptions of the binomial model, may be described by the first time yield (Y_{FT}). For those cases where the underlying assumptions of the Poisson or binomial model cannot be met, the hypergeometric model may be employed. For additional information on this particular model, the reader is directed to the bibliography.

Six Sigma Academy, Inc.

Questioning the Concept of Yield

. . . So why is scatter present in the
*   yield for a fixed DPU?*

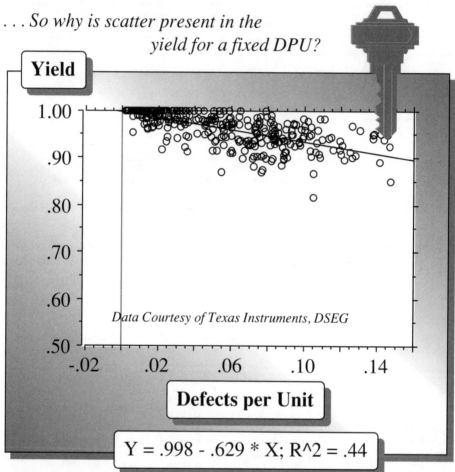

Yield

Data Courtesy of Texas Instruments, DSEG

Defects per Unit

$$Y = .998 - .629 * X; R^2 = .44$$

. . . Is yield a function of defects?
*   . . . If so, how are they related?*

THE VISION OF SIX SIGMA

σ Six Sigma Academy, Inc.   10 . 6   ®1997 Sigma Consultants, L.L.C.

Several Competing Notions of Yield

⬤ = nonconformance to standard (defect)

Yield 1 = s / u = 2 / 6 = .333 = 33.3%

where s is the number of good units and u is the total number of units

Yield 2 = (probability of a successful opportunity)^m = 4.3%

where m is the number of opportunities per unit (e.g., m = 5)

Yield 3 = f (defects) . . . *should this relation hold true?*

The Two Types of Defect Models

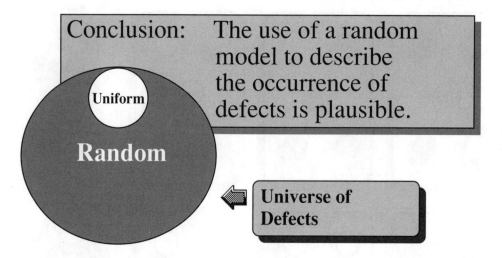

Conclusion: The use of a random
model to describe
the occurrence of
defects is plausible.

Uniform

Random

Universe of
Defects

Uniform Defect: *The same type of defect appears
within a unit of product; e.g., wrong type of steel.*

Random Defect: *The defects are intermittent and
unrelated; e.g., flaw in surface finish.*

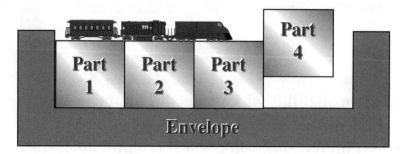

σ Six Sigma Academy, Inc.   10 . 8   ® 1997 Sigma Consultants, L.L.C.

The Widget Application

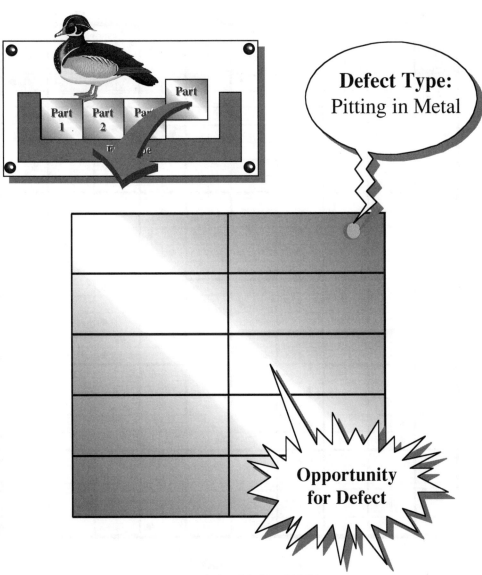

The Widget Production

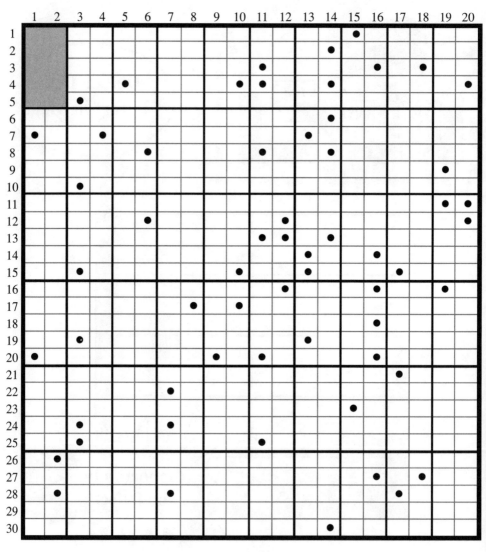

● = Defect   ☐ = Opportunity   ▨ = Unit of Product

THE VISION OF SIX SIGMA

Nature of the Problem

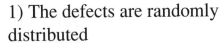

1) The defects are randomly distributed
2) 60 defects were observed out of 60 units produced
3) The defects-per-unit is 1.0
4) There are 10 opportunities for defect per unit of product

Given the facts, what is the likelihood of producing a part with zero defects? In turn, this guarantees no rework or repair.

Defects-per-Opportunity

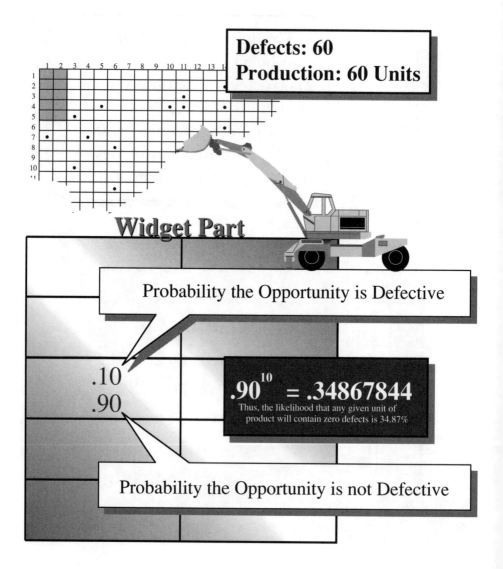

Defects: 60
Production: 60 Units

Widget Part

Probability the Opportunity is Defective

.10
.90

$$.90^{10} = .34867844$$

Thus, the likelihood that any given unit of
product will contain zero defects is 34.87%

Probability the Opportunity is not Defective

THE VISION OF SIX SIGMA

σ Six Sigma Academy, Inc.   10 . 12   ®1997 Sigma Consultants, L.L.C.

Opportunities and DPU

(based on DPU=1.0 example)

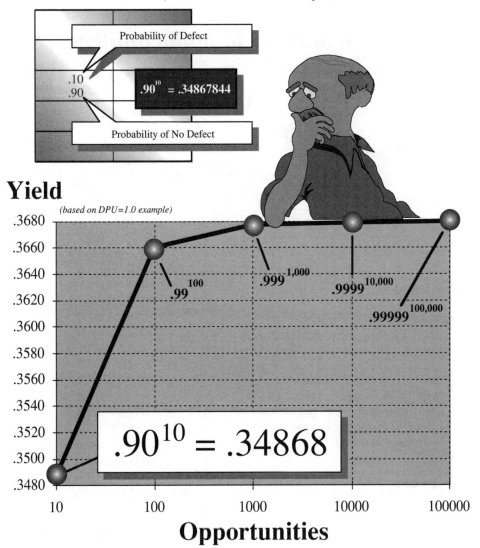

Probability of Defect

.10
.90

$.90^{10} = .34867844$

Probability of No Defect

Yield

(based on DPU=1.0 example)

.99 ^{100}

.999 ^{1,000}

.9999 ^{10,000}

.99999 ^{100,000}

$$.90^{10} = .34868$$

Opportunities

THE VISION OF SIX SIGMA

Six Sigma Academy, Inc.   10 . 13   ®1997 Sigma Consultants, L.L.C.

The Poisson as a Defect Model

(based on DPU=1.0 example)

As the number of opportunities approaches infinity we observe that the yield approaches

$$e^{-1} = .36788$$

r	p(r)
0	0.3678794412
1	0.3678794412
2	0.1839397206
3	0.0613132402
4	0.0153283100
5	0.0030656620
6	0.0005109437
7	0.0000729920
8	0.0000091240
9	0.0000010138
10	0.0000001014
11	0.0000000092
12	0.0000000008
13	0.0000000001
14	0.0000000000
Σ	1.0000000000

$$Y = \frac{(d/u)^r e^{-d/u}}{r!}$$

where d/u is the defects-per-unit and r is the number of occurrences . Thus, when r=0, we have the probability of zero defects, or "rolled-throughput yield." Note that this is different from the classical notion of yield; i.e., number of good units divided by the number of units tested/inspected.

$$Y = e^{-d/u}$$

Notes on the Poisson Approximation

☐ Generalizing from Grant and Leavenworth (1980) we note that the Poisson approximation may be applied when the number of opportunities for nonconformance (n) is large and the probability (p) of an event (r) is small. In fact, as n increases and r decreases, the approximation by the Poisson model improves.

☐ To further extend some of the criteria for applying the Poisson model, Juran (1979) stated that when the sample size is at least 16, the population size is at least 10 times that of the sample, and the probability of an event on each trial is less than 10 percent, the Poisson distribution can be used.

☐ In most industrial applications, the Poisson distribution can be fruitfully applied because the number of defect opportunities is usually quite numerous. Furthermore, the assumption of independence is usually met (in a reasonable way) owing to the nature of manufacturing. These factors, when taken together, set the stage for establishing the Poisson distribution as a viable tool in the quest for Six Sigma.

THE VISION OF SIX SIGMA

σ Six Sigma Academy, Inc.   10 . 15   ®1997 Sigma Consultants, L.L.C.

Analyzing the Poisson Model

r	p(r)	Expected Units	Observed Units	Chi Square
0	.36788	22	20	0.18
1	.36788	22	25	0.41
2	.18394	11	10	0.09
3	.06131	4	5	0.25
4	.01533	1	0	1.00
5	.00307	0	0	0.00
Σ	.99941	60	60	1.93

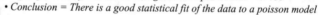

• *Alpha probability associated with given chi-square value = .7486*
• *Conclusion = There is a good statistical fit of the data to a poisson model*

P(r)

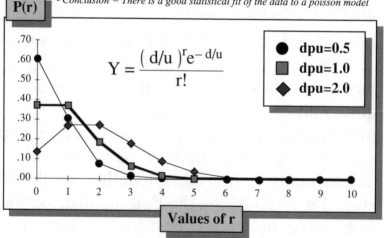

$$Y = \frac{(d/u)^r e^{-d/u}}{r!}$$

● dpu=0.5
■ dpu=1.0
◆ dpu=2.0

Values of r

THE VISION OF SIX SIGMA

σ Six Sigma Academy, Inc.   10 . 16   ®1997 Sigma Consultants, L.L.C.

Comparison of Distributions

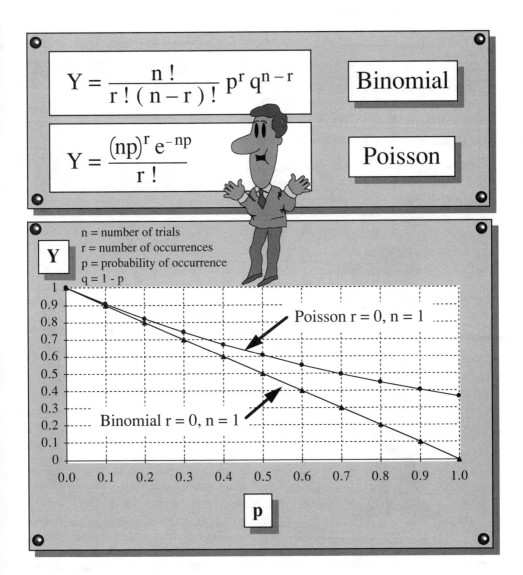

$$Y = \frac{n!}{r!\,(n-r)!}\, p^r q^{n-r}$$

Binomial

$$Y = \frac{(np)^r\, e^{-np}}{r!}$$

Poisson

n = number of trials
r = number of occurrences
p = probability of occurrence
q = 1 - p

Poisson r = 0, n = 1

Binomial r = 0, n = 1

Application Example 1

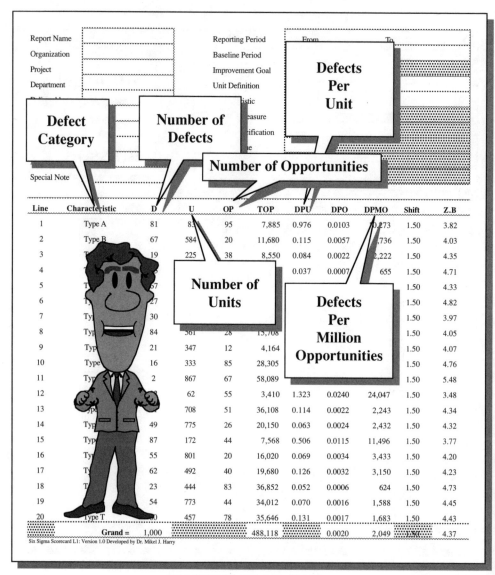

Report Name		Reporting Period	From	To
Organization		Baseline Period		
Project		Improvement Goal		
Department		Unit Definition		

Defects Per Unit

Defect Category

Number of Defects

Number of Opportunities

Special Note

Line	Characteristic	D	U	OP	TOP	DPU	DPO	DPMO	Shift	Z.B
1	Type A	81	83	95	7,885	0.976	0.0103	10,273	1.50	3.82
2	Type B	67	584	20	11,680	0.115	0.0057	5,736	1.50	4.03
3		19	225	38	8,550	0.084	0.0022	2,222	1.50	4.35
4						0.037	0.0007	655	1.50	4.71
5		67							1.50	4.33
6		27							1.50	4.82
7	Ty	30							1.50	3.97
8	Typ	84	561	28	15,708				1.50	4.05
9	Typ	21	347	12	4,164				1.50	4.07
10	Type	16	333	85	28,305				1.50	4.76
11	Ty	2	867	67	58,089				1.50	5.48
12			62	55	3,410	1.323	0.0240	24,047	1.50	3.48
13			708	51	36,108	0.114	0.0022	2,243	1.50	4.34
14	Ty	49	775	26	20,150	0.063	0.0024	2,432	1.50	4.32
15	Typ	87	172	44	7,568	0.506	0.0115	11,496	1.50	3.77
16	T	55	801	20	16,020	0.069	0.0034	3,433	1.50	4.20
17	T	62	492	40	19,680	0.126	0.0032	3,150	1.50	4.23
18	T	23	444	83	36,852	0.052	0.0006	624	1.50	4.73
19		54	773	44	34,012	0.070	0.0016	1,588	1.50	4.45
20	Type T		457	78	35,646	0.131	0.0017	1,683	1.50	4.43
	Grand =		1,000		488,118		0.0020	2,049	1.50	4.37

Number of Units

Defects Per Million Opportunities

Six Sigma Scorecard L1: Version 1.0 Developed by Dr. Mikel J. Harry

THE VISION OF SIX SIGMA

σ Six Sigma Academy, Inc.   10 . 18   ®1997 Sigma Consultants, L.L.C.

Charting the DPU Metric

Currently, and in the recent past there has been much discussion concerning a quality measure commonly referred to as defects-per-unit or "DPU." The purpose of this paper is to discuss DPU and its implications, not to debate the merits, restrictions, or implications of other indices of quality.

Let's clear the air on the mechanics, myths, and misconceptions related to DPU. This particular index (DPU) is nothing more than the total number of defects in a sample (c) divided by the total number of units in the sample (n). Over a period of time, the individual computations (u) are averaged to form a summary figure known as the "average defects per unit" ($\bar{u}$). The computation involves nothing more than simple arithmetic. If one is looking for mathematical mystique or wizardry, it simply is not there … just a solid measure of product quality that is clean, simple, and to the point. For example, consider the following information presented in Figure 1.

Sample No.	Total Defects in Sample	Defects per Unit u
1	17	1.7
2	14	1.4
3	6	0.6
4	23	2.3
5	5	0.5
6	7	0.7
7	10	1.0
8	19	1.9
9	29	2.9
10	18	1.8
11	25	2.5
12	5	0.5
13	8	0.8
14	11	1.1
15	18	1.8
16	13	1.3
17	22	2.2
18	6	0.6
19	23	2.3
20	22	2.2
21	9	0.9
22	15	1.5
23	20	2.0
24	6	0.6
25	24	2.4
TOTAL	375	37.5

Figure 1. Example Data for DPU Computation*

*Source: Adapted from Juran, J.M. (1979). Quality Control Handbook (Third Edition). New York: McGraw-Hill Book Company.

THE VISION OF SIX SIGMA

Six Sigma Academy, Inc.   10 . 19   ®1997 Sigma Consultants, L.L.C.

By sequentially plotting the individual DPU measurements across time, the "quality behavior" of the product emerges as displayed in Figure 2.

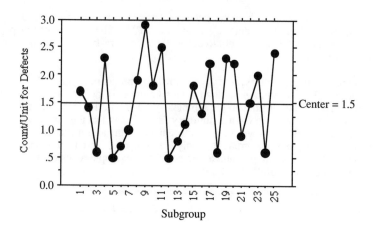

Figure 2. Example Plot of Defects Over Time

If sample number 11 was considered, what should management do? It would appear that some form of action should be taken! Right? ... after all, it is almost the "worst case." What should be the focus of that action ... The process? ... Material? ... People?

Let us now turn our attention to probability. What is the likelihood that observation number 11 could have resulted strictly by chance? If it was not a chance event (e.g., an "assignable" reason exists), then some form of corrective action would be desirable and justified. On the other hand, if it (sample 11) was a chance event, then any action taken to correct the "problem" would not be justified since it was just "random variation" (e.g., the increase in DPU was due to random causes which would not be economical to isolate and remove). In other words, the likelihood of decision error would remain unknown without the knowledge of random chance probability.

Figure 3 presents the same data in the same format but with upper and lower "statistical control limits" added to the graph. The dotted line on the graph indicates the upper and lower "3 sigma limits" of the sampling distribution which, in turn, provides an estimate of the "universe" limits. In other words, the two dotted lines depict the maximum and minimum DPU which could be expected given random variation.

THE VISION OF SIX SIGMA

Six Sigma Academy, Inc.   10 . 20   ®1997 Sigma Consultants, L.L.C.

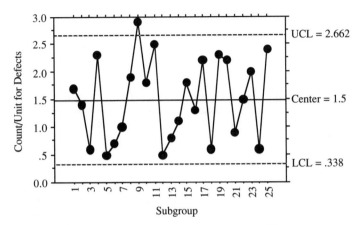

Figure 3. Example Defects per Unit (u) Chart

With this new knowledge (the addition of upper and lower control limits), it is now readily apparent that the DPU associated with sample number 11 was, in all likelihood, due to random variation in one or more of the manufacturing and/or material parameters (assuming no changes in the product design). Furthermore, it is reasonable to assert that it would not be economical to track down and eliminate the source of variation associated with sample number 11 since the variation was of a "random" nature.

The latter conclusion does not appear to hold true for sample number 9. This particular observation is beyond the "3 sigma" high water mark. In other words, there is a very low probability that the variation inherent to sample number 9 could have resulted by chance; therefore, some form of corrective action should be taken. In addition, such action would be initiated with a known degree of "probabilistic confidence" e.g., assurance of not reacting to a "false alarm."

An added feature of the statistical control limits is the ability to make a sound determination as to when the "universe" has shifted to some higher undesirable level or the range has increased. Conversely, it would be nice to know when improvement is nonrandom! Perhaps organizational resources should be expended to isolate these reasons as well as when an "unfavorable out-of-control" situation exists.

The next logical question would be: "Now that I know this stuff, what can I do with it?"...

Six Sigma Academy, Inc.   10 . 21   ®1997 Sigma Consultants, L.L.C.

The following points illustrate the practical utility of DPU charts:

• DPU is additive (assuming the defects are independent). This is important because module DPU's can be summed to create a DPU for the associated assembly. In turn, the assembly DPU's can be merged to create a system DPU ... and so on, all the way to the corporate level.

• The latter point is important because when a higher level (e.g., system, project, division, etc.) u chart displays an "out of control" condition or some nonrandom pattern, the problem can be "source traced" to the lowest levels of manufacture (if it would be necessary to "pareto-ize" that low to isolate the source). This capability serves as the "springboard" for conducting higher resolution statistical work aimed at identifying and removing unwanted sources of costly product and process variation (efficiency is also improved tremendously).

• Inherent simplicity. Unless everyone understands the output, the process is moot! As this writer has heard on several occasions, "If splitting a board is the goal, then why measure it with a micrometer ... just mark it with chalk, and then cut it with a chainsaw." During the initial stages of problem solving, simplicity is the rule. Seven digit precision is not only a burden ... it is too expensive! The more people who understand what is going on, the bigger the bandwagon will be!

• Ease of interpretation. Trends, shifts, cycles, and out-of-control points are readily apparent ... "what you see is what you did!"

• Ease of compilation. Sophisticated forms of data collection and recording are not necessary. Remember, the simpler the system, the greater the likelihood the data will be valid and representative of the universe ... not to mention the fact that the system would be used and appropriately maintained!

• Bonus point ... It doesn't take a "bunch of statistical Ph.D.'s" to make it work!

Now the question becomes: "O.K., I'm sold, but what do I need to do right now to get it off the ground?" Again, the answer is simple and straight forward ...

Step 1: Define what it is you want to know.
Since we want to know how good our quality is in terms of "nonconformance to requirements," then DPU is what we want to know!

Step 2: Determine how you want to see what it is you want to know.
Since DPU is compiled most conveniently in graphical form, then this step is already complete.

Step 3: Identify the type of data it takes to create the defined graph.
Make a list of all possible types of defects (both test and inspect). These categories are the "pigeon holes" that are used to separate the "good guys" from the "bad guys." In all likelihood, all or most of these categories are already defined, so this step is behind us.

Step 4: Identify how the numbers are to be "crunched."
As already indicated, all that is necessary to create and use the u chart is basic arithmetic. Just compute the average DPU and control limits and you are in business. The steps are summarized below:

4a. Compute DPU for each sample.
Note: a sample size of 25 is recommended before the first chart is constructed (the reason for this has to do with the "statistics of the thing").

4b. Compute u bar (average DPU for the sample).

4c. Compute upper and lower control limits.

4d. Construct graph.

4e. Interpret graph.

4f. Take appropriate corrective action as required.

Step 5: Identify where the required type of data can be collected.
Such locations become "monitoring gates." We must all recognize that DPU measures symptoms, not problems. If DPU is high, then this is a symptom of a more intrinsic problem within the "underlying cause system." In this situation, the problem is rooted in the nonrandom variation exhibited by the causal variables ... not the fact that DPU is "going out the roof." It is the causal variables which must be identified with diagnostic and experimentation tools and then controlled across time with statistical process control charts designed for continuous data (e.g., $\overline{X}$ and R charts).

There are no "knobs" to turn which can lower DPU; however, there are "knobs" to turn which controls factors such as wave height, solder flux specific gravity, temperature, etc. Direct control can be exerted over the "knob" variables! DPU is not the resultant measurement ... it is not a variable ... only an index of quality generated by the effects of process, material, design, environmental, and human factors. By systematically "back-tracking" through sub-level DPU charts, one can get very close to the root cause! If the data collection points are not properly established, then the "back-tracking" can lead "up the proverbial creek" ... so great care should be exercised when executing this step ... you know, "no pain, no gain" and all that stuff!

In summary, this writer would like to conclude by saying that virtually all organizations have the talent and resources to take advantage of the DPU concept. As with most things that are worthwhile, they take time and patience. Initially, the DPU method may be somewhat cumbersome. Recognize that transitioning to a "statistical way of doing business "is like" swallowing a bitter pill;" however, like modern medicine, the rewards are great.

THE VISION OF SIX SIGMA

σ Six Sigma Academy, Inc.   10 . 23   ®1997 Sigma Consultants, L.L.C.

Normal Transformation

CHAPTER ELEVEN

Breakthrough

Breakthrough

THE VISION OF SIX SIGMA

The Reciprocal Nature of Data

We will recall that the normal distribution, as previously discussed, can tell us the number of events to be expected when the distribution parameters are known or estimated. For example, we could determine (from the normal distribution) how many defects to expect within any continuous interval extending from x = a to x = b. Extending this line of reasoning, Taylor (1982) stated that

> *In practice, the observed number [within the interval x = a to x = b] is seldom exactly the expected number. Instead it fluctuates in accordance with the Poisson distribution. In many situations it is reasonable to expect numbers to be distributed approximately according to the Poisson distribution. The approximation is called the Gaussian approximations to the Poisson. It is analogous to the corresponding approximation for the binomial distribution and is useful under the same conditions, namely,*
>
> *when the parameters involved are large. In fact, it can be proved that as μ -> ∞, the Poisson distribution becomes steadily more symmetrical and approaches the Gauss [normal] distribution with the same mean and standard deviation.*

To illustrate the practical implications of this relation, let us postulate that a given, normally distributed response characteristic (say p1, as related to our widget example) has a capability such that the specification limits are μ ±3σ. Such a capability would translate to a first-time yield of .9973, or 2700 ppm in terms of a defect rate.

Based on this, we could report the process capability in either form so long as the corresponding distributional assumptions are reasonably adhered to. In this case, we may say that a ppm value of 2700 is directly equivalent, for all practical purposes, to a normal distribution, which is ±3σ in relation to the bilateral specification limits. As a consequence, it is possible to align the various discrete metrics to those measures of capability based on continuous data, and vice-versa.

Such "metric interconnectivity" will take on immense value and applied meaning in subsequent discussions; however, for now, let us simply recognize the existence of interconnectivity between the Poisson and normal distribution, as well as the binomial model.

THE VISION OF SIX SIGMA

The Idea of Data Interchange

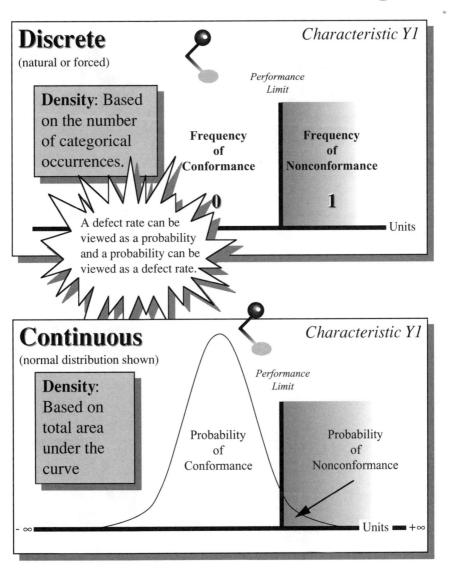

Discrete
(natural or forced)

Characteristic Y1

Density: Based on the number of categorical occurrences.

Performance Limit

Frequency of Conformance

Frequency of Nonconformance

0

1

Units

A defect rate can be viewed as a probability and a probability can be viewed as a defect rate.

Continuous
(normal distribution shown)

Characteristic Y1

Density: Based on total area under the curve

Performance Limit

Probability of Conformance

Probability of Nonconformance

- ∞

Units ▬ +∞

σ Six Sigma Academy, Inc.   11.3   ®1997 Sigma Consultants, L.L.C.

Approximating the Normal

The Poisson relation:

$$Y = \frac{(np)^r e^{-np}}{r!}$$

where n is the number of trials, r is the number of occurrences , and p is the probability of occurrence . Thus, when r=0, we have the probability of zero occurrences , or "rolled-throughput yield." Note that this is very different from the classical notion of yield; i.e., number good divided by the total number.

The poisson distribution is an approximation to more exact distributions and applies when the sample size is at least 16, the population is at least 10 times the sample size, and the probability of occurrence p on each trial is less than 10 percent. In practice, these assumptions are often met.

For n = unity and r = 0,

$$Y = e^{-p}$$

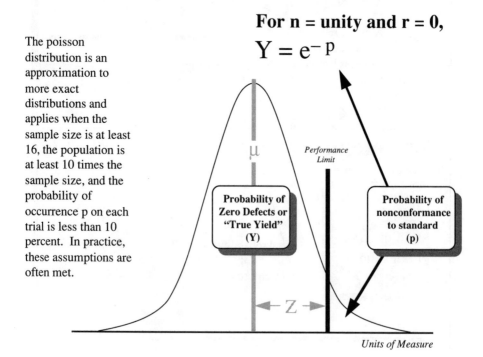

μ

Performance Limit

Probability of Zero Defects or "True Yield" (Y)

Probability of nonconformance to standard (p)

← Z →

Units of Measure

THE VISION OF SIX SIGMA

σ Six Sigma Academy, Inc.   11 . 4   ®1997 Sigma Consultants, L.L.C.

Example Application of the Poisson

A certain engineer observed 1 particular type of defect out of 346 production units. The defects-per-unit was computed as dpu = 1/346 = .00289. Hence,

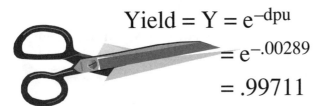

$$\text{Yield} = Y = e^{-dpu}$$
$$= e^{-.00289}$$
$$= .99711$$

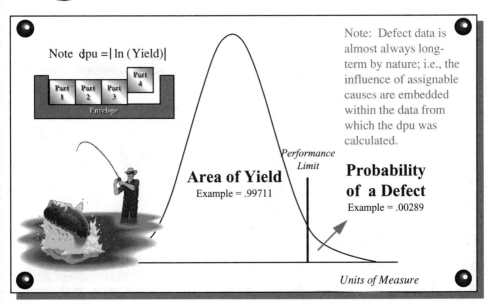

Note dpu = | ln (Yield)|

Note: Defect data is almost always long-term by nature; i.e., the influence of assignable causes are embedded within the data from which the dpu was calculated.

Performance Limit

Area of Yield
Example = .99711

Probability of a Defect
Example = .00289

Units of Measure

THE VISION OF SIX SIGMA

Six Sigma Academy, Inc.   11 . 5   ®1997 Sigma Consultants, L.L.C.

The Normal or "Z" Approximation

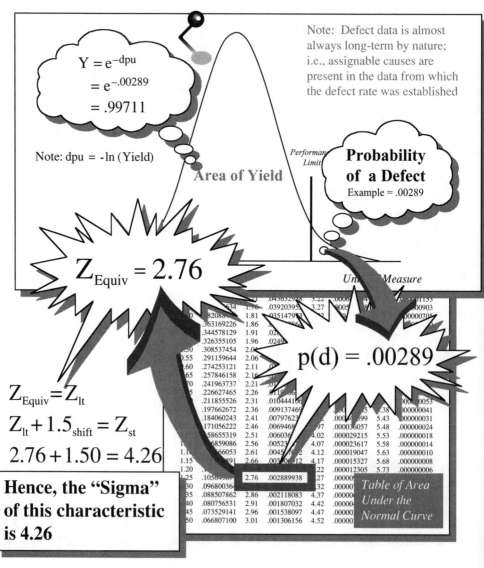

THE VISION OF SIX SIGMA

Six Sigma Academy, Inc. 11 . 6 ®1997 Sigma Consultants, L.L.C.

Comments on the Z Approximation

✔ The rate at which defects are produced must be relatively stable to utilize the Z approximation.

✔ Generally speaking, substantial time must pass to observe a stable rate of defects.

✔ The defect rate will change whenever there is a change in the short-term capability of a process, due to a change in process spread or an alteration of the design limits. In addition, the defect rate will change whenever there is a change in the process mean relative to the design limits.

✔ If, during the course of data collection, a substantial amount of time has elapsed, it is reasonable to assume that the process mean has shifted or drifted over this time interval -- due to changes in material, tool wear, operator differences, etc.

✔ Therefore, if the design and process technology has remained constant over a large interval of time, it is reasonable to assume that the influence of shifts and drifts in μ is fully embodied within the defect data. Hence, the defect data would be considered "long-term" by nature and, as a consequence, reflect random errors within the process as well as nonrandom sources of error.

✔ To assess the short-term capability of a process, it is necessary to remove the nonrandom influences from the data. If the data were based on a simple count of defects, then we must subtract

THE VISION OF SIX SIGMA

σ Six Sigma Academy, Inc.   11 . 7   ®1997 Sigma Consultants, L.L.C.

Using the Sigma Scale of Measure

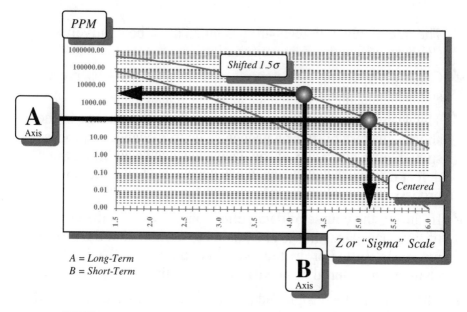

A = Long-Term
B = Short-Term

A	If you start with defect data, then compute the PPM per opportunity and enter along the "A" axis. Next, project the "A" value to the "B" axis. The resulting number is an estimate of the short-term Z value, or "sigma" as it is called.
B	If you start with a Z or "sigma" value, then enter along "B" axis. Next, project the "B" value to the "A" axis. The resulting number is an estimate of the long-term PPM.

THE VISION OF SIX SIGMA

σ Six Sigma Academy, Inc.   11 . 8   ®1997 Sigma Consultants, L.L.C.

Computing a Probability

It is often the case that we desire to compute the tail area probability associated with a given Z or "sigma" value. Of course, this can be easily accomplished using a standard table of area under the normal curve. However, we can compute the value in an electronic spreadsheet by way of the following equation:

$$\boxed{\text{Eq. 11.1}}$$

$$P = \left[\left(1 + C_1 Z + C_2 Z^2 + \ldots + C_6 Z^6 \right)^{-16} \right] / 2$$

Notes:
1) Z and P are one-tailed
2) Z is the standard normal deviate
3) P is the tail area probability
4) A4 is an arbitrary spreadsheet cell location

Constants

```
=(((((((1+0.049867347*ABS(A4))+
0.0211410061*ABS(A4^2))+
0.0032776263*ABS(A4^3))+
0.0000380036*ABS(A4^4))+
0.0000488906*ABS(A4^5))+
0.000005383*ABS(A4^6))^-16/2)
```

$C1 = 0.0498673470$
$C2 = 0.0211410061$
$C3 = 0.0032776263$
$C4 = 0.0000380036$
$C5 = 0.0000488906$
$C6 = 0.0000053830$

Computing the "Sigma" Value

In many situations, a Z or "sigma" value can be easily ascertained using a standard table of area under the normal curve. However, it is often desirable to directly compute the value in an electronic spreadsheet. This task may be accomplished using the following equation:

$$\boxed{\text{Eq. 11.2}}$$

$$Z = \lambda - \frac{C_1 + C_2\lambda + C_3\lambda^2}{1 + C_4\lambda + C_5\lambda^2 + C_6\lambda^3}$$

$$\lambda = \sqrt{\ln\left(1 / P^2\right)}$$

Notes:
1) Z and P are one-tailed
2) Z is the standard normal deviate
3) P is the tail area probability
4) E8 is an arbitrary spreadsheet cell location

Constants

```
=SQRT(LN(1/(1-E8)^2))-((2.515517
+0.802853*(SQRT(LN(1/(1-E8)^2)))
+0.010328*(SQRT(LN(1/(1-E8)^2)))^2))
/((1+1.432788*(SQRT(LN(1/(1-E8)^2)))
+0.189269*(SQRT(LN(1/(1-E8)^2)))^2
+0.001308*(SQRT(LN(1/(1-E8)^2)))^3))
```

$C1 = 2.515517$
$C2 = 0.802853$
$C3 = 0.010328$
$C4 = 1.432788$
$C5 = 0.189269$
$C6 = 0.000308$

THE VISION OF SIX SIGMA

σ Six Sigma Academy, Inc.   11 . 10   ®1997 Sigma Consultants, L.L.C.

The Sigma Conversion Guidelines

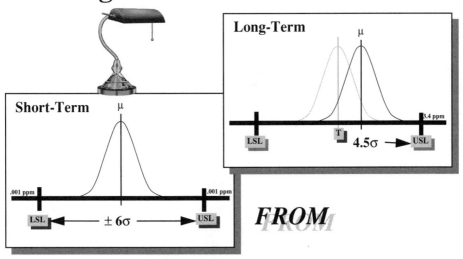

FROM

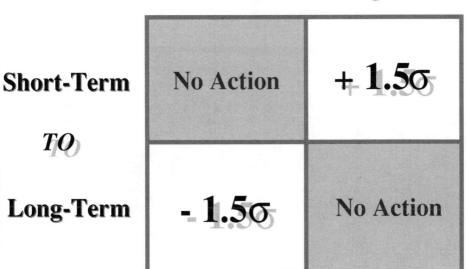

	Short-Term	**Long-Term**
Short-Term	No Action	**+ 1.5σ**
Long-Term	**- 1.5σ**	No Action

TO

THE VISION OF SIX SIGMA

σ Six Sigma Academy, Inc.   11 . 11   ®1997 Sigma Consultants, L.L.C.

PPM Conversion Table

Z	PPM	Z	PPM	Z	PPM
0.00	933,193	2.20	241,964	4.40	1,866
0.05	926,471	2.25	226,627	4.45	1,589
0.10	919,243	2.30	211,856	4.50	1,350
0.15	911,492	2.35	197,663	4.55	1,144
0.20	903,199	2.40	184,060	4.60	968
0.25	894,350	2.45	171,056	4.65	816
0.30	884,930	2.50	158,655	4.70	687
0.35	874,928	2.55	146,859	4.75	577
0.40	864,334	2.60	135,666	4.80	483
0.45	853,141	2.65	125,072	4.85	404
0.50	841,345	2.70	115,070	4.90	337
0.55	828,944	2.75	105,650	4.95	280
0.60	815,940	2.80	96,800	5.00	233
0.65	802,338	2.85	88,508	5.05	193
0.70	788,145	2.90	80,757	5.10	159
0.75	773,373	2.95	73,529	5.15	131
0.80	758,036	3.00	66,807	5.20	108
0.85	742,154	3.05	60,571	5.25	89
0.90	274,253	3.10	54,799	5.30	72
0.95	291,160	3.15	49,471	5.35	59
1.00	308,537	3.20	44,565	5.40	48
1.05	326,355	3.25	40,059	5.45	39
1.10	344,578	3.30	35,930	5.50	32
1.15	363,169	3.35	32,157	5.55	26
1.20	382,088	3.40	28,717	5.60	21
1.25	401,294	3.45	25,588	5.65	17
1.30	420,740	3.50	22,750	5.70	13
1.35	440,382	3.55	20,182	5.75	11
1.40	460,172	3.60	17,865	5.80	9
1.45	480,061	3.65	15,778	5.85	7
1.50	500,000	3.70	13,904	5.90	5
1.55	480,061	3.75	12,225	5.95	4
1.60	460,172	3.80	10,724	6.00	3
1.65	440,382	3.85	9,387		
1.70	420,740	3.90	8,198		
1.75	401,294	3.95	7,143		
1.80	382,088	4.00	6,210		
1.85	363,169	4.05	5,386		
1.90	344,578	4.10	4,661		
1.95	326,355	4.15	4,024		
2.00	308,537	4.20	3,467		
2.05	291,160	4.25	2,980		
2.10	274,253	4.30	2,555		
2.15	257,846	4.35	2,186		

Note: This table includes a 1.5σ shift for all listed values of Z.

THE VISION OF SIX SIGMA

Six Sigma Academy, Inc.   11 . 12   ®1997 Sigma Consultants, L.L.C.

The Widget Example Data

g	X1	X2	X3	X4	X5
1	1.242	1.239	1.239	1.242	1.240
2	1.240	1.241	1.240	1.239	1.242
3	1.239	1.239	1.239	1.239	1.240
4	1.241	1.240	1.240	1.240	1.241
5	1.240	1.241	1.240	1.238	1.241
6	1.241	1.240	1.240	1.240	1.239
7	1.237	1.240	1.240	1.237	1.238
8	1.240	1.242	1.240	1.240	1.238
9	1.240	1.239	1.240	1.239	1.242
10	1.239	1.239	1.241	1.239	1.240
11	1.239	1.238	1.242	1.238	1.240
12	1.239	1.241	1.239	1.239	1.242
13	1.239	1.242	1.239	1.239	1.240
14	1.240	1.239	1.240	1.239	1.241
15	1.241	1.240	1.240	1.240	1.240
16	1.240	1.239	1.240	1.240	1.240
17	1.241	1.239	1.238	1.240	1.240
18	1.239	1.239	1.241	1.241	1.239
19	1.240	1.239	1.240	1.238	1.242
20	1.241	1.240	1.241	1.239	1.240

Sampling Strategy: 5 consecutive parts were selected every hour (X_1, ... , X_N). Each group (g) of parts was labeled and set aside for careful measurement of dimension "B." The location of measurement was arbitrarily chosen by the inspector.

Widget Characterization - 2a

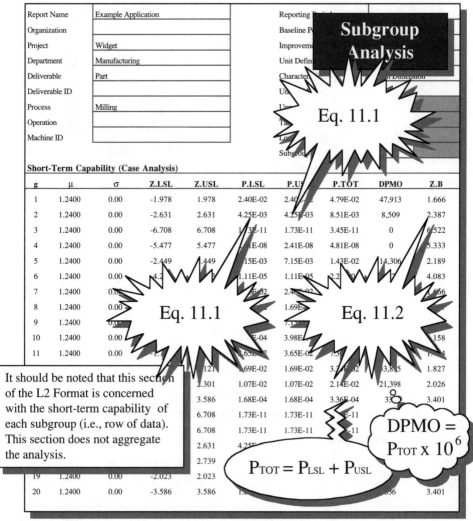

Report Name	Example Application
Organization	
Project	Widget
Department	Manufacturing
Deliverable	Part
Deliverable ID	
Process	Milling
Operation	
Machine ID	

Reporting Period
Baseline Period
Improvement
Unit Definition
Character...
U...
...
Ta...
Lo...
Subgroup...

Subgroup Analysis

Eq. 11.1

Short-Term Capability (Case Analysis)

g	μ	σ	Z.LSL	Z.USL	P.LSL	P.USL	P.TOT	DPMO	Z.B
1	1.2400	0.00	-1.978	1.978	2.40E-02	2.40E-02	4.79E-02	47,913	1.666
2	1.2400	0.00	-2.631	2.631	4.25E-03	4.25E-03	8.51E-03	8,509	2.387
3	1.2400	0.00	-6.708	6.708	1.73E-11	1.73E-11	3.45E-11	0	6.522
4	1.2400	0.00	-5.477	5.477	2.41E-08	2.41E-08	4.81E-08	0	5.333
5	1.2400	0.00	-2.449	2.449	7.15E-03	7.15E-03	1.43E-02	14,306	2.189
6	1.2400	0.00	-4.2		1.11E-05	1.11E-05	2.2		4.083
7	1.2400	0.0				2.4			.66
8	1.2400	0.00				1.69E-			
9	1.2400	0.0				7.1			
10	1.2400	0.00			04	3.98E-			158
11	1.2400	0.00	-1.		.65E-02	3.65E-02	7.3		1. 4
			121		.69E-02	1.69E-02	3. .E .2	3,8 5	1.827
			2.301		1.07E-02	1.07E-02	2.14E-02	21,398	2.026
			3.586		1.68E-04	1.68E-04	3.36E-04	33	3.401
			6.708		1.73E-11	1.73E-11		-11	
			6.708		1.73E-11	1.73E-11		-11	
			2.631		4.25				
			2.739						
19	1.2400	0.00	-2.023	2.023					
20	1.2400	0.00	-3.586	3.586	1.		36		3.401

Eq. 11.1

Eq. 11.2

It should be noted that this section of the L2 Format is concerned with the short-term capability of each subgroup (i.e., row of data). This section does not aggregate the analysis.

$$DPMO = P_{TOT} \times 10^6$$

$$P_{TOT} = P_{LSL} + P_{USL}$$

Format L2

THE VISION OF SIX SIGMA

Six Sigma Academy, Inc.   11 . 14   ®1997 Sigma Consultants, L.L.C.

Widget Characterization - 2b

Short-Term Capability (Cumm Analysis)

g	μ	SS	σ	Z.LSL	Z.USL	P.LSL	P.USL	P.TOT	DPMO	Z.B
1	.2400	.000009	.00152	-1.978	1.978	2.40E-02	2.40E-02	4.79E-02	47,913	1.666
2	00	.000014	.00134	-2.236	2.236	1.27E-02				.954
3	1.	.000015	.00113	-2.666	2.666	3.84E-03				424
4	1.2	.000016	.00101	-2.?63	2.963	1.52E-03				743
5	1.240				2.835	2.29E-03				606
6	1					1.46E-03				756
7										.503
							4.25E-03	8.51E-03	8,509	2.387
11										
13	1.2?			469	2.469	6.78E-0				
14	1.2?0	.000?0	.19	-2.?6	2.516	5.93E-0				
15	1.2400	.000080	.116	-2.59?	2.592	4.78E-0				
16	1.2400	.000081	.00113	-2.663	2.663	3.87E-0				
17	1.2400	.000086	.00113	-2.661	2.661	3.89E-0				
18	1.2400	.000091	.00113	-2.666	2.666	3.84E-0				
19	1.2400	.000100	.00115	-2.615	2.615	4.46E-0				
20	1.2400	.000103	.00113	-2.646	2.646	4.07E-03	4.07E-03	8.13E-03	8,133	2.403

Cumulative Short-Term Analysis

Z.B for the cumulative short-term analysis is computed in the same manner as that given for the case-wise short-term analysis

It should be noted that this section of the L2 Format is concerned with the cumulative short-term capability. For each new subgroup (i.e., row of data), the $Z.st$ value is recomputed using all of the previous data. This particular analysis is based on the nominal specification (i.e., target value).

THE VISION OF SIX SIGMA

Six Sigma Academy, Inc.   11 . 15   ®1997 Sigma Consultants, L.L.C.

Widget Characterization - 2c

g	μ	SS	σ	Z.LSL	Z.USL	P.LSL	P.USL	P.TOT	DPMO	Z.B	Z.shift
1	2404	.000009	.00152	-2.242	1.714	1.25E-02	4.32E-02	5.57E-02	55,713	1.592	0.074
2	404	.000014	.00126	-2.688	2.055	3.59E-03	1.99E-02	2.35E-02	23,511	1.987	-0.032
3		.000020	.00120	-2.510	2.510	6.04E-03	6.04E-03				
4	1.	.000022	.00107	-2.894	2.707	1.90E-03	3.39E-03				
5	1.24	.000028	.00108		2.711	2.12E-03	3.35E-03				
6	1.240				2.890	1.26E-03	1.92E-03				
7						1.04E-02	4.80E-03				
8							5.25E-03	1.50E-02	15,552	2.150	0.251
							26E-03				
10							24E-03				
							02				
							1.09E-02				
13							1.07E-02				
						5	28E-03				
	1.23				2.7		7.30E-03				
16	1.2	.00		11	2.799	6.02E-03					
17	1.2398	.000 06	113	-2	2.823	6.05E-03					
18	1.2398	.000111	.00112	-2.52	2.843	5.78E-03	2.23E-03	8.01E-03	8,010	2.409	0.015
19	1.2398	.000120	.00113	-2.497	2.814	6.26E-03	2.45E-03	8.70E-03	8,704	2.378	-0.009
20	1.2398	.000123	.00112	-2.543	2.830	5.49E-03	2.33E-03	7.82E-03	7,817	2.418	-0.014

Long-Term Capability (Cumm Analysis)

Cumulative Long-Term Analysis

Z.B for the cumulative long-term analysis is computed in the same manner as that given for the case-wise short-term analysis.

It should be noted that this section of the L2 Format is concerned with the cumulative long-term capability . For each new subgroup (i.e., row of data), the Z.lt value is recomputed using all of the previous data. This particular analysis is based on the process mean.

Application Example 2d

Report Name

Organization

Project

Department

Deliverable

Deliverable ID

Process

Step

Machine ID

Special Note

Reporting Period   From   To

Baseline Period   From   To

...nt Goal

Remember, defects per opportunity (dpo) is treated as a probability for purposes of applying Eq. 11.1

Eq. 11.1

Defects Per Opportunity

Line	Characteristic			TOP	DPU	DPO	DPMO	Shift	Z.B
1	Type A	83	95	7,885	0.976	0.0103	10,273	1.50	3.82
2	Type B		584	20	11,680	0.115	0057	5,736	1.50	4.03
3	T	19	225	38	8,550	0.084	022	2,222	1.50	4.35
4	T		884	57	50,388	0.037	0007	655	1.50	4.71
5	T	57	774	37				2,340	1.50	4.33
6	T	27	669	91				444	1.50	4.82
7	Typ	30	86	51				6,840	1.50	3.97
8	Typ	84	561	28				5,348	1.50	4.05
9	Typ	21	347	12				5,043	1.50	4.07
10	Type	16	333	85	28,305	0.048	0.0006	565	1.50	4.76
11	Typ	2	867	67	58,089	0.002	0.0000	34	1.50	5.48
12			62	55	3,410	1.323	0.0240	24,047	1.50	3.48
13	yp		708	51	36,108	0.114	0.0022	2,243	1.50	4.34
14	Typ	49	775	26	20,150	0.063	0.0024	2,432	1.50	4.32
15	Typ	87	172	44	7,568	0.506	0.0115	11,496	1.50	3.77
16	Ty	55	801	20	16,020	0.069	0.0034	3,433	1.50	4.20
17	T	62	492	40	19,680	0.126	0.0032	3,150	1.50	4.23
18	T	23	444	83	36,852	0.052	0.0006	624	1.50	4.73
19		54	773	44	34,012	0.070	0.0016	1,588	1.50	4.45
20	Type T		457	78	35,646	0.131	0.0017	1,683	1.50	4.43
	Grand =	1,000			488,118		0.0020	2,049	1.50	4.37

Six Sigma Scorecard L1: Version 1.0 Developed by Dr. Mikel J. Harry

THE VISION OF SIX SIGMA

σ Six Sigma Academy, Inc.   11 . 17   ®1997 Sigma Consultants, L.L.C.

Guidelines for the Mean Shift

Guideline 1: If a metric is computed on the basis of data gathered over many cycles or time intervals, the resultant value should be regarded as a long-term measure of performance. Naturally the long-term metric must be converted to a probability. Once expressed as a probability, Z.lt value may be established by way of a table of area-under-the-normal-curve, or any acceptable computational device. If we seek to forecast short-term performance (Z.st), we must add a shift factor (Z.shift) to Z.lt so as to remove time related sources of error which tend to upset process centering. Recognize that the actual value of Z.shift is seldom known in practice; therefore, it may be necessary to apply the accepted convention and set Z.shift = 1.50. As a consequence of this linear transformation, the final Z value reflects only random sources of error and, therefore, is a projection of short-term performance. Thus, we are able to artificially remove the effect of nonrandom influences (i.e., normal process centering errors) from the analysis via the transform Z.st = Z.lt + Z.shift.

Guideline 2: If a metric is computed on the basis of data gathered over a very limited number of cycles or time intervals, the resultant value should be regarded as a short-term measure of performance. Naturally, the short-term metric must be converted to a probability. Once expressed as a probability, Z.st may be established by way of a table of area-under-the-normal-curve, or any acceptable computational device. If we seek to forecast long-term performance, we must subtract Z.shift from Z.st so as to approximate the long-term capability. Recognize that the actual value of Z.shift is seldom known in practice; therefore, it may be necessary to apply the accepted convention and set Z.shift = 1.50. As a consequence of this linear transformation, the final Z value reflects both random and nonrandom sources of error and, therefore, is a projection of long-term performance. Thus, we are able to artificially induce the effect of nonrandom influences (i.e., normal process centering errors) into the analysis by way of Z.st - Z.shift = Z.lt

Guideline 3: In general, if the originating data is discrete by nature, the resulting Z transform should be regarded as long-term. The logic of this guideline is simple; a fairly large number of cycles or time intervals is often required to generate enough nonconformities from which to generate a relatively stable estimate of Z. Hence, it is reasonable to conclude that both random and nonrandom influences are reflected in such data. In this instance, guideline 1 would be applied.

Guideline 4: In general, if the originating data is continuous by nature and was gathered under the constraint of sequential or random sampling across a very limited number of cycles or time intervals, the resulting Z value should be regarded as short-term. The logic of this guideline is simple; data gathered over a very limited number cycles or time intervals only reflects random influences (white noise) and, as a consequence, tends to exclude nonrandom sources of variation, such as process centering errors.

Guideline 5: Whenever it is desirable to report the corresponding "sigma" of a given performance metric, the short-term Z must be used. For example, let us suppose that we find 6210 ppm defective. In this instance, we must translate 6210 ppm into its corresponding "sigma" value. Doing so reveals Z.lt = 2.50. Since the originating data was long-term by nature, guidelines 1 and 3 apply. In this case, Z.lt + Z.shift = 2.5 + 1.5 = 4.0. Since no other estimate of Z.shift was available, the convention of 1.5 was employed.

THE VISION OF SIX SIGMA

Nature of Opportunities

CHAPTER TWELVE

Breakthrough

Breakthrough

THE VISION OF SIX SIGMA

The Role of Complexity

➤ Producibility and quality are closely coupled because both are essentially the resultant or integrated effect of a myriad of diverse and complex interactions between the product and the manufacturing processes which produce it within a complex environment.

➤ These interactions involve all components of the manufacturing system. Inattention to these interactions during the design phase generally results in poor product quality, costly production problems, and a steady stream of engineering change notices (ECNs) during the production phase. Conversely, quality during the production phase is the result of a "producible design" created during the design phase.

➤ A producible design results from paying close attention to product/process interactions and seeking to minimize these interactions and their impact by designing the product and process as a coordinated system. In this sense, producibility can be thought of as "quality during the design phase."

Stoll, H., Kumar, A., and Maas, D. (Date Unknown).
Producibility Measurement: Key to the Design of Producible Products.
Unpublished paper. pp 1-2. Industrial Technology Institute, Ann Arbor,
Michigan.

THE VISION OF SIX SIGMA

σ Six Sigma Academy, Inc.   12 . 2   ®1997 Sigma Consultants, L.L.C.

Dealing with Complexity

"Complexity" is a measure of how complicated something is. From a theoretical perspective, it is doubtful that we will ever be able to quantify this concept in an exacting manner. From a more practical point-of-view, we may say that notion of complexity is closely associated with the number of product and process characteristics.

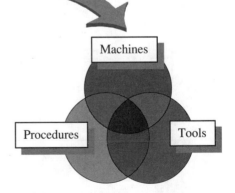

Product

Complexity

If we assume that all characteristics are independent and mutually exclusive, we may say that "complexity" can be reasonably estimated by a simple count.

Process

In terms of quality, each product and process characteristic represents a unique "opportunity" to either add or subtract value.

Complexity and Capability

The goal should be to reduce the total number of opportunities and concurrently increase the capability of each opportunity which remains.

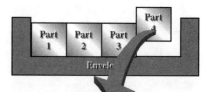

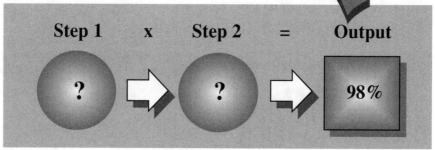

Sigma Capability (with 1.5s shift)

. . . The following graph displays the Sigma Capability which must be maintained (for X number of process steps) in order to produce 98% of the products defect free.

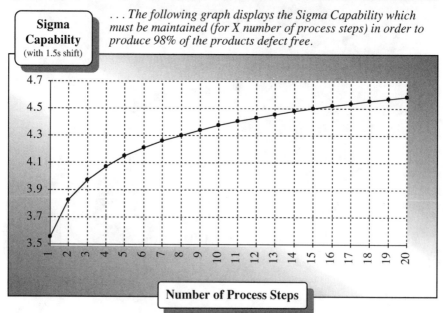

Number of Process Steps

THE VISION OF SIX SIGMA

σ Six Sigma Academy, Inc.   12 . 4   ®1997 Sigma Consultants, L.L.C.

Complexity and Quality

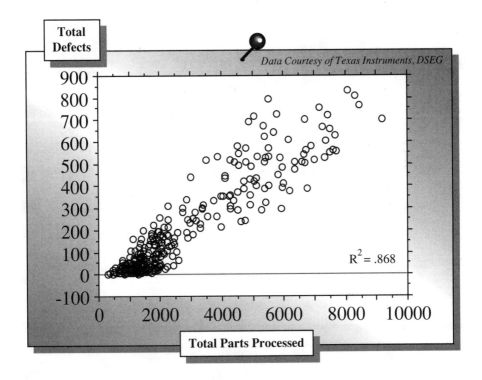

Data Courtesy of Texas Instruments, DSEG

$R^2 = .868$

Total Defects (y-axis)

Total Parts Processed (x-axis)

The data suggests that there is a strong correlation between the total number of parts processed and the total number of observed defects. Given the linear nature of this relationship, we may conclude that the process maintains a relatively stable level of capability over time.

The Opportunity Exercise

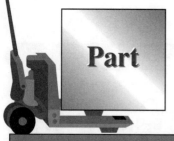

For the given widget part, identify the product opportunities.

Description of Opportunity	Count

Note: Opportunities must be independent -- one type of opportunity can not cause another type to be nonconforming to its respective standard.

Total =

 Six Sigma Academy, Inc.   12 . 6   ®1997 Sigma Consultants, L.L.C.

Example Application Format

Project	Document
Hardware A	Design
Software	Process B
Service	Proceedure

A = Object   B = Focus

Demographics

Level		Description	Legend
Complex	1	NA	F Failure
System	2	Widget Model #7	D Defect
Subsystem	3	Holdit Assembly - ABC	E Error
Component	4	Gotahavit Part #123	A Number Appraised
Element	5	x	T Total (F+D+E)

	Characteristic	F	D	E	A	T		Characteristic	F	D	E	A	T
1	Dimension		6		5	6	15						
2	Finish						16						
3	Diameter		3		3	3	17						
4	Angle		4		1	4	18						
5	Hardness	1			1	1	19						
6	Stress	1			1	1	20						
7							21						
8							22						
9							23						
10							24						
11							25						
12							26						
13							27						
14							28						
15							29						
							Total		2	13	0	11	15

THE VISION OF SIX SIGMA

σ Six Sigma Academy, Inc.   12.7   ®1997 Sigma Consultants, L.L.C.

Comments on Opportunity Counting

Nature of an Opportunity

Level	Opportunity			
	A Characteristic	B Scale	C Standard	D Density
1 Complex				
2 System				
3 Subsystem				
4 Component				
5 Element				

Note: An opportunity can exist at any level of a hierarchy

Opportunity: Set of circumstances favorable to an end

Characteristic	Distinguishing attribute, trait, property, or quality.
Scale	Relative basis for measuring a characteristic.
Standard	Criterion state, condition or model circumstance.
Density	Quantity per unit of measure.

 Six Sigma Academy, Inc.   12.9   ®1997 Sigma Consultants, L.L.C.

The Set of Circumstances

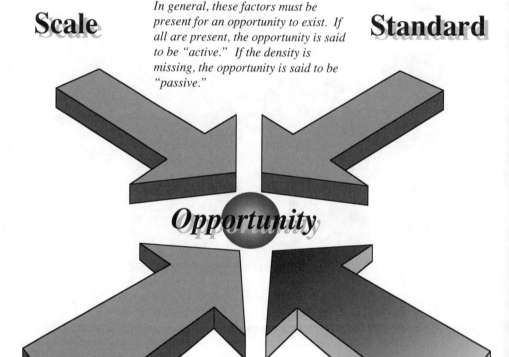

Scale

In general, these factors must be present for an opportunity to exist. If all are present, the opportunity is said to be "active." If the density is missing, the opportunity is said to be "passive."

Standard

Opportunity

Characteristic

Density

Developing Density With Data

✩ Two kinds of data can be used for establishing density. First, there is data which characterizes a product or process feature in terms of its size, weight, volts. This type of data is said to be continuous by nature. In other words, the measurement scale can be meaningfully divided into finer and finer increments of precision.

✩ Another way to look at the data is to merely count the frequency of occurrence; e.g., the number of times something happens or fails to happen. Notice that such data is not capable of being meaningfully subdivided into more precise increments and, therefore, is said to be discrete by nature.

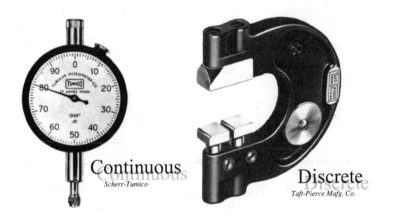

Continuous
Scherr-Tumico

Discrete
Taft-Pierce Mafg. Co.

Opportunity and Density

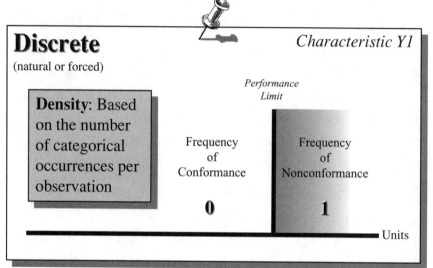

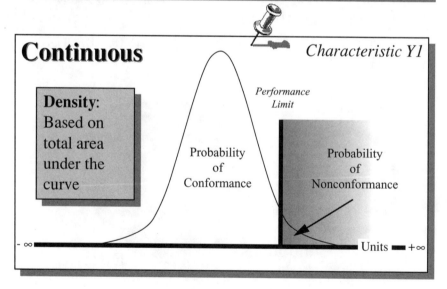

THE VISION OF SIX SIGMA

Six Sigma Academy, Inc.   12 . 12   ®1997 Sigma Consultants, L.L.C.

The Opportunity Hierarchy

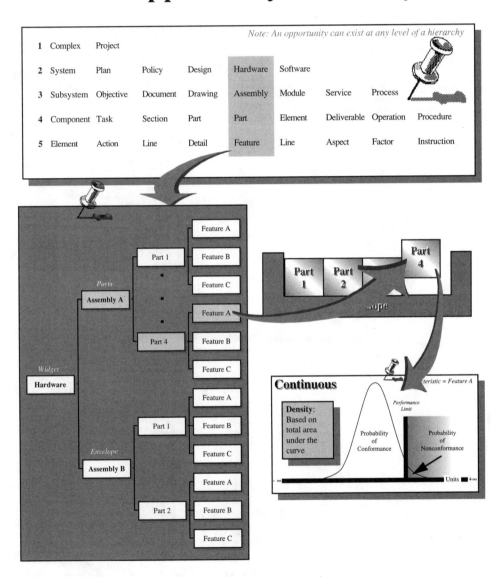

Note: An opportunity can exist at any level of a hierarchy

1	Complex	Project						
2	System	Plan	Policy	Design	Hardware	Software		
3	Subsystem	Objective	Document	Drawing	Assembly	Module	Service	Process
4	Component	Task	Section	Part	Part	Element	Deliverable	Operation	Procedure
5	Element	Action	Line	Detail	Feature	Line	Aspect	Factor	Instruction

Continuous

Characteristic = Feature A

Density: Based on total area under the curve

Performance Limit

Probability of Conformance

Probability of Nonconformance

Units

THE VISION OF SIX SIGMA

σ Six Sigma Academy, Inc.   12 . 13   ®1997 Sigma Consultants, L.L.C.

Application to the Widget

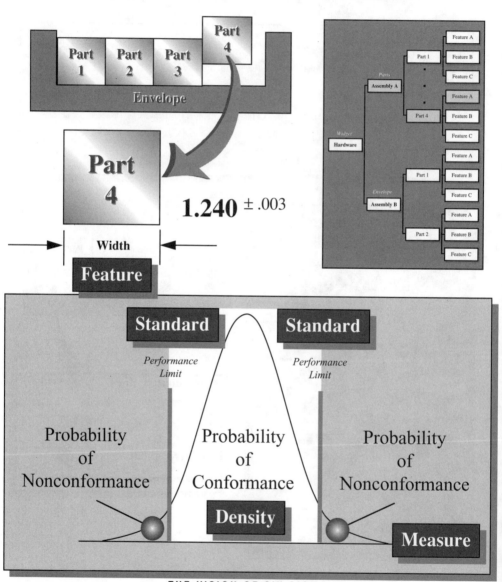

$1.240 \pm .003$

The States of an Opportunity

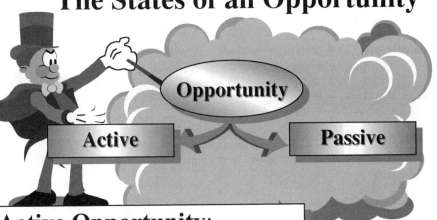

Active Opportunity:
The chance for conformance to standard is assessed.

Passive Opportunity:
The chance for conformance to standard is not assessed.

For a typical product, what proportion of the total opportunities do you suppose are active? If all of the passive opportunities were to become active, do you suppose the "sigma" would change much?

In short, any product characteristic which is measured to a standard should be classified as an "active defect opportunity." Any process characteristic which impacts a given product characteristic constitutes a "control opportunity." Taken together, such opportunities govern the likelihhood of customer satisfaction.

THE VISION OF SIX SIGMA

 Six Sigma Academy, Inc.   12 . 15   ®1997 Sigma Consultants, L.L.C.

Active and Passive Exercise

Let us suppose that a certain organization determines that process ABC has m = 100,000 opportunities for nonconformance to standard. However, during the normal course of process operation, only 1,000 of these opportunities are assessed and recorded. We will further suppose that TDPU = 10.

General Rule: An opportunity is an opportunity only if it is measured.

What is the defects-per-opportunity and what "sigma" capability should be declared?

If we employ 100,000 opportunities which exist, we compute:

$$DPO = \frac{TDPU}{M} = \frac{10}{100,000} = .0001$$ **Active + Passive**

This converts to 3.72σ. Since the originating data was long-term by nature, we must remove the influence of process shift and drift by adding 1.50σ to the result. Doing so, we discover the short-term opportunity capability is 5.22σ. Such performance is approaching world-class.

If we employ the 1,000 opportunities we assessed , we compute:

$$DPO = \frac{TDPU}{M} = \frac{10}{1,000} = .01$$ **Active Only**

This converts to 2.33σ. After adding 1.5σ to the result, we discover the short-term opportunity capability is 3.83σ. Such performance is slightly below average. Obviously, this is the "true" capability of the process

As we can see, the inclusion of those opportunities which were not assessed makes a big difference in the stated process capability.

σ   Six Sigma Academy, Inc.   12 . 16   ©1997 Sigma Consultants, L.L.C.

The Classes of Nonconformance

Fault: Results when a <u>characteristic</u> does not <u>perform</u> to standard.

Defect: Results when a <u>characteristic</u> does not <u>conform</u> to standard.

Error: Results when an <u>action</u> does not <u>comply</u> with standard.

Note: A failure can only be detected upon the application of energy. The detection of a defect or error is not energy dependent.

The Moving Van Example

	Active	Passive
Fault		
Defect		
Error		

The Basic Model for Failures

A failure at any given level of the opportunity hierarchy can be attributed to the independent or joint occurrence of defects, faults, or errors at one or more of the subordinate levels associated with that hierarchy .

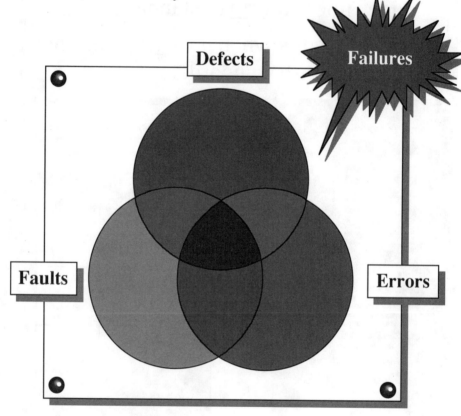

THE VISION OF SIX SIGMA

σ Six Sigma Academy, Inc.   12 . 18   ®1997 Sigma Consultants, L.L.C.

Extending the Basic Model

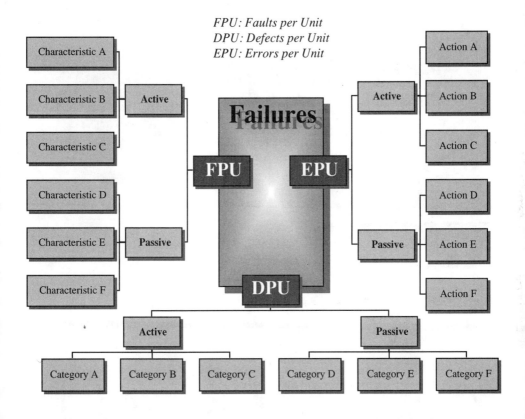

FPU: Faults per Unit
DPU: Defects per Unit
EPU: Errors per Unit

Characteristic A
Characteristic B — Active
Characteristic C
Characteristic D
Characteristic E — Passive
Characteristic F

Failures

FPU   **EPU**

DPU

Active   Passive

Category A   Category B   Category C   Category D   Category E   Category F

Action A
Action B
Action C
Action D
Action E
Action F

Active
Passive

Six Sigma Academy, Inc.   12 . 19   ®1997 Sigma Consultants, L.L.C.

Translating Needs into Requirements

The vital needs of the customer are translated into critical-to-satisfaction characteristics (CTS's).

$$CTS_1, \ldots, CTS_K$$

The CTS's are translated into critical requirements related to quality, delivery, and cost.

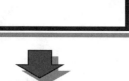

$$CTQ_1, \ldots, CTQ_L$$
$$CTD_1, \ldots, CTD_M$$
$$CTC_1, \ldots, CTC_N$$

Note: Any CTQ, CTD, or CTC would, by definition, constitute an opportunity for nonconformance, so long as it is actively measured and reported. Recognize that such characteristics are often targeted as black belt improvement projects (following the breakthrough strategy).

Defining the CTY (Product) Tree

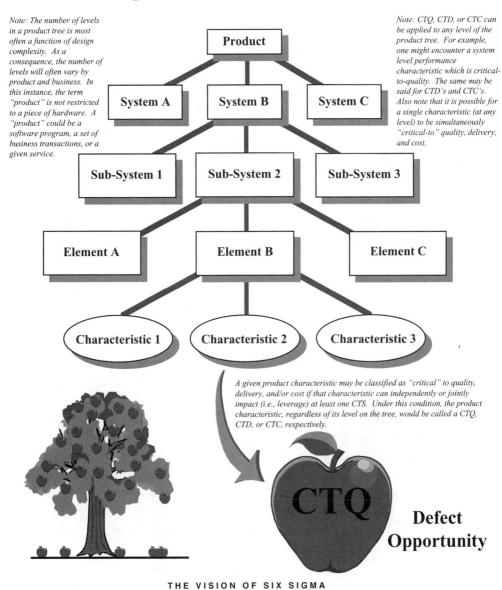

Note: The number of levels in a product tree is most often a function of design complexity. As a consequence, the number of levels will often vary by product and business. In this instance, the term "product" is not restricted to a piece of hardware. A "product" could be a software program, a set of business transactions, or a given service.

Note: CTQ, CTD, or CTC can be applied to any level of the product tree. For example, one might encounter a system level performance characteristic which is critical-to-quality. The same may be said for CTD's and CTC's. Also note that it is possible for a single characteristic (at any level) to be simultaneously "critical-to" quality, delivery, and cost.

Product

System A   System B   System C

Sub-System 1   Sub-System 2   Sub-System 3

Element A   Element B   Element C

Characteristic 1   Characteristic 2   Characteristic 3

A given product characteristic may be classified as "critical" to quality, delivery, and/or cost if that characteristic can independently or jointly impact (i.e., leverage) at least one CTS. Under this condition, the product characteristic, regardless of its level on the tree, would be called a CTQ, CTD, or CTC, respectively.

CTQ

Defect Opportunity

THE VISION OF SIX SIGMA

Defining the CTX (Process) Tree

Note: The number of levels in a process tree is most often driven by design complexity and the available manufacturing technologies. As a consequence, the number of levels will often vary by product and business.

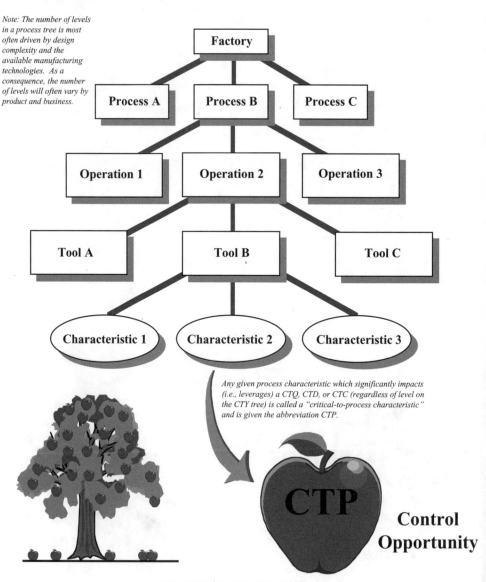

Any given process characteristic which significantly impacts (i.e., leverages) a CTQ, CTD, or CTC (regardless of level on the CTY tree) is called a "critical-to-process characteristic" and is given the abbreviation CTP.

CTP

Control Opportunity

THE VISION OF SIX SIGMA

Developing the CT Matrix

Product (Y) Tree

Process (X) Tree

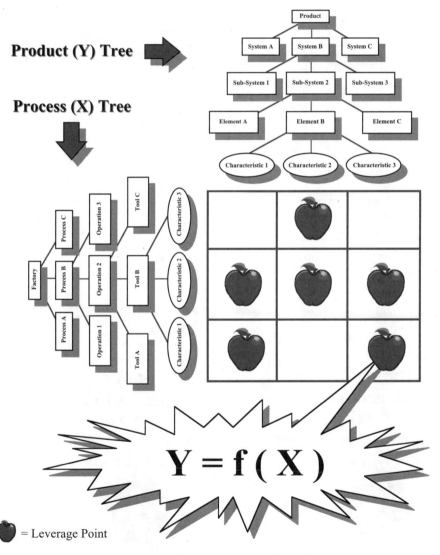

$$Y = f(X)$$

= Leverage Point

"Critical-To" Characteristics

The variation inherent to any dependent variable (Y) is determined by the variations inherent to each of the independent variables.

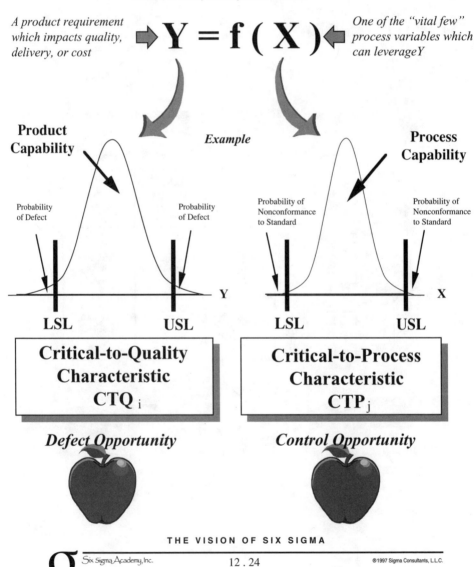

A product requirement which impacts quality, delivery, or cost ➡️

$$Y = f (X)$$

⬅️ *One of the "vital few" process variables which can leverage Y*

Product Capability

Example

Process Capability

Probability of Defect

Probability of Defect

Probability of Nonconformance to Standard

Probability of Nonconformance to Standard

LSL   USL   Y

LSL   USL   X

Critical-to-Quality Characteristic CTQ$_i$

Critical-to-Process Characteristic CTP$_j$

Defect Opportunity

Control Opportunity

Performance Metrics

CHAPTER THIRTEEN

Breakthrough

Breakthrough

THE VISION OF SIX SIGMA

The Need for Performance Metrics

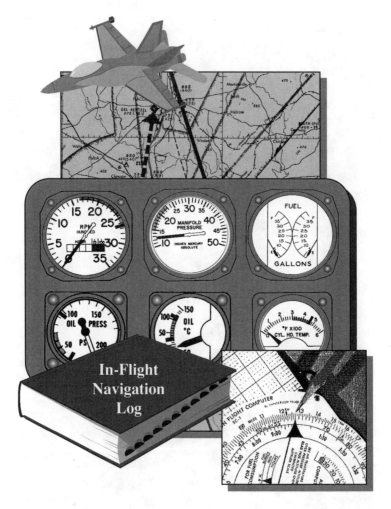

*. . . So what do these things have in common
with business. . . What are the implications?*

Best Quality Management Practice

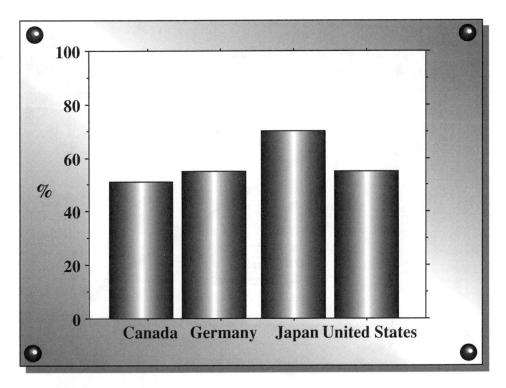

"How often does senior management evaluate information regarding the business consequences of quality performance; that is, gains in market share or profit resulting from quality improvements"

Source: *The Definitive Study of the Best International Quality Management Practices*
Ernst & Young 1991

THE VISION OF SIX SIGMA

 Six Sigma Academy, Inc.   13 . 3   ® 1997 Sigma Consultants, L.L.C.

Nature of Performance Metrics

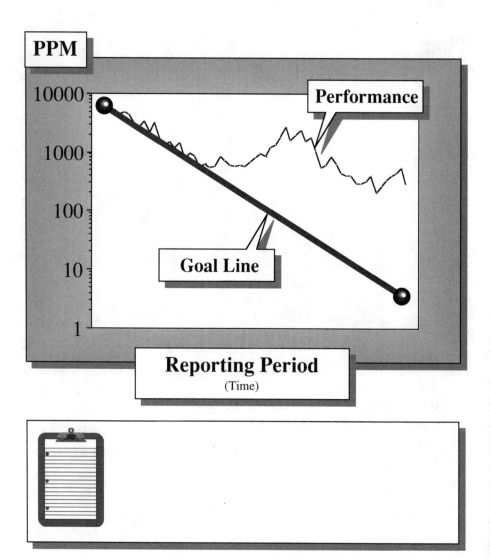

 Six Sigma Academy, Inc.   13 . 4   ®1997 Sigma Consultants, L.L.C.

Using the Log Scale for Graphs

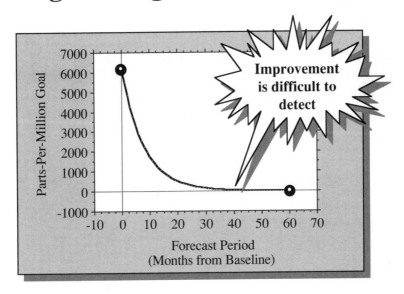

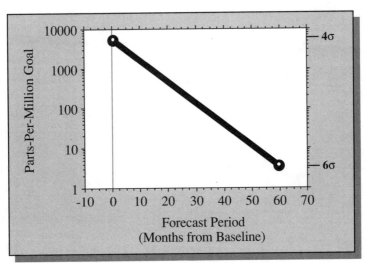

Six Sigma Academy, Inc.   13 . 5   ®1997 Sigma Consultants, L.L.C.

Guiding the Business with Metrics

The benefit of performance metrics can not be understated. Use of metrics is a proven means to guide the basic operations of business. Performance metrics provide feedback and ensure a focus on business fundamentals.

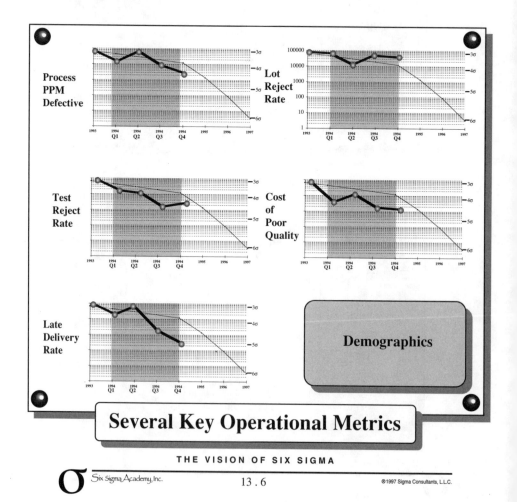

Several Key Operational Metrics

Six Sigma Academy, Inc.   13 . 6   ®1997 Sigma Consultants, L.L.C.

Business Metrics Report Summary

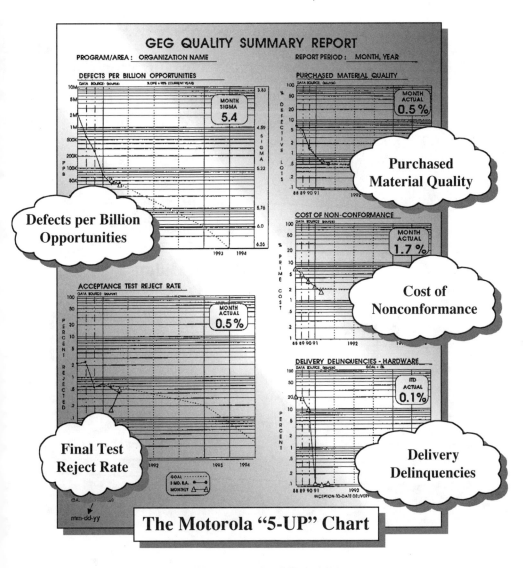

GEG QUALITY SUMMARY REPORT

Defects per Billion Opportunities

Purchased Material Quality

Cost of Nonconformance

Final Test Reject Rate

Delivery Delinquencies

The Motorola "5-UP" Chart

THE VISION OF SIX SIGMA

Six Sigma Academy, Inc.   13 . 7   ®1997 Sigma Consultants, L.L.C.

Hierarchical Reporting

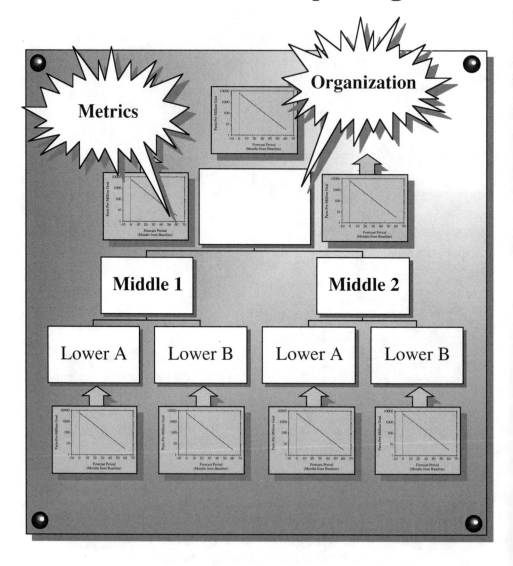

Six Sigma Academy, Inc.   13.8   ®1997 Sigma Consultants, L.L.C.

Example Performance Metrics

Motorola Factory

Metrics Report	QSR 5-UP	Goal	Baseline Period
Acceptance/Realiabiltiy Test Rejects	A	68% IPY	1988 average
Cost of Nonconformance	A	25% IPY	1988 average
Cost of Quality		18% IPY	1988 average
Defects per Cost Proposal		68% IPY	1988 average
Defects per Million Opportunities-Assembly		68% IPY	1st & 2nd Q, 1990
Defects per Million Opportunities-Manufacturing		68% IPY	1st & 2nd Q, 1989
Defects per Million Opportunities-Solder		68% IPY	1st & 2nd Q, 1990
Defects per Million Opportunities-Test and Inspection	A	68% IPY	1988 average
Delivery Delinquencies-CDRLs		0 Delinquencies	N/A
Delivery Delinquencies-Hardware	A	0 Delinquencies	N/A
First-Time Test Reject-Subassemblies		25% IPY	1st & 2nd Q, 1989
First-Time Test Reject Rate-Systems		25% IPY	1st & 2nd Q, 1989
Method Bs (QDR)		0 QDRs	N/A
MRB Actions		0 MRB Actions	N/A
MRB Items-Number Processed		0 MRB Items	N/A
Productivity		10% IPY	1st Q of meas.
Purchased Material Quality-Project Responsibility	P	0 Defects	N/A
Purchased Material Quality-QSM Responsibility		0 Defects	N/A
Purchased Material Quality	G	50% IPY	1987 average
Quality Summary Report		N/A	N/A
Software-Total Defect Containment Effectiveness		100% by 1992	1st Q, 1988
Standard Repairs		68%	4th Q, 1989
Technical Documentation Accuracy		68% IPY	4th Q, 1987
Time Card /Time Sheet Accuracy		68% IPY	1987 average
Waivers		0 Waivers	N/A

IPY = Improvement Per Year

N/A = Not Applicable

A = This report is included in the Program, Division, and Group Quality Summary Reports (5-Up)

G = This report is included in the Division and Group Quality Summary Reports (5-Up)

P = This report is included in the Program Quality Summary Report (5-Up)

THE VISION OF SIX SIGMA

Six Sigma Academy, Inc.   13.9   ®1997 Sigma Consultants, L.L.C.

Example Metrics Reporting

Motorola Factory

Metrics Report	QSR 5-UP	Operations Review	Division Review	Group Review	Corp Review
Acceptance/Realiabiltiy Test Rejects	A	X	X	X	X
Cost of Nonconformance	A	X	X	X	X
Cost of Quality			X	X	
Defects per Cost Proposal			X	X	X
Defects per Million Opportunities-Assembly		X			
Defects per Million Opportunities-Manufacturing		X	X		
Defects per Million Opportunities-Solder		X			
Defects per Million Opportunities-Test and Inspection	A	X	X	X	X
Delivery Delinquencies-CDRLs		X	X	X	X
Delivery Delinquencies-Hardware	A	X	X	X	X
First-Time Test Reject-Subassemblies		X			
First-Time Test Reject Rate-Systems		X			
Method Bs (QDR)				X	X
MRB Actions		X	X	X	
MRB Items-Number Processed		X	X	X	
Productivity		X	X	X	
Purchased Material Quality-Project Responsibility	P	X	X	X	
Purchased Material Quality-QSM Responsibility			X	X	
Purchased Material Quality	G		X	X	X
Quality Summary Report		X	X	X	X
Software-Total Defect Containment Effectiveness		X	X	X	
Standard Repairs		X	X		
Technical Documentation Accuracy			X	X	
Time Card /Time Sheet Accuracy			X	X	X
Waivers		X	X	X	

IPY = Improvement Per Year

N/A = Not Applicable

A = This report is included in the Program, Division, and Group Quality Summary Reports (5-Up)

G = This report is included in the Division and Group Quality Summary Reports (5-Up)

P = This report is included in the Program Quality Summary Report (5-Up)

Note 1. Operations Reviews are not required by the Strategic Electronics Division.

Note 2. Purchased Material Quality-Supplier Responsibility is reported by the Quality Supply Management organization.

Six Sigma Academy, Inc.

13 . 10

Performance Metrics Manual

Standardization of documentation and reporting formats is a major key to successful application

THE VISION OF SIX SIGMA

σ Six Sigma Academy, Inc.   13 . 11   ®1997 Sigma Consultants, L.L.C.

Creating Performance Metrics

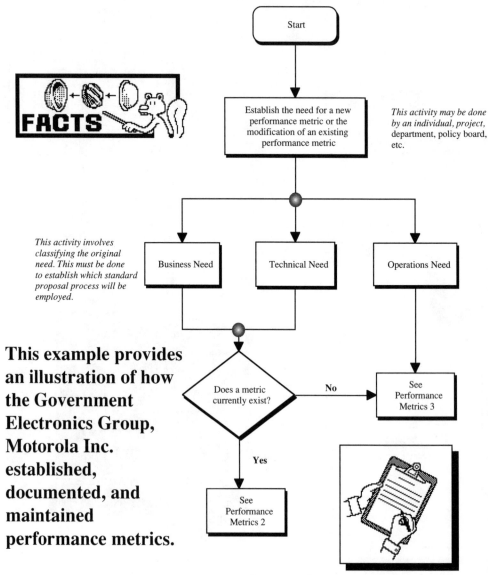

This activity may be done by an individual, project, department, policy board, etc.

This activity involves classifying the original need. This must be done to establish which standard proposal process will be employed.

This example provides an illustration of how the Government Electronics Group, Motorola Inc. established, documented, and maintained performance metrics.

Performance Metrics: Option 2

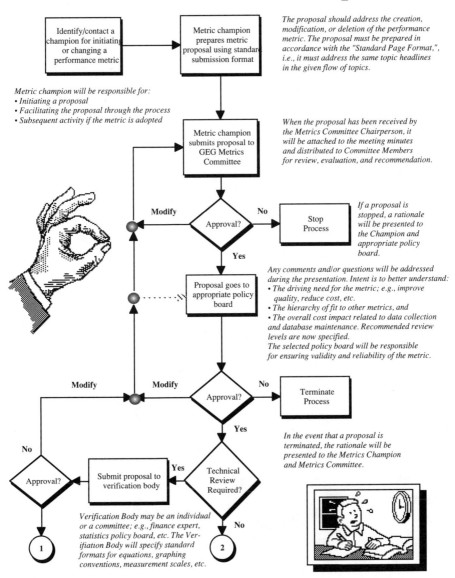

Identify/contact a champion for initiating or changing a performance metric

Metric champion prepares metric proposal using standard submission format

The proposal should address the creation, modification, or deletion of the performance metric. The proposal must be prepared in accordance with the "Standard Page Format,", i.e., it must address the same topic headlines in the given flow of topics.

Metric champion will be responsible for:
• Initiating a proposal
• Facilitating the proposal through the process
• Subsequent activity if the metric is adopted

Metric champion submits proposal to GEG Metrics Committee

When the proposal has been received by the Metrics Committee Chairperson, it will be attached to the meeting minutes and distributed to Committee Members for review, evaluation, and recommendation.

Modify

Approval?

No

Stop Process

Yes

If a proposal is stopped, a rationale will be presented to the Champion and appropriate policy board.

Proposal goes to appropriate policy board

Any comments and/or questions will be addressed during the presentation. Intent is to better understand:
• The driving need for the metric; e.g., improve quality, reduce cost, etc.
• The hierarchy of fit to other metrics, and
• The overall cost impact related to data collection and database maintenance. Recommended review levels are now specified.
The selected policy board will be responsible for ensuring validity and reliability of the metric.

Modify   Modify

Approval?

No

Terminate Process

Yes

In the event that a proposal is terminated, the rationale will be presented to the Metrics Champion and Metrics Committee.

No

Approval?

Submit proposal to verification body

Yes

Technical Review Required?

No

Verification Body may be an individual or a committee; e.g., finance expert, statistics policy board, etc. The Verifiation Body will specify standard formats for equations, graphing conventions, measurement scales, etc.

1

2

Six Sigma Academy, Inc.   13.13   ®1997 Sigma Consultants, L.L.C.

Performance Metrics: Option 3

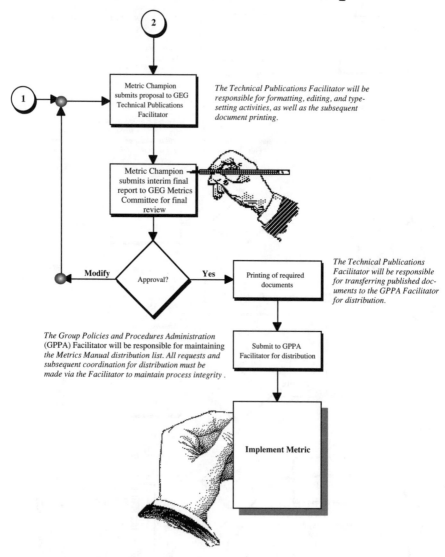

2

Metric Champion submits proposal to GEG Technical Publications Facilitator

The Technical Publications Facilitator will be responsible for formatting, editing, and type-setting activities, as well as the subsequent document printing.

1

Metric Champion submits interim final report to GEG Metrics Committee for final review

Modify — Approval? — **Yes** — Printing of required documents

The Technical Publications Facilitator will be responsible for transferring published doc-uments to the GPPA Facilitator for distribution.

The Group Policies and Procedures Administration (GPPA) Facilitator will be responsible for maintaining the Metrics Manual distribution list. All requests and subsequent coordination for distribution must be made via the Facilitator to maintain process integrity .

Submit to GPPA Facilitator for distribution

Implement Metric

Establishing Performance Goals

$$Y_G = B \left(10^{\log[(1-R)/12]} \right)^N$$

		Y = Goal value for the forecast period
		B = Baseline performance for given metric
B	6,210	R = Desired annual improvement rate
R	78.00	N = Number of months since baseline period

N	Y.G	N	Y.G	N	Y.G
0	6209.7				
1	5473.6	21	438.8	41	35.2
2	4824.7	22	386.8	42	31.0
3	4252.8	23	341.0	43	27.3
4	3748.7	24	300.5	44	24.1
5	3304.3	25	264.9	45	21.2
6	2912.6	26	233.5	46	18.7
7	2567.3	27	205.8	47	16.5
8	2263.0	28	181.4	48	14.5
9	1994.7	29	159.9	49	12.8
10	1758.3	30	141.0	50	11.3
11	1549.9	31	124.3	51	10.0
12	1366.1	32	109.5	52	8.8
13	1204.2	33	96.5	53	7.7
14	1061.4	34	85.1	54	6.8
15	935.6	35	75.0	55	6.0
16	824.7	36	66.1	56	5.3
17	726.9	37	58.3	57	4.7
18	640.8	38	51.4	58	4.1
19	564.8	39	45.3	59	3.6
20	497.9	40	39.9	60	3.2

If the baseline capability is 4σ, the corresponding ppm = 6210. Given an improvement rate of 78% per year, the goal for the 60th month would be Y.G = 3.2 ppm, or 6σ.

Annual Rate of Improvement

$$Y_A = 1 - \left(10^{\log(C/B)/N}\right)^{12}$$

Y = Improvement rate for the given month
B = Baseline performance for given metric
C = Performance for current month
N = Number of months since baseline period

B	6,210
C	233

N	Y.A	N	Y.A	N	Y.A
1	1.0000	21	0.8469	41	0.6176
2	1.0000	22	0.8333	42	0.6087
3	1.0000	23	0.8198	43	0.6001
4	0.9999	24	0.8064	44	0.5917
5	0.9996	25	0.7933	45	0.5835
6	0.9986	26	0.7804	46	0.5755
7	0.9964	27	0.7677	47	0.5677
8	0.9927	28	0.7553	48	0.5600
9	0.9875	29	0.7431	49	0.5526
10	0.9806	30	0.7312	50	0.5453
11	0.9722	31	0.7195	51	0.5383
12	0.9625	32	0.7082	52	0.5313
13	0.9518	33	0.6971	53	0.5246
14	0.9401	34	0.6862	54	0.5180
15	0.9277	35	0.6757	55	0.5116
16	0.9148	36	0.6654	56	0.5053
17	0.9016	37	0.6553	57	0.4991
18	0.8880	38	0.6455	58	0.4931
19	0.8743	39	0.6360	59	0.4873
20	0.8606	40	0.6267	60	0.4815

If the baseline capability is 4σ, the corresponding ppm = 6210. If after the 60th month ppm = 233, the rate of improvement per year would be Y.A = 48.15%.

Note: In order to achieve a 10X reduction in defects every two years, Y.A = 68.37%. This learning curve is currently employed by Motorola. Thus, the goal is a 100X reduction in defects every 4 years.

THE VISION OF SIX SIGMA

Six Sigma Academy, Inc.   13 . 16   ®1997 Sigma Consultants, L.L.C.

Monthly Rate of Improvement

R	Y.M
.00	.00000
.05	.00427
.10	.00874
.15	.01345
.20	.01842
.25	.02369
.30	.02929
.35	.03526
.40	.04168
.45	.04860
.50	.05613
.55	.06438
.60	.07352
.65	.08377
.70	.09546
.75	.10910
.80	.12551
.85	.14623
.90	.17460
.95	.22092

$$Y_M = 1 - \left(10^{\,[\log(1-R)]/12} \right)$$

Y = Monthly rate of improvement
R = Desired annual improvement rate

If the annual improvement rate is 70%, the monthly rate is 10.9%.

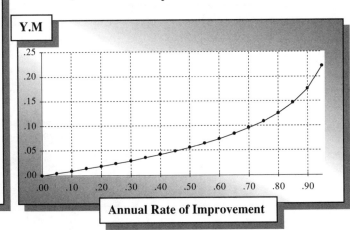

Annual Rate of Improvement

THE VISION OF SIX SIGMA

Six Sigma Academy, Inc.   13 . 17   ®1997 Sigma Consultants, L.L.C.

Computing the "Sigma" Value

Short-term data is free of assignable causes, thus it represents the effect of random causes only.

Long-term data reflects the influence of random causes as well as assignable phenomena.

If the yield or defect data were gathered over many intervals of production, consider the situation to be long-term; otherwise, assume it to be short-term.

FROM

	Short-Term	Long-Term
Short-Term	No Action	**+ 1.5σ**
Long-Term	**- 1.5σ**	No Action

TO

Equations

$$P = \left[\left(1 + C_1 Z + C_2 Z^2 + \ldots + C_6 Z^6\right)^{-16}\right]/2$$

Constants

$C1 = 0.0498673470$
$C2 = 0.0211410061$
$C3 = 0.0032776263$
$C4 = 0.0000380036$
$C5 = 0.0000488906$
$C6 = 0.0000053830$

Equations

$$Z = \lambda - \frac{C_1 + C_2\lambda + C_3\lambda^2}{1 + C_4\lambda + C_5\lambda^2 + C_6\lambda^3}$$

Notes:
1) Z and P are one-tailed
2) Z is the standard normal deviate
3) P is the tail area probability

$$\lambda = \sqrt{\ln\left(1 / P^2\right)}$$

Constants

$C1 = 2.515517$
$C2 = 0.802853$
$C3 = 0.010328$
$C4 = 1.432788$
$C5 = 0.189269$
$C6 = 0.000308$

THE VISION OF SIX SIGMA

Creating a Benchmarking Chart

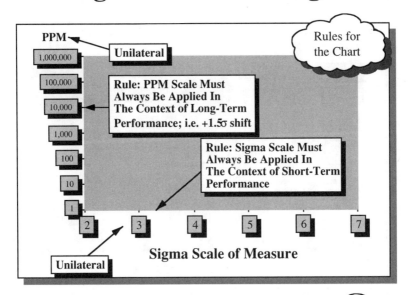

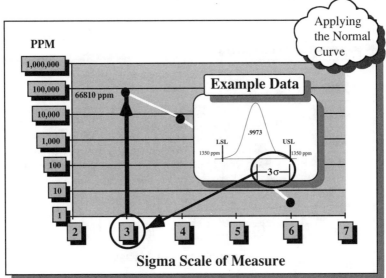

Creating a Benchmarking Chart

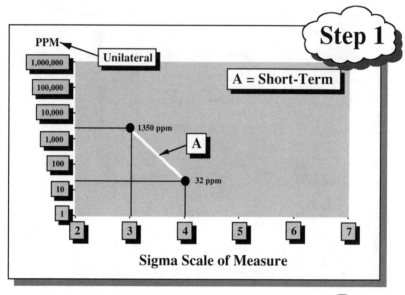

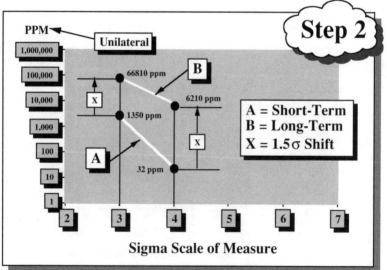

Creating a Benchmarking Chart

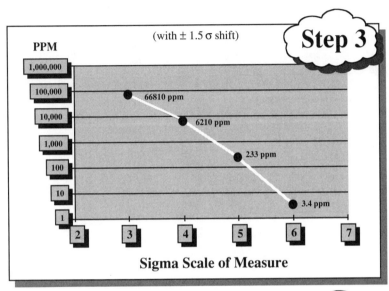

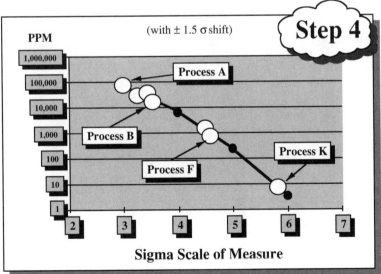

THE VISION OF SIX SIGMA

Six Sigma Academy, Inc.   13 . 21   ®1997 Sigma Consultants, L.L.C.

Rolled-Throughput Yield

CHAPTER FOURTEEN

Breakthrough

Breakthrough

THE VISION OF SIX SIGMA

The Classical Perspective of Yield

$$Y_{final} = \frac{s}{u}$$

Where:

Y_{final} = final yield

s = number of units that pass

u = number of units tested

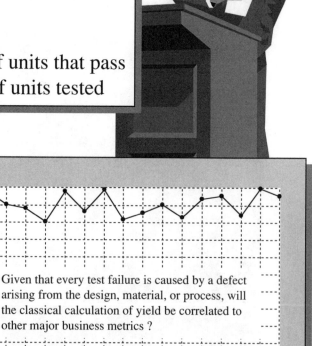

$Y_{.final}$

Given that every test failure is caused by a defect arising from the design, material, or process, will the classical calculation of yield be correlated to other major business metrics ?

Reporting Period

Questioning Basic Beliefs

Data: Jan 92 through Dec 92

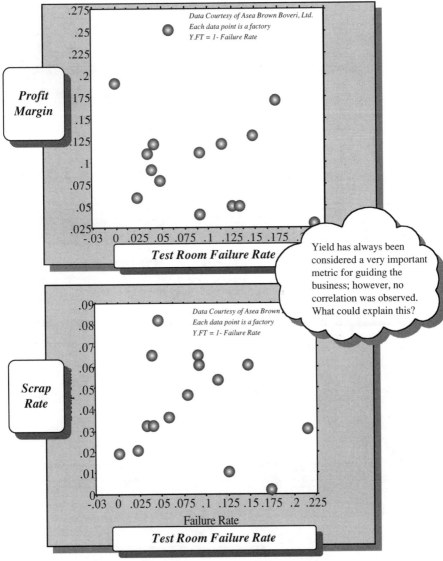

Data Courtesy of Asea Brown Boveri, Ltd.
Each data point is a factory
Y.FT = 1- Failure Rate

Profit Margin

Test Room Failure Rate

Data Courtesy of Asea Brown
Each data point is a factory
Y.FT = 1- Failure Rate

Scrap Rate

Failure Rate

Test Room Failure Rate

Yield has always been considered a very important metric for guiding the business; however, no correlation was observed. What could explain this?

THE VISION OF SIX SIGMA

Six Sigma Academy, Inc.   14 . 3   ®1997 Sigma Consultants, L.L.C.

The Dilemma of Classical Yield

. . . Obviously, there is a correlation between process capability and final yield. However, if we hold the process capability at a constant level, say 3.2σ, we observe that the final yield varies from about 92% to 100%. Why is this so? We also observe that this range decreases as the process capability improves. What is happening to cause this phenomenon?

$$Y_{final} = \frac{s}{u}$$

Where:
Y_{final} = final yield
s = number of units that pass
u = number of units tested

Given that every test failure is caused by a defect arising from the design, material, or process, will the classical calculation of yield be correlated to other major business metrics ?

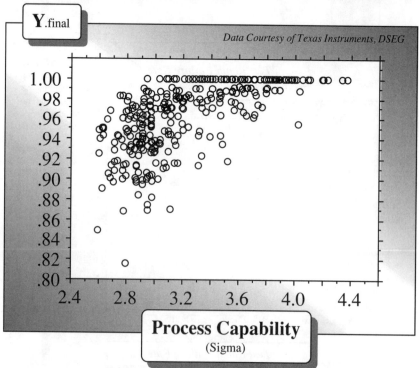

Y.final

Data Courtesy of Texas Instruments, DSEG

Process Capability
(Sigma)

THE VISION OF SIX SIGMA

Six Sigma Academy, Inc.   14.4   ®1997 Sigma Consultants, L.L.C.

The Idea of Rolled-Throughput Yield

Suppose we say that there are 5 key characteristics which must be executed (without error) in order to successfully complete the event. In this case, what is the probability of accomplishing the task error free?

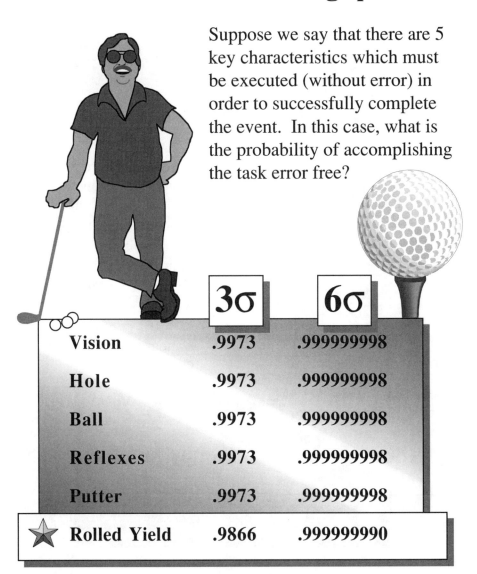

	3σ	6σ
Vision	.9973	.999999998
Hole	.9973	.999999998
Ball	.9973	.999999998
Reflexes	.9973	.999999998
Putter	.9973	.999999998
⭐ Rolled Yield	.9866	.999999990

THE VISION OF SIX SIGMA

 Six Sigma Academy, Inc.   14 . 5   ®1997 Sigma Consultants, L.L.C.

Extension of the Application

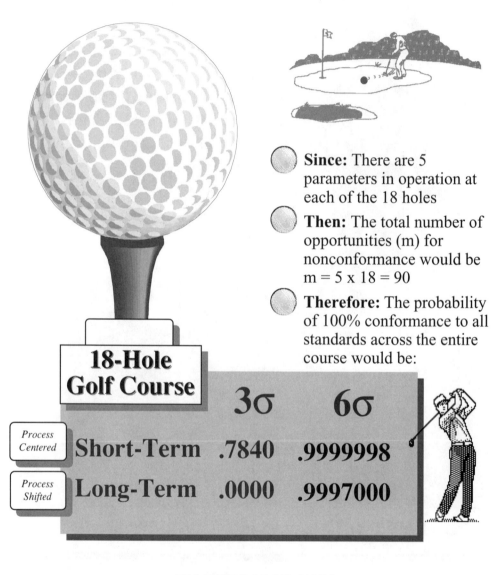

Since: There are 5 parameters in operation at each of the 18 holes

Then: The total number of opportunities (m) for nonconformance would be m = 5 x 18 = 90

Therefore: The probability of 100% conformance to all standards across the entire course would be:

18-Hole Golf Course

	3σ	6σ
Process Centered **Short-Term**	.7840	.9999998
Process Shifted **Long-Term**	.0000	.9997000

THE VISION OF SIX SIGMA

 Six Sigma Academy, Inc.   14.6   ®1997 Sigma Consultants, L.L.C.

Comparison of the Yield Models

For Example:

$$Y_{final} = \frac{s}{u} = \frac{90}{100} = .90, \text{ or } 90\%$$

$$Y_{tp} = e^{-dpu} = e^{-1.0} = .3679, \text{ or } 37\%$$

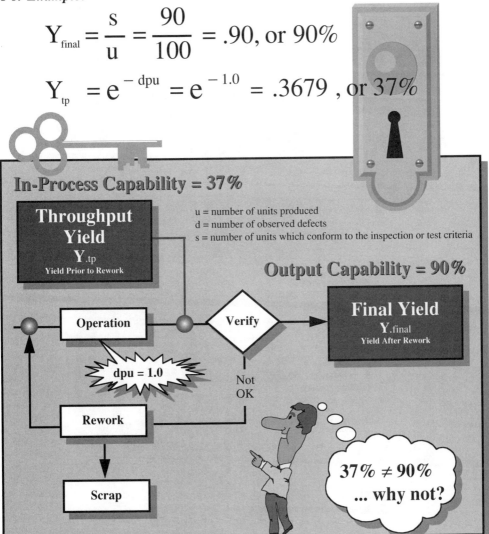

In-Process Capability = 37%

Throughput Yield
$Y_{.tp}$
Yield Prior to Rework

u = number of units produced
d = number of observed defects
s = number of units which conform to the inspection or test criteria

Output Capability = 90%

Final Yield
$Y_{.final}$
Yield After Rework

Operation

Verify

dpu = 1.0

Not OK

Rework

Scrap

37% ≠ 90% ... why not?

THE VISION OF SIX SIGMA

σ Six Sigma Academy, Inc.   14 . 7   ®1997 Sigma Consultants, L.L.C.

The Hidden Operation

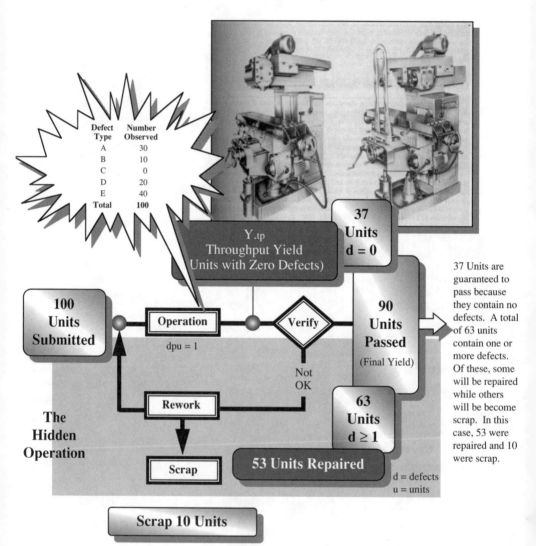

Defect Type	Number Observed
A	30
B	10
C	0
D	20
E	40
Total	**100**

Y.tp
Throughput Yield
(Units with Zero Defects)

37 Units d = 0

100 Units Submitted

Operation
dpu = 1

Verify

Not OK

90 Units Passed
(Final Yield)

63 Units d ≥ 1

Rework

The Hidden Operation

Scrap

53 Units Repaired

d = defects
u = units

Scrap 10 Units

37 Units are guaranteed to pass because they contain no defects. A total of 63 units contain one or more defects. Of these, some will be repaired while others will be become scrap. In this case, 53 were repaired and 10 were scrap.

The Root of Defects

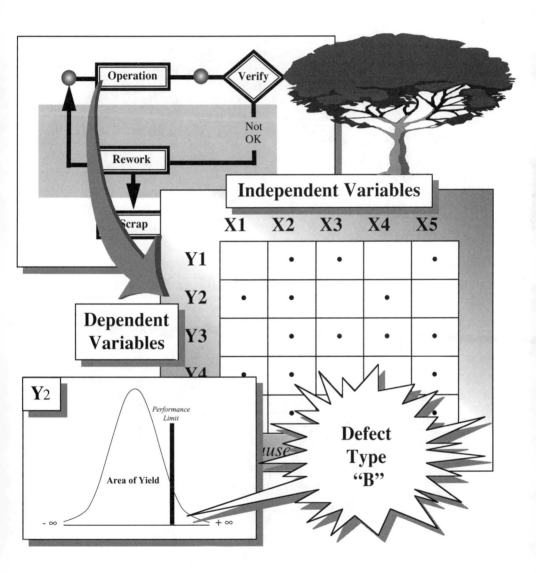

Six Sigma Academy, Inc.   14 . 9   ®1997 Sigma Consultants, L.L.C.

A New Perspective of the Factory

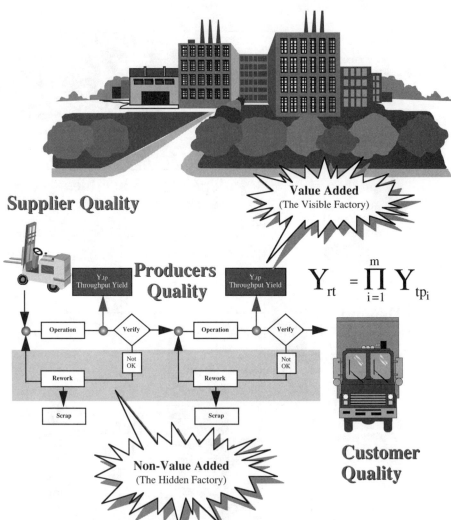

$$Y_{rt} = \prod_{i=1}^{m} Y_{tp_i}$$

To decrease defects-per-unit means to increase rolled-throughput yield which, in turn, improves product reliability and customer satisfaction.

Extending the Concept

A given process has two operations. Each operation has a throughput yield of 99%. The rolled-throughput yield equals:

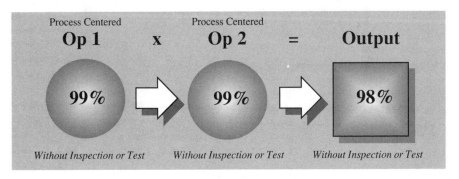

Process Centered   Process Centered

Op 1   x   Op 2   =   Output

99%   99%   98%

Without Inspection or Test   Without Inspection or Test   Without Inspection or Test

. . . There is an 98% probability that any given unit of product could pass through both operations defect free.

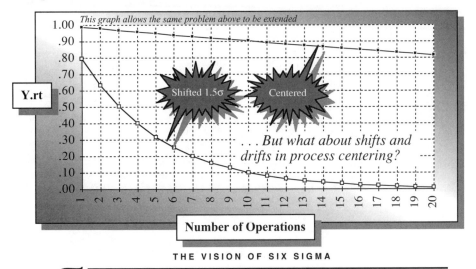

This graph allows the same problem above to be extended

Y.rt

Shifted 1.5σ   Centered

. . . But what about shifts and drifts in process centering?

Number of Operations

THE VISION OF SIX SIGMA

Application of Rolled Yield

Rolled-Throughput Yield

$$\mathbf{Y}_{rt} = \mathbf{Y}_{tp;1} * \mathbf{Y}_{tp;2} * , \ldots, * \mathbf{Y}_{tp;m}$$

where: Y.rt is the rolled-throughput yield, "m" is the number of
categories, and "tp" is the throughput yield of any given category.

Interpretation
of Y.rt for the
example data:
There is a 35.8%
likelihood that
all m = 10
categories will
simultaneously
yield.

Spreadsheet Format

	A	B	C	D	E	F
1			Cumulative	Cumulative	Cumulative	umulative
2	Category	Y.tp	Y.rt	Y.norm	Y.rt	norm
3	1	.928	.928	.928	=PRODUCT(B$3:B3)	=C3^(1/A3)
4	2	.805	.747	.864		
5	3	.816	.610	.848		
6	4	.970	.591	.877		
7	5	.915	.541	.884		
8	6	.940	.509	.893		
9	7	.885	.450	.892		
10	8	.848	.382	.887		
11	9	.998	.381	.898		
12	10	.940	.358	.902	=PRODUCT(B$3:B12)	=C12^(1/A12)

Note: The rolled-throughput yield of .358 may not be converted to a "sigma" value.

THE VISION OF SIX SIGMA

σ Six Sigma Academy, Inc.   14 . 12   ®1997 Sigma Consultants, L.L.C.

The Flip Side of Rolled Yield

Normalized Yield

$$Y_{norm} = (Y_{rt})^{1/m}$$

where: "Y.norm" is the normalized yield, "m" is the number of categories, and "Y.rt" is the rolled-throughput yield.

Interpretation of Y.norm for the example data: Given a rolled-throughput yield of 35.8% over the m = 10 categories, the normalized yield (i.e., average or "typical" categorical yield) would be 90.2%

Spreadsheet Format

	A	B	C	D	E	F
1			Cumulative	Cumulative	Cumulative	Cumulative
2	Category	Y.tp	Y.rt	Y.norm	Y.rt	Y.norm
3	1	.928	.928	.928	=PRODUCT(B$3:B3)	=C3^(1/A3)
4	2	.805	.747	.864		
5	3	.816	.610	.848		
6	4	.970	.591	.877		
7	5	.915	.541	.884		
8	6	.940	.509	.893		
9	7	.885	.450	.892		
10	8	.848	.382	.887		
11	9	.998	.381	.898		
12	10	.940	.358	.902	=PRODUCT(B$3:B12)	=C12^(1/A12)

Note: The normalized yield of .902 may be converted to a "sigma" value, or an equivalent Z as some would say. However, the resulting Z value would most likely have to be adjusted to compensate for the influence of long-term process centering error. To do this, we would simply add 1.5 to the given Z value. In this manner, we convert the long-term Z to its short-term equivalent. At the risk of redundancy, it should be pointed out that when converting yield data into a standard normal deviate, the resulting Z value is an "equivalent Z" and, as a consequence, should be viewed as a performance metric and not taken or interpreted as a statistic.

THE VISION OF SIX SIGMA

 Six Sigma Academy, Inc.   14 . 13   ®1997 Sigma Consultants, L.L.C.

The Impact of Complexity

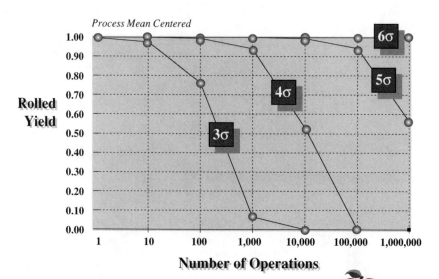

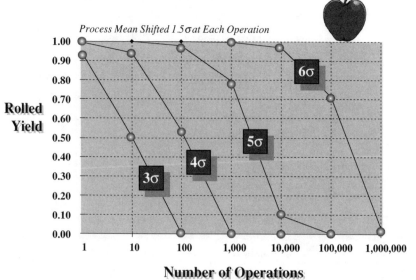

Chocolate Manufacturing Process

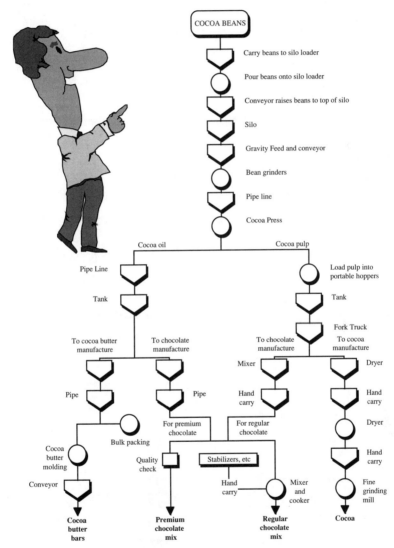

COCOA BEANS

Carry beans to silo loader

Pour beans onto silo loader

Conveyor raises beans to top of silo

Silo

Gravity Feed and conveyor

Bean grinders

Pipe line

Cocoa Press

Cocoa oil — Cocoa pulp

Pipe Line

Load pulp into portable hoppers

Tank — Tank

To cocoa butter manufacture — To chocolate manufacture — To chocolate manufacture — To cocoa manufacture

Fork Truck

Mixer — Dryer

Pipe — Pipe — Hand carry — Hand carry

For premium chocolate — For regular chocolate — Dryer

Bulk packing

Cocoa butter molding — Quality check — Stabilizers, etc — Hand carry

Conveyor — Hand carry — Mixer and cooker — Fine grinding mill

Cocoa butter bars — **Premium chocolate mix** — **Regular chocolate mix** — **Cocoa**

From Edward H. Bowman and Robert B. Fetter, Analysis for Production and Operations Management, 3rd Edition (Homewood, IL : Richard D. Irwin, Inc., 1961), pp. 38-39

THE VISION OF SIX SIGMA

Rolled-Throughput Yield Case Study

$$Y_{rt} = e^{-dpu} \quad \text{Rolled-Throughput Yield}$$

$$Y_{final} = \frac{s}{u} \quad \text{Classic Final Yield}$$

Classical Yield

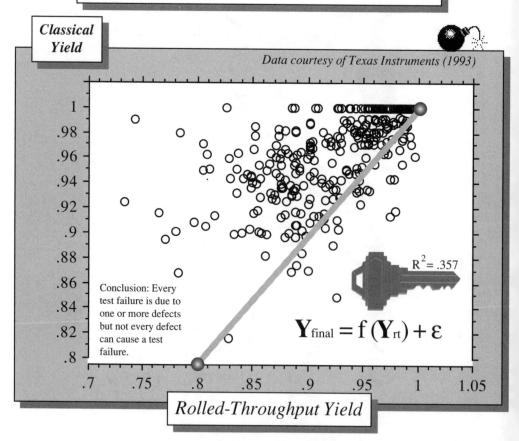

Data courtesy of Texas Instruments (1993)

Conclusion: Every test failure is due to one or more defects but not every defect can cause a test failure.

$R^2 = .357$

$$Y_{final} = f(Y_{rt}) + \varepsilon$$

Rolled-Throughput Yield

THE VISION OF SIX SIGMA

Six Sigma Academy, Inc.   14 . 16   ®1997 Sigma Consultants, L.L.C.

Improving Rolled-Throughput Yield

Which factor(s) should be the central focus of a sustained effort to improve the rolled-throughput yield of a typical manufacturing process?

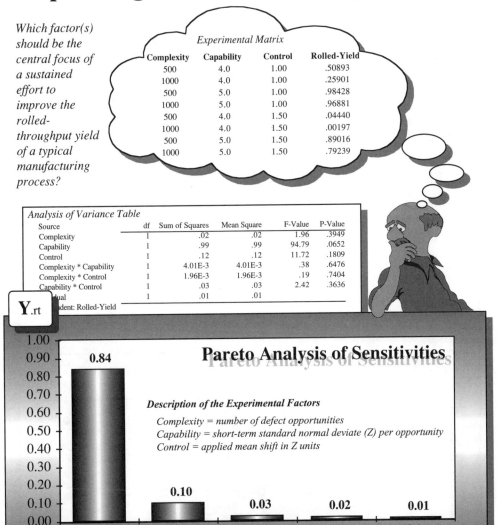

Experimental Matrix

Complexity	Capability	Control	Rolled-Yield
500	4.0	1.00	.50893
1000	4.0	1.00	.25901
500	5.0	1.00	.98428
1000	5.0	1.00	.96881
500	4.0	1.50	.04440
1000	4.0	1.50	.00197
500	5.0	1.50	.89016
1000	5.0	1.50	.79239

Analysis of Variance Table

Source	df	Sum of Squares	Mean Square	F-Value	P-Value
Complexity	1	.02	.02	1.96	.3949
Capability	1	.99	.99	94.79	.0652
Control	1	.12	.12	11.72	.1809
Complexity * Capability	1	4.01E-3	4.01E-3	.38	.6476
Complexity * Control	1	1.96E-3	1.96E-3	.19	.7404
Capability * Control	1	.03	.03	2.42	.3636
Residual	1	.01	.01		

dependent: Rolled-Yield

Y.rt

Pareto Analysis of Sensitivities

Capability 0.84, Control 0.10, Capab x Control 0.03, Complexity 0.02, Other 0.01

Description of the Experimental Factors

Complexity = number of defect opportunities
Capability = short-term standard normal deviate (Z) per opportunity
Control = applied mean shift in Z units

Understanding the Factor Effects

The ordinate of each graph corresponds to rolled-throughput yield.

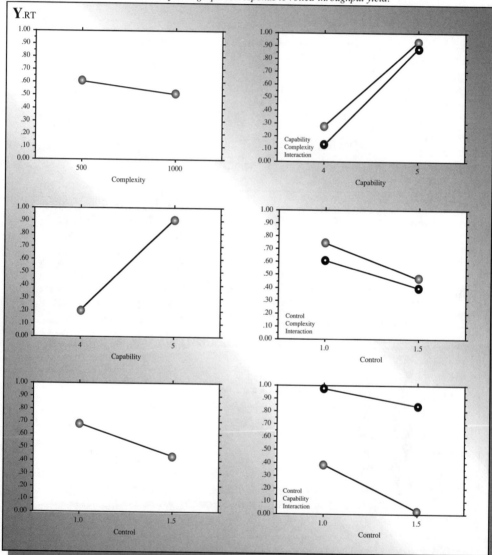

THE VISION OF SIX SIGMA

Six Sigma Academy, Inc.   14 . 18   ®1997 Sigma Consultants, L.L.C.

Simulation of a Typical Process

Note: One opportunity per operation

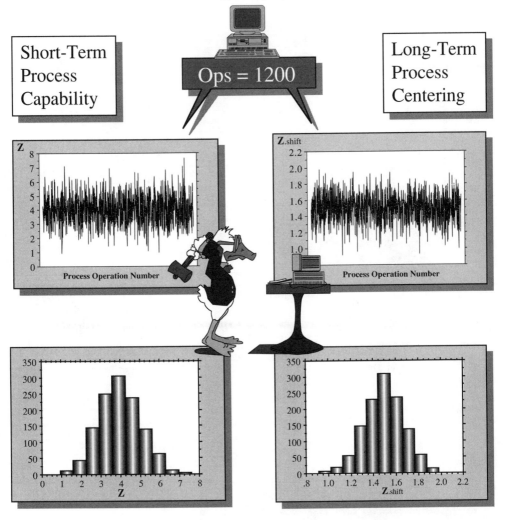

Results of Computer Simulation

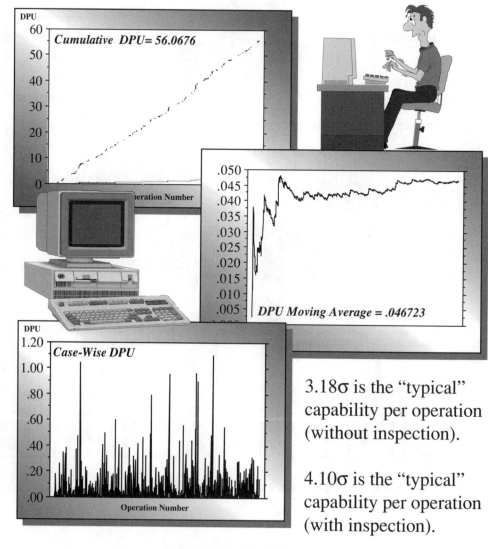

Cumulative DPU= 56.0676

DPU Moving Average = .046723

Case-Wise DPU

3.18σ is the "typical" capability per operation (without inspection).

4.10σ is the "typical" capability per operation (with inspection).

THE VISION OF SIX SIGMA

Six Sigma Academy, Inc.   14 . 20   ®1997 Sigma Consultants, L.L.C.